A DEVELOPMENTAL APPROACH TO PROBLEMS OF ACTING OUT

Revised Edition

A DEVELOPMENTAL APPROACH TO PROBLEMS OF ACTING OUT

Revised Edition

Edited by

EVEOLEEN N. REXFORD

INTERNATIONAL UNIVERSITIES PRESS, INC.

New York

Library of Congress Cataloging in Publication Data

Rexford, Eveoleen N., ed.
    A developmental approach to problems of acting out.

    Bibliography: p.
    Includes index.
    1. Acting out (Psychology)—Addresses, essays, lectures. 2. Juvenile delinquency—Addresses, essays, lectures. 3. Psychoanalysis—Addresses, essays, lectures. I. Title.
RC569.5.A25R49   362.7'4   77-17666
ISBN 0-8236-1221-X

Manufactured in the United States of America

CONTENTS

CONTRIBUTORS

Suzanne Taets van Amerongen, M.D.
Clinical Professor of Child Psychiatry, Boston University School of Medicine
Training and Supervising Analyst, Boston Psychoanalytic Society and Institute, Inc.

David A. Balla, Ph.D.
Associate Professor, Department of Psychology, Yale University and Yale University Child Study Center

Bernard Bandler, M.D.
Professor Emeritus in Psychiatry, Boston University School of Medicine

Peter Blos, Ph.D.
Faculty of Columbia University Center for Psychoanalytic Training and Research
Faculty, New York Psychoanalytic Institute

Helene Deutsch, M.D.
Honorary Professor of Psychiatry, Boston University School of Medicine

George E. Gardner, M.D.
Professor Emeritus in Psychiatry, Harvard School of Medicine

D. Wells Goodrich, M.D.
Professor of Psychiatry and Pediatrics, University of Rochester
Chairman, Division of Child, Adolescent, and Family Psychiatry, University of Rochester

Phyllis Greenacre, M.D.
  Faculty, New York Psychoanalytic Institute
  Emeritus Clinical Professor of Psychiatry, Cornell Medical
    College

Samuel Kaplan, M.D.
  Clinical Professor of Child Psychiatry, Boston University
    School of Medicine
  Training and Supervising Psychoanalyst, Boston Psycho-
    analytic Institute

Dorothy Otnow Lewis, M.D.
  Associate Clinical Professor of Psychiatry, Yale University
    Child Study Center

Theodore Lidz, M.D.
  Sterling Professor of Psychiatry, Yale University School of
    Medicine
  National Institute of Mental Health Career Investigator,
    Yale University

Elizabeth Makkay, M.D.
  Associate Clinical Professor of Psychiatry, Tufts University
    Medical School

Charles A. Malone, M.D.
  Professor and Director, Division of Child Psychiatry, Case
    Western Reserve University School of Medicine and
    University Hospitals of Cleveland

Beata Rank
  Deceased. Formerly Co-Director, James J. Putnam Chil-
    dren's Center
  Honorary Professor in Psychiatry, Boston University School
    of Medicine

David E. Reiser, M.D.
  Clinical Director of Children's Services, Granite Mental
    Health Center, Salt Lake City, Utah

Eveoleen N. Rexford, M.D.
   Professor Emeritus in Psychiatry and Child Psychiatry,
      Boston University School of Medicine
   Instructor, Boston Psychoanalytic Institute

Gregory Rochlin, M.D.
   Professor of Psychiatry, Harvard Medical School
   Training and Supervising Analyst, Boston Psychoanalytic
      Institute

Maxwell J. Schleifer, Ph.D.
   Professor of Psychology, University of Massachusetts

Shelley S. Shanok, M.P.H.
   Associate in Research, Yale University Child Study Center

Henry Wermer, M.D.
   Deceased. Formerly Chief of Child Psychiatric Unit, Beth
      Israel Hospital
   Faculty, Boston Psychoanalytic Institute

FOREWORD TO THE
ORIGINAL MONOGRAPH

Bernard Bandler, M.D.

This monograph consists of the proceedings of a symposium on
A Developmental Approach to Problems of Acting Out presented by the Division of Psychiatry, Boston University School
of Medicine, and its affiliate, the Douglas A. Thom Clinic for
Children, in Boston, Massachusetts, June 15 and 16, 1962.
The Thom Clinic Anniversary Symposium was planned to cel-
ebrate the 40th year of continuous operation of the Clinic as a
child psychiatric facility for service, training, and research in
the Boston area. It was the third in a series presented by the
Division of Psychiatry: the first, on research in child development and the second, on psychopharmacology.

Both the problems and the theoretical concepts regarding
acting out appear to us sufficiently important and confusing to
warrant the publication of the Symposium in a form available
to students and practitioners in psychiatry and the allied professional groups. Dr. Irene M. Josselyn, Editor of the *Journal of
the Academy of Child Psychiatry*, in which the Symposium was
published in January, 1963, suggested the addition of an extended survey of the pertinent literature to make available to
monograph readers a more detailed review of the background
of the contributions of the Symposium. The papers are pre-

sented as they were given in Boston in June, 1962; highlights of
the recorded discussions follow each presentation.

When the Symposium Committee[1] began to plan the program in 1961, the choice of the topic of problems of acting out
emerged naturally from the Thom Clinic research interest in
antisocial young children and their parents, a study begun by
its founder, Douglas A. Thom, in 1947. These research activities have ranged from case studies of the children and certain
of their mothers to a more recent investigation of family interactions and attitudes toward help to effect change in the antisocial grade school child. The implications of this work for acting-out behavior in a more general and varied sense have been
suggested by clinical experiences with children of other age
groups and with adolescents and adults in psychotherapy and
analysis.

The Symposium Committee noted that while many psychoanalysts reserve the term acting out for a special phenomenon
observed in the course of analysis, professional observers from
a number of fields place the label acting out today on a wide
variety of behaviors. Even within the psychoanalytic literature
there are frequent discrepancies in terminology which undoubtedly reflect differences and confusions in concepts.
While acting-out phenomena have been described and discussed in a series of papers since 1901, the Committee felt that
clinical experiences and theoretical formulations had not been
brought together in an adequate conceptual scheme which did
justice to the potentialities of the studies carried out or pointed
the way to fruitful areas of investigation in the future.

The theme of a developmental approach to problems of
acting out evolved in the Symposium Committee discussions as
a unifying concept which would reflect our own point of view
and provide in itself a stimulus for discussion and debate. The
program was arranged to focus upon four specific phases of the

---

[1] Drs. Bernard Bandler, Eleanor Pavenstedt, Eveoleen N. Rexford,
Maxwell Schleifer, and Suzanne T. van Amerongen.

life cycle in sequence: the preschool years, the latency period, adolescence, and adulthood. We invited papers from psychiatrists and analysts who have contributed to our understanding of this area or who had access to clinical material with direct bearing upon the topic. The discussants similarly spoke from clinical and research experiences bearing upon different aspects of the topic. The work described was carried out in various types of settings: a settlement house, child psychiatric clinics, and private offices. Two of the papers presented data derived from psychoanalyses, one from the clinical program of a child psychiatric clinic, three from a clinic research study, and one from a demonstration research project in a low-income urban community.

We were exceedingly appreciative of the willingness of the participants to bring their experience, theories, speculations, and questions to this Symposium. It was our hope that they, the audience, and later readers, would be stimulated to further clinical and conceptual efforts so that five years hence we would find ourselves with clearer concepts of the phenomena we were discussing and more effective therapeutic measures to counter them. We are grateful to Mrs. Lottie Newman of International Universities Press for her assistance and suggestions in the preparation of this monograph.

FOREWORD TO REVISED EDITION

Eveoleen N. Rexford, M.D.

In this revised edition we have brought up to date the survey on the literature on acting out. We have, in addition, added articles to round out what was presented and discussed at the original Symposium. The Boston University-Thom Clinic symposium dealt scantily with two issues that seemed important: delinquency in girls and the fathers of antisocial children and youth.

Studies of antisocial behavior, during the ensuing years, however, have been even more infrequent than prior to the Symposium. The papers in the child and adolescent field were apt to be statistical and superficial in nature, adding little to the considerations we had tried to build up in the concepts of a developmental approach to problems of acting out within the life cycle.

Peter Blos's classic paper on delinquency in girls brought together clinical materials from different milieux and placed them in a theoretical framework valuable to a generation of clinicians faced with adolescent girls who were involved in "sexual acting out."

We turned to Dr. Blos for his perspective upon female delinquency twenty years after he had published his well-known paper. What evidence had he accumulated which bore upon the issue of the changing cultural attitudes toward expressions of sexuality among adolescents? Would he alter his earlier formulations and adapt his recommendations for therapeutic management accordingly? We are fortunate indeed to be able to publish not only his original paper, but a Postscript to it as well.

The 1962 Symposium indicated that data regarding the mothers of delinquent children have been more commonly available than those concerning the fathers. The study by Dorothy Lewis et al. helps to fill that gap. In the Lewis study of a sizable number of families, the firm association between paternal criminality and paternal psychiatric treatment contrasted with the possible statistical association between maternal criminality and psychiatric treatment. It is encouraging to find the Lewis group pursuing many questions about antisocial behavior which have seemed to lie fallow for over a decade.

A DEVELOPMENTAL CONCEPT OF THE PROBLEMS OF ACTING OUT

Eveoleen N. Rexford, M.D.

In his "Psychopathology of Everyday Life" (1901), Freud first recorded and discussed the psychological significance of actions, many of which we would now call acting out. By 1914, the phenomenon of acting out in the transference in which analytic patients substituted action for recall was a subject of such frequent discussion that Freud devoted considerable attention to it in his technical paper "Remembering, Repeating and Working-Through." Acting out as a special form of remembering which replaces associations in the course of analysis, neurotic acting out in everyday life of instinctual urges, the defenses against the instinctual urges, or the affects connected with them, and chronic character disorders in which impulsive acting-out behavior is a way of living having been described in a series of psychoanalytic papers familiar to all of us. I wish as an introduction to this Symposium on Problems of Acting Out to sketch briefly the commonly held concepts of the nature, origin, and development of these phenomena and to indicate a few of the special contributions to our understanding of them.

Otto Fenichel in 1945 defined neurotic acting out as follows: "Obviously, all 'neurotic acting out' has the following in common: It is an acting which unconsciously relieves inner

1

tension and brings a partial discharge to warded-off impulses
(no matter whether impulses express instinctual demands, or
reactions to original instinctual demands, e.g., guilt feelings):
the present situation, somehow associatively connected with
the repressed content, is used as an occasion for the discharge
of repressed energies; the cathexis is displaced from the repressed memories to the present 'derivative,' and this displacement makes the discharge possible" (p. 296). Fenichel discussed factors involved in acting-out phenomena, such as the
mobilization of unconscious tendencies in the course of psychoanalysis, the weakening of defenses against the instinctual expression in action in response to life circumstances, and a basic
psychic structure which predisposes to habitual patterns of acting out. He formulated the preconditions for acting out as (1)
an alloplastic readiness; (2) fixations on orality, high narcissistic need, and intolerance toward tension; and (3) early
traumata.

Phyllis Greenacre, in her paper "General Problems of
Acting Out" (1950b) observed, "It would seem that in acting
out there may be special problems of (a) specific problems in
the immediate real situation; (b) special persistence of memories of earlier disturbing experiences; or (c) an inadequate sense
of reality" (p. 225). She noted a compulsion to reproduce repetitively a total experience or episode rather than to select a
small part of it as a token representative. In her consideration
of the genesis of the habitual acting-out pattern, Greenacre
accepted as of undoubted importance the preconditions Fenichel described and added two others: "a special emphasis on
visual sensitization producing a bent for dramatization" and a
largely unconscious belief in the magic of action. Furthermore, Greenacre introduced another element from her long
experience with chronically acting-out analysands, "It may be,
however, that the common genetic situation which combines
with or sometimes partly produces these characteristics, and
the accompanying general tendency to act out, consists in a
distortion in the relation of action to speech and verbalized

thought, arising most often from severe disturbances in the second year and showing its effects in the following months as well" (p. 227).

In 1956 the American Psychoanalytic Association held a panel on "Acting Out and Its Relation to Impulse Disorders" (see Kanzer, 1957a). Michaels characterized acting on impulse as a more primary, more malignant phenomenon, one closer to the psychosomatic pattern than the traditional acting out, which he saw as linked rather to highly evolved neurotic conflicts. Primary acting out, associated with narcissism and the primary process, is more generalized; however, he believed a continuum between the two exists. Frosch described the evolution of mechanisms of delay of impulse expression from the built-in neurological to the fully evolved psychological patterns and attempted to devise a nosology of impulse disorders on the basis of such a scheme. Hanna Fenichel and Greenson stressed the primitive nature of the identifications in acting-out patients whose impulse controls are often dependent upon the fantasy of being part of the body of another person. Since controls are externalized to such an extent, a possible separation from this person is especially threatening. Ultimately, Hanna Fenichel believed, the problem is the trauma of separation from the mother. Edith Jacobson (1957) in her studies of borderline patients has emphasized the relationship of their acting out to pervasive denial and distortion of reality.

The literature provides us with a conception of manifestations of acting out which may be arranged on a continuum: transient, highly specific acting out in the transference, more pervasive acting out within or outside analysis in persons so disposed, and, finally, the chronic acting-out pattern of living. The authors who have sought to explain the evolution of the acting-out character structure (Fenichel, Greenacre, Greenson, Altman, and others) ascribe its origin to faulty development during the first two years of life, early and repeated traumata, and a disharmony in the maturational sequences of the motor system and speech. The implication of disturbances in

the early mother-child relationship is clear in all of these formulations: from the transference phenomena and from un-
covered memories of adult analysands, the nature of the disturbance has been inferred, as by Altman (1957), who remarked that the transference is superior to any other form of
history taking.

Adelaide Johnson, S. Szurek, and their colleagues, in a
series of papers (Szurek et al., 1942; Johnson, 1949; Johnson
and Szurek, 1952; Litin et al., 1956) brought into the area of
investigation the role of the current parent-child relationship
in promoting and maintaining the child's acting-out behavior.
Their acting-out child patients, most of them adolescents, and
their parents underwent psychiatric treatment concomitantly;
and from a series of such collaborative therapies, Johnson and
her co-workers have concluded: (1) the causes of the child's delinquent behavior can be deduced by a study of family interrelationships as with any other type of emotional disturbances;
(2) parental neurotic difficulties are expressed in the child's
delinquent behavior; and (3) the child frequently acts out the
parents' unconscious antisocial wishes and is aided and abetted
in his activies by them. Bird (1957) noted with approval Johnson's thesis that antisocial acting out in a child is initiated, fos-
tered, and sanctioned by the parents; in his opinion, it is the
specific peculiarity of all acting out that it involves an interaction between two people in which unconscious incitements
and responses accomplish a specific purpose for the partners in
the interaction.

The study of acting-out children offers the opportunity to
investigate the development of the acting-out pattern from
both vantage points, that of the child at different ages and that
of the parent-child relationship. The possibility of studying the
emotional climate of the home in which the child is growing
up, the personalities of each parent, the nature of the psychic
equilibrium within the family, and the part the child and his
behavior play in the maintenance of that balance can provide
us with a more precise understanding of those factors operative

in the evolution of the child's psychic structure which encourage or militate against the acting-out propensity.

The development of every boy and girl presents us with a case history of the evolution of impulse controls, the gradual mastery over direct instinctual expression under the influence of the growing relationships with those important and dear to him, maturing ego functions, and an increasing grasp of reality. Impulse controls are normally attained over a wide-ranging battleground, with recurrent skirmishes won and lost; major battles fought over a period of months and years with inevitable retreats to former strongly entrenched positions under the impact of too great stress. These are familiar chapters in the life story of every child.

The development of impulse controls presents such difficulties for some little boys and girls that they become unmanageable and their parents seek out professional help for them at an early age. Those of us at the Putnam Children's Center during the 1940's recall vividly the group of aggressive, destructive little boys from two and a half to four years who occasioned much lively discussion of their current status and probable future course.

The largest group of acting-out children who come to the attention of psychiatrists are referred for antisocial behavior in their grade school or adolescent years. Aichhorn (1925) explained delinquency as "an interplay of psychic forces, which has created the distortion which we call dissocial behavior," and distinguished between the symptoms of delinquency and the fundamental problem underlying delinquency.

Kate Friedlander (1947) described the various crucial steps in the development of the child's social adaptation, highlighting the key roles of his early relationship to his mother, the nature of his oedipal conflicts, the formation of the superego, and group formation in his family. She defined the antisocial character formation as follows: this formation "shows the structure of a mind where instinctive urges remain unmodified and therefore appear in great strength, where the Ego, still

under the dominance of the pleasure-principle and not supported by an independent Super-Ego, is too weak to gain control
over the onrush of demands arising in the Id. This character
formation is at the basis of the condition which Aichhorn calls
'the state of latent delinquency' and it will depend upon the
various factors exerting their influence in the latency period
and puberty whether delinquent behaviour becomes manifest
or not" (p. 94).

These authors, then, as did Fenichel in considering adults
who act out, distinguish between the psychic structure underlying acting out and the actual occurrence of spontaneous
acting-out behavior. While many of the studies in the
literature deal either with the classical episodic or isolated instances of acting out in the transference or with the habitual
life pattern of the person with a chronic character disorder, we
know from our clinical experiences with both children and
adults that, spontaneously and in treatment, problems of
acting out occur which must be placed somewhere between
these two extremes.

Such problems may be discerned in the life history of different individuals during one specific developmental phase
and then disappear from view; they may occur repetitively in
response to very specific life situations, often in the setting of a
unique interpersonal relationship. Acting out may appear,
particularly in children, in response to a highly traumatic experience; in play or interaction with others, the child strives repetitively to master actively what he experienced passively.
Acting out may occur as an expression of a highly specific instinctual wish or defenses against that wish, and not in relation to other instinctual urges. The episode of acting out may
involve a more widespread instinctual expression or the
defenses or affects connected with the drives.

Problems of acting out wear many faces, and the disappearance of the pattern confronts us with interesting questions. We know, for instance, that many children who over a
period of years have displayed an aggressive, destructive pat-

tern do not necessarily continue chronic acting out in their adolescent and adult life even in response to considerable stress. When, in 1955, we followed up a group of fifty-seven antisocial young children of grade-school age who had been observed or treated at the Thom Clinic, we found that thirty-two of the forty-eight treated were not displaying evidence of delinquent behavior and six of those who had not been treated were also nondelinquent, as far as we could tell from our investigations. On the other hand, two of the treated children had relapsed into antisocial behavior under the impact of puberty (Rexford et al., 1956).

The fathers of many of the antisocial boys whom we have seen over the years also evoke the question of what influences, internal and external, may lead to a spontaneous curbing of acting-out behavior. A great majority of the fathers gave a history of rather sustained antisocial behavior during their grade-school years and occasionally into adolescence, and yet, so far as we could ascertain, were law-abiding and conforming as adults. That the acting-out tendencies were present was suggested by their encouragement of their son's acting out and the obvious gratification they received from the boy's behavior.

The significance of a constitutional predilection for motor expression of instinctual urges is one we cannot evaluate with certainty. Our impression of aggressive, destructive children of preschool and latency age seen in the clinics is that they tend to be sturdy, well-developed. muscular boys. The Gluecks (1956) included a detailed examination of body types in their studies of five hundred delinquent and five hundred nondelinquent boys, and the mesomorphic type showed the highest potential for delinquency. It is interesting to note that they found these traits more seriously involved in the delinquency of the boys of mesomorphic build, namely, low verbal intelligence, a feeling of not being taken care of, and marked oral-receptive trends.

Central-nervous-system damage from prenatal or perinatal causes has been indicted by some observers as the principal etiological agent in antisocial behavior of children. While many of our research children at the Thom have shown minor neurological abnormalities and atypical electroencephalographic findings, this has also been true for only slightly fewer of the neurotic children. Difficulties in impulse controls are undoubtedly compounded when central-nervous-system damage exists, but evidence that it is a primary factor or even implicated in the majority of children presenting chronic patterns of acting out is not available to us.

The generally accepted formulations of the genesis and evolution of the acting-out pattern imply that these individuals have been subjected to early and probably long-continuing experiences which have militated against the development of ego functions and object relations adequate to the task of impulse control. William Healy's pioneering study of individual delinquents (1915) was the first of many to demonstrate the frequency of early severe disruptions in the lives of such children: separation of the children from the parents, loss of affection for or confidence in the parents, prolonged absence or death of parents, repeated changes in foster homes and institutional life which provides no opportunity for the development of personal attachments. Bowlby (1944), Kaufman (1955), and others have stressed the etiological role of early separation from the mother. The typical life history of the young delinquent or predelinquent seen in our clinics and casework agencies reveals such gross emotional and social deprivation that studies of the impact of the interplay of the parents' conscious and unconscious attitudes toward this specific child with his developing personality have not been feasible.

Since 1947, we at the Thom Clinic have carried out a series of studies of antisocial young children, mostly boys, from six to ten years of age who came to the attention of the Clinic because of habitually impulsive, destructive-aggressive behavior over a period of two years or more, which rendered them unmanageable at home, at school, and in the neighborhood. These studies (see Rexford, 1959) have led us from the area of psychodynamic descriptions of the child's personality structure and appropriate treatment techniques for him to a consideration of the parent-child relationships, and, finally, to a study of the processes of interactions whereby these family members deal with one another and with outsiders.

One of these investigations, a psychotherapeutic study of a group of mothers (Rexford and van Amerongen, 1957), demonstrated the influence of unsolved maternal oral conflicts upon impulsive acting out in their young children. The four mothers, although varying widely in their levels of personality organization, presented in a strikingly similar way their problems with the child brought to the clinic. All four shared the central conflict of unresolved oral demands which influenced their children's development in the direction of persistent impulsive acting out in several important ways. Because of their feelings that their own oral-dependent wishes had not been met, these women were handicapped in giving love and affection to their children. They did not reject them as babies, nor were they indifferent or entirely hostile to their offspring, but they could not provide a consistently satisfying milieu for the child when they themselves felt chronically deprived of vital oral supplies. The young child's strong hostile feelings are not sufficiently overcome so that he can move on to a capacity for true object relations. He is not withdrawn from the world, but his relationship to it remains a predominantly hostile one. Because these mothers feel they did not get enough love, they are unable to set limits and to frustrate the child in a constructive fashion. The unresolved oral conflicts carry over in supporting the self-oriented pleasure principle rather than the other-oriented reality principle. In the second place, these women fear that lack of gratification can lead only to intolerable tension and destructive retaliation upon the source of frustration, the parents. This fear inhibits still further their educating the child by dosed frustration to tolerate delay and by finding substitutive formations for direct instinctual gratification. Hence, the child does not build up a strong ego, his reality

testing and sublimations are limited, he must repeatedly resort
to action to master tension and anxiety. In the third place, the
mother's pattern of changing her love object in a persistent
search for the person who will meet her infantile needs
involves the child, particularly when his oedipal wishes focus
her attention upon his so-called adult demands. Lastly, when
he encounters the outside world in school, his behavior meets
with punishment and censure which increase his tension and
his hostile acting out. His mother's identification with him
supports his aggressive behavior as she repeatedly displays her
vicarious enjoyment of his nonconforming ways.

When the opportunity was given to us by The National
Institute of Mental Health in 1956 to pursue our investigations
more systematically, we took as the focus of our research a
group of families with an antisocial young child, families who
did not present the familiar picture of overwhelming social
and emotional pathology obscuring the details of the interplay
of conscious and unconscious parental attitudes and the child's
developing personality. We hypothesized that the parental attitudes toward frustration and control of instinctual impulses
in the child who demonstrates the antisocial patterns would
differ significantly from the parental attitudes toward these
same issues in the neurotically inhibited or overcontrolled
child, and, similarly, that the two groups of children would
differ significantly in their attitudes toward gratification and
frustration of instinctual urges. By studying ongoing processes
of interaction among family members and of family members
with the research staff, we hoped to learn of the parents' current attitudes toward their child's instinctual gratification and
frustration, while their reports of the child's development and
their ways of handling his various maturational problems
would give us relevant information about his upbringing.

Our findings indicate that the two groups of parents and
children were significantly differentiated in respect to the
issues of attitudes toward gratification and frustration of instinctual urges.

When we scrutinized our material at the end of an eighteen-month pilot study, we saw that we had tapped an important source of information in the attitudes of the parents and children toward the various staff members. The reality is that families who come to a child psychiatric clinic are motivated by a wish for help in changing a child whose problems have occasioned them considerable frustration, for they have been unable either to alter the child's behavior or to control him. The clinic offers them the possibility for a gratification of that wish, but it imposes in turn certain frustrations which are implicit in the kind of help obtainable from modern psychiatric treatment methods. We therefore incorporated the concept of "help toward change" in the next phase in the research.

The analysis of the data collected over a period of four and a half years indicates that the families with an antisocial child present a pattern of interactions among themselves and with the clinic staff which has been remarkably consistent and which has differed significantly from that of the comparison group of families. We have been able in this clinical research study to achieve a clearer understanding of the emotional climate of the home in which the child was growing up. The antisocial child's parents seem to be primarily concerned with the control and suppression of the boy's misbehavior in order to avoid the criticism of outsiders. They have not welcomed the opportunity to think about the child or to try to understand his feelings and behavior. They want to do something, and they demand from the clinic staff devices which will magically stop the criticized acts.

Although treatment was not part of the formal research plan, we have taken all the families from both groups into our regular clinic therapy when the parents wished such assistance following the research diagnostic study. These therapeutic experiences with the antisocial families corroborated the original clinical findings and provided us with a rich yield of additional data.

Notwithstanding that all of the antisocial children had

histories of persistent acting-out behavior over a period of many months—often years—and of earlier developmental problems before the behavioral disorder was predominant, we found, not unexpectedly, that they did not present an identical personality structure. The children of the two groups, one with the presenting problems of fears, inhibitions, learning blocks, and the other with the manifest antisocial problems, could be placed upon a diagnostic continuum, with well-defined neurosis at one extreme and antisocial character disorder at the other. Whereas the members of each group could be differentiated from those of the other, many of the antisocial children did not present the picture of the typical character disorder, but rather an admixture to varying degrees of internalization and externalization of their conflicts. Within the antisocial group itself, there were readily discernible differences in the pervasiveness of motoric expression of impulses, in the impression of "drivenness" which they conveyed, in the variety and maturity of their defenses, and in their ways of relating to the staff members. Similarly, certain of the neurotic children displayed clear evidence of difficulty in controlling their impulses and of a tendency toward erupting into action under stress.

Nor can the parents of the antisocial children be placed in any one diagnostic category. The fathers resemble one another more closely than the mothers, and display a strikingly similar attitude toward their sons. They tend to be passive-aggressive men with a high degree of dependency needs and confused sexual identifications. The diagnoses of the mothers ranged from moderately severe neurosis to severe character disorder. They resembled one another in the frequent finding of evidences of regression under the abrasive influence of the sadomasochistic relationship with their sons, but the variety of personality structures in this group of mothers parallels the findings in our smaller sample of four studied psychotherapeutically. What is common to them is their inability to see the needs of this particular child as separate from their own and to provide him with reasonably consistent warmth and appropriate limit-setting at the different developmental phases.

These studies illustrate the traumatic impact of certain chronic parental attitudes upon the development of libidinal and ego capacities in the child. Two processes of interaction appear to mingle with and reinforce each other: (1) the parents', and particularly the mother's, ambivalent and inconsistent ways of dealing with the child's conflicts and anxieties at each maturational phase; and (2) the parents' continuing encouragement of direct instinctual expression. In one family, there may have been more difficulty with the child about one particular developmental stage than another; in other families, each new maturational task for the child seemed to add another insurmountable problem to the group of previous conflicts which the child had mastered only minimally. The critical problems in the mother-child relationship tend to emerge during the second year of life around the issues of activity and control; whereas the infant-mother relationship may have been far from ideal, the situation tends to deteriorate with the child's growing self-assertion and motor skills. It is the combination of minimal ego education at each step of the child's development with persistent undermining of his somewhat uncertain controls through overstimulation and encouragement to acting out that appears significant to us in these families.

In summary, problems of acting out include a wide range of phenomena having dynamic, structural, and economic features in common. They appear in childhood, adolescence, and adult life, in acute transient form in response to a specific stress or a sudden shift in psychic balance, in episodic sequences over a period of months or years, and as a chronic pattern of living. Acting out is rooted in oral conflicts, in heightened narcissism, an intolerance for drive frustration, and an inadequate grasp of reality.

These psychological traits characterize the psychic struc-

ture of chronic acting-out individuals, but the structure may
be present without spontaneous acting out, except under specific circumstances which shift the balance of drive and defense, as during psychoanalysis. The developmental history of
acting-out individuals reveals early emotional disturbances,
particularly problems in the second year when the issues of
autonomy, control, and self-assertion arise.

Studies of the emotional climate in which the child was
brought up have been made by elucidation of the transference of adult acting-out analysands and by investigation of
the family milieu of acting-out children. These different approaches provide us with an increasing understanding of the
origin of problems of acting out and of influences which may
encourage and perpetuate this pattern of behavior.

DISCUSSION

Dr. George E. Gardner:

Dr. Rexford has given us a very succinct overview of the
response mechanisms or syndrome designated as "acting out"
as it is detailed in the literature, and as she herself has observed its emergence in her clinical experience with both children and adults. Her very excellent paper is directed principally to the problem of placing as accurately as possible, in a
chronological sense, the origins or the beginnings and the development of this behavioral deviation. Significantly, to my
mind, she draws attention to immaturations in development
that relate to the second year of life.

Without repeating a summarization of Dr. Rexford's findings, I should like to emphasize first another failure in development or in maturation that is closely allied to, and that in
fact not infrequently accompanies or complicates, the acting
out or delinquent behavior that we see in children. I refer
here to word-usage immaturation or verbal symbolization
failure that is noted in children with marked learning disa-

bilities. Our researches in this area would seem to us to indicate that these two disabilities — acting out and word-usage disabilities — are embedded in time and in type in the same developmental matrix and sequence. A crucial and critical task for us is to be able to account eventually for the persistence of one disability and not the other or for their disassociation in expression in the individual case. This task of the differentiation and modification of these allied developmental failures, however, must wait upon more research data than any of us possess at this moment.

Nonetheless, in respect to the acting-out syndrome, I would conjecture that basically this immaturation is evidenced by three factors. First, in these children there is an observable persistent and continued *somatization* (particularly in respect to motility) of the thought processes and of the words or verbalizations used in the thought process. Secondly, I think that there is seen in the not-infrequent subtle combination of these two disabilities of which I speak a marked failure in the achievement of *impersonalization* of aggression. Thirdly, there seems to be a failure in the establishment or the incorporation within the child of a *verbalized* adversary or "opponent," as described by Bessie Sperry in a recent paper (1962) — a verbalizing adversary that acts as an ever-present check on, or evaluator of, the individual's decisional thinking referable to actions and reality. Of greatest significance to us, however, is that these task-failures in development are allied and are evidenced in both the acting-out syndromes and in the verbal learning disabilities and that they are posited for solution by the child at the same time chronologically, that is, in the second year of life.

We have as yet but a hint as to the critical difference in the persistence of one type of immature behavior and not the other. If we posit, as we must (and as Dr. Rexford does), a basic experientially inculcated fear of annihilation, coupled with the threat of the emergence of forbidden instinctual impulses, we can assume, I think, that in the child when the thought processes are essentially nonverbalized or inadequately governed by words, the only methods available to the child for mastering anxiety are (1) mobility in action, or (2) pictographic anxiety-reduction fantasy to an inordinate and disabling degree. As we attempt to understand these children, it is our tentative notion that the disabling defense in the acting-out child is primarily the persistence of motility and action as substitutes for the expected but nonutilized verbalized thought processes, and that in the child with a marked learning deficit the defense of choice is primarily an embracive, all-consuming reliance upon anxiety-reducing fantasy. Only future research, as I have said, will tell us whether these hints are correct. Nonetheless, whether correct or incorrect, to my mind it is no accident (as demonstrated in symptoms and as seen to be phasically allied developmentally) that these two childhood behavioral deviations are seen not infrequently to exist in the same child.

In conclusion, let me again congratulate Dr. Rexford for her splendid overview of the literature in reference to the acting-out response in children. It sets the matrix for what I am sure will be an earnest and profitable examination of this disability in our symposium. It is Dr. Rexford's emphasis upon the importance of the developmental approach to this problem that I feel is so salutary, and my remarks were assembled to expand and extend this approach in the light of our clinical observations.

Dr. Theodore Lidz:

Although Dr. Rexford intended her paper to be primarily an introduction to the Symposium, it has also made a distinct contribution of its own. I was very pleased to note in her paper as well as in some that will be presented later an emphasis that differs from most of the recent contributions to psychoanalytic ego psychology. She specifically takes into account the positive influences required to assure the child's integrated ego development rather than tacitly implying that without notable pathological influences the child's development will unfold normally as a consequence of the inherent genetic make-up. An emphasis is placed upon the positive developmental guidance and positive influences required to shape the child's personality.

Both the project at the Thom Clinic and our project at Yale have been interested in seeking to delineate what essentials in the family structure and family interactions are necessary to promote the development of a stable ego structure in children. How does the parental interaction influence the family structure; and, in turn, how does the family structure relate to the developing ego structure of the child? What do parents have to communicate of the adaptive techniques of the culture? How do they carry out the process of acculturation? How does the family communicate the instrumental techniques of adaptation that the culture has built up over countless ages and which the child must assimilate in order to become a functioning adult in the society? How do they influence the way the child learns to communicate, categorize, and conceptualize?

I would like to comment briefly on Dr. Gardner's remarks about the relationship between language development and the learning of ego control. It is, I believe, a topic that transcends the problems of acting-out children and the particular type of linguistic problem that Dr. Gardner has designated. We are going to hear more and more about the development of meanings and category and concept formation in schizophrenia in general and in childhood schizophrenia in particular, and how the family transactions influence and can cause profound distortions of meanings. Linguistic functions, and particularly the learning of valid meanings, play a central role in "autonomous ego functions." Without learning instrumentally valid meanings of words, a person is capable of very little ego control. The learning of language is not simply a matter of teaching the child words by repetition or even by proper reinforcement. The process starts very early in life when the child seeks to solve problems even before his language develops: starting with gaining a mutuality with the mother through her responses to the child's cues, the child learns that her cues are meaningful. Gaining the essential ability to defer or relinquish immediate gratification of needs may well become confused in very early childhood in acting-out children because signals do not seem to solve problems for them. The ability to communicate verbally should lead to more focused efforts at problem solving, but it may lead to only increased misunderstandings.

A great deal that we usually take for granted goes into learning verbal communication, but in the few minutes available I can merely touch upon this intriguing topic. The attainment of trust in the utility and reliability of verbal communications is essential to the learning of reality testing and to problem solving in general. The relationship between language and ego functioning becomes apparent when we realize that we require words to categorize our experiences and that, unless we categorize properly, we live in a completely aleatory world. Language provides the child with a reference system by which the culture in which he lives categorizes experiences. It is preformed for him, and he must learn this system to obtain a foundation for his own individual ways of grouping things together. Words simplify our environment and our lives by grouping together things and events with common attributes. Without such grouping or categorization, each event remains an isolated never-recurring experience. Further, the meaning of a word has a predictive capacity. If something is termed a "chair," we are predicting that it is something that can be sat upon; if it is termed a "pencil," we anticipate that it can be used for writing. It is only through the certainty of meanings that the child gains an ability to cope with the future. Unless words have reasonably consistent meanings to the child, there can be very little ego control at all. I cannot expand on this complicated topic. I simply wish to focus attention on the relationship between acting out, impulsivity, and language development in general, and to emphasize that basic meanings are learned in the family and reflect parental ways of thinking and of relating.

I wish to mention one other topic. Dr. Rexford talked about *boys*. We must be cautious about assuming that studies of acting out in boys can be extended to apply to girls as well. Acting out in adolescent boys and girls is usually quite different symptomatically. It is, for example, difficult to find a sociopathic girl in whom the primary complaint does not concern promiscuity, whereas, in boys, the complaints center about stealing or flagrant aggressivity. While we have reason to believe that there are similarities in the family configurations that relate to sociopathic tendencies in children of both sexes, it is quite possible that there may also be significant differences in the configurations and that some families are more apt to have delinquent sons and other families are more likely to have delinquent daughters.

SOME OBSERVATIONS ON CHILDREN
OF DISORGANIZED FAMILIES
AND PROBLEMS OF ACTING OUT

Charles A. Malone, M.D.

Two years ago, the South End Family Project was established to explore the development of techniques of effective service to a small group of highly pathologic families with only pre-school children, living in a skid-row slum area. We selected families that had failed, or never attempted, to use constructively any organized community health or social work facilities. In view of the high cost, both human and economic, of the repetitive patterns of family disorganization and severe pathology, our goal has been to alter the outlook for these young children and families. Our observations and impressions derive from the clinical process of work with the families in their homes, and the children in our therapeutic nursery school. The data from which this paper is drawn are therefore descriptive, and center around the relationships of the family members with each other and with the members of the project staff.

The families with whom we work show many forms of severe psychosocial pathology: alcoholism, neglect, brutality, illegitimacy, delinquency, and crime. The children grow up in an environment in which impulses are not merely fantasied, but are real because they are lived out. Petty crime, prostitution, sights such as degraded alcoholics urinating in the streets and vicious fights are witnessed by the children as part of their daily lives. They exist in a rather hopeless, normless world where actions speak louder than words and impulsivity is dominant, where people live from day to day with weak ties to a meaningful past and little investment in the future. What is most striking about the children is that, as the result of their gross deprivation, they show little investment in or enjoyment from themselves or others, a markedly diminished capacity to sustain interest, and a relative lack of stable inner structure. Their energies and ego functions are diverted and preoccupied with the task of searching for reliable, satisfying contact with people, avoiding pain, and compensating for deficient inner growth. Their efforts give way easily under stress and tension is discharged motorically.

Although this paper focuses on pathology, it would be misleading to emphasize solely this aspect of the families. The children are attractive, sturdy, well coordinated, and appealing. By virtue of their skill in reading cues they orient themselves quickly to the externals of a situation. They are capable of accomplishing rather grown-up tasks, such as doing the family shopping. Importantly for our work with them, their affect hunger and longing for an object are not complicated by bitterness. Their parents, though highly disturbed and showing inconsistent, neglectful, seductive, and aggressive behavior toward their children, cannot be simply categorized as "bad" or "rejecting." They are concerned about their children, want them to look nice and to have a better life than they had, struggle to raise them properly, and often blame themselves for their child's difficulties.

Most of the children do not show the extreme aggressive, destructive behavior at a preschool age that is usually described in discussions of children with antisocial character (e.g., Rexford, 1959). What does emerge from our observations, however, are certain characteristics, described later, which, combined with the model of their parents' impulsivity and the asocial quality of their neighborhood, may predispose them in a basic way to later chronic acting out and impulse disorder.

Since Freud's (1914) original definition of acting out as the compulsive repeating of the past in action instead of remembering, the term acting out has often been broadened beyond its original intended limitation to psychoanalytic therapy. It has been used to describe a wide range of behaviors and pathologic states whose characteristic feature is failure to control impulses. This paper will be concerned with this latter, broader meaning of the term acting out. As the definitions of acting out which have arisen in analytic practice refer to specific, complex, organized units of behavior, they *do not* seem applicable to the behavior observed in our children. The particular quality noted in the children is the direct, massive discharge in action of affects, tension, and impulses. Michaels's designation (1959) "acting upon impulse" is the most suitable term to describe this rather nonspecific unorganized behavior. The children do not fit into the diagnostic category "hyperkinetic," however.

The characteristics seen in many children in our nursery school seem to fit with the general descriptions of types of severe impulsive character disorders. The clinical features in our children may be presented schematically as follows: low frustration tolerance, impulsivity and unreliable controls, dominant use of motor action for discharge, language retardation, tendency to concrete thinking, need-satisfying object relations, little evidence of constructive play or use of fantasy in play, poor sense of identity, and marked use of imitation.

This clinical description (and many such descriptions in the literature) can be condensed. What is being described is a primitive, poorly differentiated personality dominated by primary-process thinking, with strong pregenital fixation (mainly oral), a narcissistic need-satisfying orientation to objects, and ego weakness, particularly with reference to the synthetic function and the capacity for internalization.

Although our children are similar to other children with
severe ego impairment, they differ in several ways. They are
not withdrawn and do not attempt to become independent
people and directly gratify component instincts, as Rank
(1949b) noted in her study of atypical children. Rather they
are hypersensitive to and almost constantly oriented to people
in their efforts to obtain attention and interest and avoid
pain.

This paper will focus on the developmental delay seen in
these children as it appears related to certain gross disturbances in the mother-child relationship. Three interrelated
areas of delay will be stressed: (1) the transition to secondary-
process thinking; (2) the capacity for stable internalization;
and (3) the dominant use of action rather than words. These
areas will be related to the topic of this symposium in the
sense that these lags in development interfere with the capacity to control impulses and result in a tendency to act upon
impulse. Some of the children's attempts to compensate for
their deficiencies will be noted. To illustrate these features
condensed clinical extracts of three children and their
mothers will be presented.[1] The material concentrates on the
initial months of nursery-school observations.

CASE PRESENTATIONS

Carol and her Mother

Carol is a tall, almost constantly active, appealing
four-year-old Negro girl with facile friendliness and enthusi-
asm. She is the kind of little girl people smile at and for
whom they produce candy out of their pockets. Her masklike
smile is broken only rarely by a look of confusion and despair.

---

[1] I am indebted to members of the project staff (Mrs. Mattick, Miss
Weisenbarger, Miss White, Mr. Devlin, and Dr. Blackwell) for use of their
clinical records in preparing these clinical extracts.

Carol's mother is an attractive, moody nineteen-year-old woman with two illegitimate children, who comes from a background of deprivation, neglect, and confused values and identity. The illegitimate child of a Negro prostitute and a white father, she was abandoned by her mother and placed at the age of six months in the foster home of Mrs. G., a chronic alcoholic. In adolescence, Carol's mother was a member of a gang involved in delinquency, drinking, and promiscuity; the latter resulted in her becoming illegitimately pregnant with Carol when she was fifteen. During Carol's first three years, her mother continued her gang activities and escapades. Sporadically, she left her child to the foster mother's indulgent, unreliable care. Frequent conflicts between the two "mothers" arose over Carol's upbringing, and we have reports of violent scenes between them, with Carol standing crying and confused, or actually being pulled back and forth in a kind of human tug of war. Carol was weaned at the age of three, only after her mother had moved to her own apartment with the children of her new boy friend.

Her mother generally insists on immediate compliance from Carol and this is often coupled with outbursts of aggressive punishment. Carol's mother is distressed by her loss of control and occasionally plagued by fears that Carol will be seriously injured in a fall. Yet her aggression toward Carol also seems pleasurable. She frequently teases Carol, reducing her to tears and helplessness, or provoking expressions of anxiety. It is our impression that in this manner she uses her child to express affects which she feels but cannot acknowledge. During periods of depression, she becomes more hostile toward Carol and has to "get away"; she "dumps" her children at her foster mother's while she goes out with her girl friends.

At other times Carol's mother is more successful in her efforts to care for her children. She aspires to a higher social status for Carol, wanting her to attend the same Christian

Science Sunday School that she went to as a child, and to "make something of herself." She shows pleasure when Carol uses "big words," even though Carol does not know their meaning and says them to gain attention. The mother involves herself in Carol's play, but mainly to control it and to encourage Carol to entertain her (for example, by dancing). Indeed, the mother's narcissistic gratification is the dominant mode of their relationship, and Carol is expected to recognize and meet the mother's needs.

Carol entered school with boundless energy and indiscriminate, fleeting "interest" in everything. She separated from home easily, and, for some months, did not show any indication of separation anxiety. There was, however, often a quality of restless searching about her, of traveling but never arriving. She was almost continually in motion—climbing, running, skipping—and tension and frustration were tolerated poorly and readily discharged in bodily activity. In fact, her only genuine pleasure appeared during gross motor activity. Although she was something of an acrobat, Carol occasionally fell; at those times she did not seek comfort. Her play consisted of picking up, handling and discarding materials and toys, without sustained interest or sign of enjoyment. She did not balk at routines and readily accepted limitations. There was a similar compliance in her faithful repeating after her teacher the names of colors or animals in a book without learning them. Aggression toward other children took the form of impulsive grabbing of toys, and she often provoked them to chase her, to which she responded with excited shrieks.

Although she related in a shallow, indiscriminate way to her teacher and classmates, Carol readily imitated and took on their activities and gestures. She was extremely sensitive to the moods and intentions of others. For example, if her teacher went to switch on the lights, Carol was already there, turning them on. If a child looked to the doll corner, Carol immediately had a doll in her hand. Rarely initiating any play, her choices were determined by what someone else was doing. Sometimes, when imitating another child, she asked softly, "Do you like me?"

For Carol, anything or anybody out of sight seemed gone —a toy that could not be seen was not searched for. When the teacher put on gloves Carol looked bewildered and exclaimed, "Where your hands? They lost." Similarly, when playing peek-a-boo, Carol wandered off as soon as her teacher was out of sight.

More recently (during Carol's second year in nursery school) after a period of stability in her home life and the development of some meaning and trust in her relationship with her teacher, Carol began hiding in order to be discovered over and over by her teacher. She expressed the wish to control the presence of her teacher and requested her to repeat the same enjoyable play. Traveling in the car to and from school, comfortably settled in her teacher's lap, Carol with an intent, serious look often asked, "Did you miss me?" or "Will you come back?" Gradually her fear of being left was stated and restated, and regularly she was reassured. Dramatic play developed along the same lines. In such play she was the angry, demanding, scolding mother, shouting at her child, "Stay in the house all by yourself and cry." Carol used dramatic play to punish other children who had been "bad," and to express anger toward her teacher. Finally, one day when her mother was not at home after school, she slowly, with the teacher's help, acknowledged her feelings in relation to this event and allowed her teacher to comfort her. When her mother was found, she was able to say to her, "I called and called, but you were not there." Carol no longer obediently tolerated being shifted around and increasingly wanted to take matters in her own hands. Lately, she has expressed anger toward her mother over disappointments and being left, to which her mother has responded with defensive annoyance.

Although decreased in amount, verbal and dramatic play

expression of her concern over separation continues. At the same time Carol's interests and self-directed play activities have broadened. She has shown more curiosity and interest in learning, has asked questions she really wants answered, and has added many words which she understands to her vocabulary. These changes are reflected in Carol's second psychological testing (one year after the first) which revealed increased verbal comprehension and capacity to handle multiple stimuli, and an I.Q. increase of almost 20 points.

Bobby and His Mother

Bobby is a tense, constricted, slender, sober-faced four-year-old boy brimming with barely concealed hostility. His mother, a small, dark, stone-faced, unmarried Negro woman, seems older than her twenty years. A rigidly compulsive woman, she ably maintains an orderly household in spite of overcrowding and the burdens of caring for her four children. She comes from a poor Southern family; her parents frequently battled and she was shifted around among the relatives. Her father died when she was thirteen, and two and a half years later her mother was hospitalized with a diagnosis of schizophrenia. At age sixteen, the birth of her unwanted son, Bobby, was followed shortly by the burdensome post-hospital care of her mother. Until recently, when Bobby's mother took her children to a new apartment and sent her mother to live with her grandparents, there were frequent battles over ownership and control of the children. Bobby, being his grandmother's favorite, often slept with her.

His mother's repeated question, "Did he do the right thing?" betrays her enormous concern over Bobby's behavior and her fear of the evaluation of others. She expects adultlike behavior from Bobby, and severely punishes any evidence of lack of control, dependence, messiness, assertiveness, or negativism. Even Bobby's showing fear of dogs is forbidden. It is our speculation that for Bobby's mother any loss of control is equated with her mother's psychotic behavior and her own devaluated image. Her attitude toward Bobby is changeable —sometimes showing concern and interest, at other times ignoring him or dismissing him with a slap. At times Bobby is devalued by his mother in front of others. For example, she said to the teacher, "He wants to go to the party, but who is he—a nobody!" Her outbursts of aggression apparently do not trouble her, and she teasingly provokes Bobby's fears. Without expression, she explains that she beat him until he could not move because "he's got to do what's right and learn who's boss!" Bobby's fear of his mother is shown when he flinches or anxiously pulls back when she yells or scolds. He responds to his mother's restrictions and expectations with compliance and indicates his resentment only by occasional passive resistance or by tantrums.

In nursery school Bobby was a contrast of restricted inactivity and restless movement. On the whole, Bobby's play consisted either of fingering objects or of an unimaginative, pleasureless repetition of the same activity, such as squeezing a sponge out over and over. Although his choice of play materials was dominated by wanting what others had, he struggled only briefly to hold on to a toy, readily relinquishing ownership and walking away, often with a defeated air. Toys that fell off the table were not retrieved or even looked for. When the children made chocolate pudding, Bobby, along with others, could not wait to eat it. After the teacher put it aside to cool, however, not one child asked for or searched for the now "forgotten" pudding at snacktime. Despite falls, Bobby's rare expressions of animation and pleasure were seen when he was running, jumping, or climbing. He attempted initially to follow his teacher's lead but could not long remain settled in his chair. Characteristically, Bobby never sat with both feet under the table; one foot was always outside, poised for action. In regard to routines and limitations, Bobby was overly obedient and tried very hard to be controlled. At times, frustration of his wishes resulted in wild tantrums or destructive dismantling of another child's block building; episodes of destructive aggression, however, occurred only occasionally in school and were rarely seen at home. If Bobby were to express destructive wishes openly at home, his mother would beat him without mercy. It appears that, in the interests of self-preservation, Bobby restrains direct expressions of aggression at home.

In relation to his teacher, Bobby was initially fearful and mistrustful. He made no direct requests, and glances had to be interpreted as indicative of wants. His sparse verbalizations contained adultlike polite phrases and he attempted to appear grown up. Accepting help was particularly difficult for him and he insisted on doing by himself things which he was unable to do. Whenever reality confronted him with his inability to do what he claimed he could, he either ran off, regressively made demands and showed how "helpless" he was, or became angry. For example, unable to draw as he insisted he could, Bobby ended up angrily scribbling, saying he was making "shit," and then indicated his name was to be put on his drawing as "Shitty Bobby."

His mother's punishments appear to have accomplished an empty and meaningless "socialization" in Bobby. *In lieu* of reliable inner control and autonomy, he pretends independence only to suffer humiliation when he becomes aware that he cannot actively master. He is reduced to passive helplessness and self-devaluation.

After months of carefully observing his teacher's responses whenever any child did something which seemed remotely daring to him, Bobby began testing out. Streams of toilet talk and defiant refusals, particularly to toilet himself, appeared. He showed increased fearfulness, especially of noises, and occasionally soiled himself. Bobby protested vehemently when taken to the bathroom. At one point, after accepting his teacher's encouragement to go to the bathroom by himself, Bobby angrily shouted, "You will leave me!" Reassured by his teacher, he then made bitter complaints about being left alone and having to take care of his siblings. Bobby seemed to express the feeling that to be grown up is to be alone and burdened, and indicated the weight of his unmet needs and of the responsibilities foisted on him. Yet he struggled to avoid his mother's punishment by meeting her expectations.

For some time, Bobby did not show any separation anxiety. Indeed, it seemed that he and his mother conspired to ignore the fact of separation. For example, whenever his mother came to the window and said "Good-by," Bobby turned his back, and whenever Bobby waved or looked for her, his mother did not notice. Later, separations were difficult for him and he made requests to remain with his teacher. He often left a piece of paper for her to hold in her purse, while he asked for something he could take home. At the same time, his mother reported with considerable annoyance and distress that Bobby was more demanding of her attention at home.

Susan and Her Mother

Susan is a small, sturdy, hyperactive, pert five-year-old, whose expressive face at times reflects unquestioning eagerness, and at other times mistrust, weariness, and dejection. Susan's mother is a thin, tired-looking twenty-two-year-old woman who compulsively tries to control and order her life. She is a contrast of painful shyness on the one hand, and masculine toughness on the other. At times she looks middle-aged under the burden of caring for her five children. In childhood she was enmeshed in a hostile, dependent relationship with her alcoholic, unreliable mother, and she still counts on her mother, only to be repeatedly disappointed. She impulsively became pregnant at age sixteen by Mr. R., whom she subsequently married. She was frightened, and totally unprepared for pregnancy and marriage. She acted as though she were not pregnant. When Susan was born she did not know what to do, and was afraid to hold her. She often became overwhelmed and gave Susan's care over to her sister or her resentful mother, with whom she lived for the first three years of Susan's life. Susan's mother's concept of child care is the minimal meeting of physical needs with very little handling or play. She was happiest when Susan was quiet, "good," and easily controlled. She was not able to cope with the more specific demands of her growing infant, which were interpreted as the baby's aggressive effort to control her and were sharply limited. In general, Susan's motor development pleased Mrs. R. and was encouraged as long as Susan did not get in her way. Although Mr. R. objected, Susan was allowed a bottle until she was four and a half years old. Mrs. R. did not see how she could take the bottle away from Susan.[2] Susan was enuretic until she was five, and did not learn to dress herself until she entered school. In contrast to her infantile ways, Susan has done shopping for the family since she was four, and her mother frequently relies on her to make decisions which the mother seems unable to make. Mrs. R. expresses the feeling that girls must not be dependent, and insists on Susan's standing "on her own two feet", yet she often interprets Susan's attempts to assert herself as aggression, and punishes them or undermines them by withdrawing. Although she is pleased by Susan's toughness, she punishes her and expresses the fear, "You will grow up to be a delinquent like your father." Susan's mother seems unable to avoid repeating her own mother's pattern of being unreliable with her children, and undermining and hostile toward her husband. Her surprising capability in running her large household is in sharp contrast to her vagueness and confusion about time and her difficulty in making plans. It is of interest in this regard to mention her difficulty in making conscious connections between herself and what she is doing or feeling.

In nursery school, Susan had a nonspecific amiable, out-

---

[2] Rexford and van Amerongen (1957) point out, in a study of four mothers of acting-out children, that the mothers are unable to set limits and, because of their own oral conflicts, fear that lack of gratification will lead to destructive retaliation against them.

going, head-on approach to everything. From the start, before she had a relationship with her, Susan repeated imitatively her teacher's words and actions. This imitation had a superficial quality. For example, Susan parroted her teacher's "Watch the cars, kids," but did not look herself. She was action-oriented, using her infantile speech mostly to attract attention rather than for communication. Sure-footed and graceful, she accomplished daring feats on the swing and climber. She seemed capable beyond her years at serving juice and setting up the sliding board and heavy climbing equipment by herself, but her demonstrated capacity was deceptive. It soon became apparent that her activities had a driven quality, were diffuse and unplanned, and did not last or develop in any consistent direction. For example, after setting up the climbing equipment skillfully, she would become overexcited, using her body only for tension discharge. At times she used poor judgment, being careless to the point of endangering herself. In fact, she, like the other children, required close supervision for her safety and months of repeated demonstrations of concern and verbalized encouragement to be careful before she protected herself. The defensive nature of Susan's exclamations that she could do for herself and needed no help soon became apparent. The intensity of her refusal to acknowledge any lack of mastery, despite her inability to sustain interest in play or to complete tasks, was striking. It became clear that Susan's busyness was a bid for attention, and that she was acutely aware of the teacher's every move, and of who was getting what from her. Often she seemed compelled to leave what she was doing and interpose herself between the teacher and another child. She usually finished even simple tasks only when the teacher gave her undivided attention. Susan's attention-getting maneuvers and manipulations were manifold and skillful, and whenever she was unsuccessful at separating the teacher from another child, she would incorporate the child and teacher as a unit and ask them both to come and "look at what me doing."

When she felt left out, Susan's attempts to be grown up gave way to aimless dashing around the room or some bid for attention. Like most of our children, Susan revealed immature qualities in her thinking. To illustrate, concepts were grasped when they were demonstrated concretely in action rather than explained verbally, pictures of furry animals were stroked, and she appeared to live from moment to moment with little sense of time. Particularly she did not expect or count on her teacher doing the same thing she had done before, even after many repetitions. Susan was bossy and controlling in her play with other children, calling them "sister" or "brother" as though they were siblings. Later, in dramatic play Susan expressed the same theme over and over again — small animals searching for their mothers, or babies crying and no one coming. The fixity of Susan's play around this theme was remarkable. Almost any inanimate object became a "mother" or a "baby." She often could not make up her mind in dramatic play whether she was the mommy, the big sister, or the baby, and alternated roles confusedly.

DISCUSSION

In the mothers described, a variety of factors, particularly their narcissistic needs, devaluated self-image, oral and anal conflicts, and impulsivity and ambivalence, interfered with their maternal efforts and resulted in gross disturbance of their relations with their children. The children showed the effects of this disturbance in the delay and imbalance of their development, which is emphasized in the disparity between their outward appearance and apparent capability and the deficiencies of their inner ego growth.

As already indicated, the discussion will center on certain influences of the disturbed mother-child relationship in three interrelated areas of developmental lag: (1) the transition from primary- to secondary-process thinking; (2) the capacity for stable, integrated internalizations; (3) the dominant use of action rather than words. An attempt will be made to relate these areas of developmental lag to the topic of this symposium in the general sense that control of impulse involves capacities for delay and detour of discharge, and that partial or temporary arrest in these areas of development interferes with the establishment of these ego capacities and results in a tendency to act upon impulse.

Transition to Secondary-Process Thinking

Piaget's sensorimotor theory of intelligence, as summarized by Wolff (1960), traces the development of the inborn potential for what we term secondary-process thinking from its earliest reflex beginnings. He describes six stages in the transformation of action into thought. Delay in progression through these stages and in other aspects of cognitive development is readily demonstrated in our children. They show concreteness and immature modes of thinking, a poor concept of time, and difficulty in comprehension and integration of multiple stimuli. To illustrate the children's delayed cognitive functioning, the lag in two steps in intellectual development (what Piaget terms "object concept" and the "concept of intention") and corresponding deficiencies in ego growth will be presented.

First, organized, self-directed activities are seldom seen in nursery school. The children do not actively initiate, but follow in a passive, imitative way, or make choices which are dominated by instinctual needs (e.g., rivalry). There is a tendency not to connect action with self, and not to take responsibility for deeds. Related to this, causality is not well established, and there are indications of magical thinking. For example, a child cleaning a table explains that he is doing it because "the table wants to be washed." To a degree the children live in a world in which things simply "happen," a capricious world beyond control. These patterns of behavior are probably related to features of the mother-child relationship. We observe that the mothers, in their effort to exert strong

controls over their children, are given to outbursts of impulsive, verbal, and physical aggression. The children's efforts toward active exploration and initiative are seen as "demands"
and as attempts to control, and are either punished or not supported. Self-help is thwarted, and motor activity inside the
overcrowded home, which is more object-directed, is sharply
restricted.

What is described in these children is a relatively weak *concept and sense of initiative and invention*. In terms of intellectual development, the concept of intention introduces cause-
and-effect behavior and counters belief in the magic of action.[3] Intentional behavior allows a child to delay immediate
ineffectual action, while exploring new means of attaining his
intended goal, and thus is crucial for adaptation; it prepares
the way for later, more truly representational forms of thought
(Wolff, 1960). For our children the environment has interfered
not only with this but with other related aspects of ego
development. The experience of the self as active and capable
of self-direction has been thwarted. Bobby's humiliation and
devaluation when he becomes aware that he cannot actively
master have already been noted. These children have not had
repeated experience of self-initiated action bringing appropriate responses from their mothers. As a result the children
have difficulty in successfully planning action in terms of pleasurable or painful results which would lead later to internalization of what is approved or disapproved, "right" or "wrong."
Importantly, awareness of intention is necessary for later
superego sense of responsibility.

Secondly, we note that the mothers' own deprivations and
narcissistic needs make it difficult for them to give to their
children in a consistent way. Extremes of frustration are
unrelieved or are alternated with overindulgence. The
children are infantilized while they are expected at the same

---

[3] Greenacre (1950b) indicates that a largely unconscious belief in the
magic of action is a regular etiologic factor in chronic acting out.

time to be adultlike in their control. The children's relationship to the teacher tends to be shallow and superficial. They
show little interest in toys (lack preferred or favorite toys) and
have minimal investment in or enjoyment from play. In addition, when toys that are played with are dropped or removed,
they are often not pursued—just as the pudding that is made
and set aside to cool is "forgotten."

These observations suggest a relatively *weak cathexis of objects*, both human and inanimate, and also a relatively poor
concept of and belief in the permanence of people and things
(or what Piaget terms "object concept"). The observations of
Provence and Ritvo (1961) on deprived, institutionalized children indicate that the strength of the cathexis of inanimate
objects depends on the strength of the cathexis of the mother
from whom it is displaced. Deprived infants appear to lack the
necessary interest to make use of their maturing potentials.
The maintenance of interest in and belief in the existence of
objects that are out of sight are vital for intellectual and ego
growth. For the child to pursue things that disappear involves
a sense of possession and the capacity to sustain the mental
image of the object (which involves delay of discharge), while
exploring means of recovery. The importance of object constancy for individuation and object relations is well known and
cannot be overstressed. Its role in the mastery of separation
anxiety has been emphasized by Fraiberg (1959) and
beautifully illustrated by Freud in *Beyond the Pleasure Principle* (1920a).

In our children the strength of instinctual fixation at pregenital levels fosters the dominance of primary-process thinking. It contributes to the delay in cognitive development by
keeping the children so bound to internal stimuli that they are
not free to explore manipulatively their environments for
learning purposes. Susan seems endlessly caught up in expressions of her fear and wish that she might still be a baby. Her
efforts to prove that she is self-sufficient frequently dissolve,
giving way to behavioral expression in stereotyped play of her

passive-oral longings, or impulsive motoric discharge. She is so dominated by her rivalrous feelings that it is difficult for her to sustain her interest in reality-oriented activities, so that the frustration of seeing her teacher with another child sets off a burst of attention-getting activity. Similarly, the sadistic punishment and teasing Bobby and Carol experience not only heighten their sadomasochistic orientation, but also result in fear of their mothers and increase the real danger from their environment. Thus, the distinction between fantasy and reality is made more difficult, and the children's preoccupation with danger militates against developing mental and personal autonomy.

Internalization

The discussions in Hendrick's paper on early identification (1951) and in Sandler's on the process of internalization (1960) imply (although they do not specifically state it) that stable internal models arise under the influence of an "average expectable environment" (Hartmann, 1939). Our children do not have such an environment. To explore the effects of this environment on the processes of internalization, several types of influence relating to impulse control, identification, and identity will be presented.

To begin with, the unreliability of the mothers' physical and emotional presence, and the inconsistency of their patterns of gratification and frustration interfere with their children's capacity to *assess* their mothers' behavior and set up realistic expectations. Thus the children are distrustful, their cathexes are tentative and readily withdrawn, and they show little evidence of planning and anticipation.

In Carol's and Bobby's response to their mothers' aggression and impulsivity, another problem appears. Both children in part try to cope with the fearful and aggressive aspects of their mothers by identification. They shout, swear, quarrel, boss, and control. On the other hand, the mothers cannot tolerate, and often punish such reflections of themselves. The children are caught in confusion between the impulsivity of the mother which they see and experience, and her verbalized expectations. If this confusion and inconsistency are internalized, they will lead to a faulty superego.

Carol's extreme sensitivity to the cues of others, imitating their actions and choices, and reflecting their moods and wishes, is of interest in terms of Greenson's views on acting out (see Kanzer, 1957a). He states that individuals who are prone to chronic habitual acting out have disorders of identity, are apt imitators, and play roles. Although our children are young and their characters are not formed, Helene Deutsch's (1942, 1955) careful delineation of the development of several extreme forms of identity and reality-testing pathology has considerable relevance for them. In this regard, the adaptive and compensatory aspects of Carol's imitation are interesting.

These characteristics in Carol appear to be an outgrowth of features in her relationship to her mother and the added confusion and contradiction between her "two mommies." Her mother frequently uses Carol narcissistically as an extension of herself. She shows pleasure when Carol meets her needs, performs for her, and entertains her. In the interests of preserving her relationship with her mother, Carol has learned to follow imitatively her mother's lead. At the same time the unreliable atmosphere in which Carol has grown up has deprived her of adequate supports for her developing individuality. In view of her mother's shifting moods, attitudes, and behavior, it behooves Carol to read cues well. What is "expectable" in her environment is that it changes. It appears that she compensates for deficiency in her inner assurance about her own identity and the permanence of her world by precocious, imitative, and cue-reading capacities.

In terms of identification we have noted that the children initially make rather facile, imitative identifications with the teacher *before* they have a meaningful relationship with her. At first their relationship is superficial and nonspecific. They

easily orient themselves to her and to the forms of school routines, in spite of lacking an inner sense of the sequence and
purpose of them. They appear to use imitativeness to adapt in
spite of (and to compensate for) a relatively weak object
cathexis. The children seem to *take on* the qualities of another
so that they appear like someone, rather than the gradual process of taking in and taking over the characteristics of another
in an integrated fashion. In view of their deprivation, these observations make us wonder about the depth of the children's
capacity to relate, and yet their longing for an object makes
them responsive in what seems a genuine way. It is a question
for further work, whether stable identifications which grow out
of, rather than precede, object relationship can be developed.
If the dominance of imitative identification is not altered,
standards and moral values may change with new objects.

There are a number of indications of rather precocious capacities in our children, such as Susan's shopping and decision
making, and Bobby's caring for his siblings. In an effort to
meet their mothers' expectations and avoid pain, they try to
appear to be grown up without feeling grown up. There is
insufficient blending of instinctual and ego maturation in the
sense that the children's attempts at self-control which defend
against dependency or objective anxiety are not matched with
and supported by experience of mastery and self-reliance.
They attempt to compensate for this lack of independence and
voluntary control by a kind of pseudo autonomy and compliance.

Another aspect of the children's self-representation and
identification can be seen in relation to repeated falling. Repeated falling without expression of affect occurs in these
children, in spite of the fact that they possess adequate and
even advanced motor skills. Yet, in the course of what
appears to be an increasingly meaningful attachment to the
teacher, during which she repeatedly shows her concern for
their welfare and encourages them to be careful of
themselves, this behavior gradually disappears. It is replaced

in play by placing themselves in "danger," an implicit call for help, and eventually they learn that they can ask for their teacher's "help," an appeal with dual meaning, since it asks for protection and also the teacher's manifestation of interest.

It appears that these children demonstrate in *action* their failure to experience comfort and protection from their mothers, as though identified with the neglectful aspect of their mothers. They have not developed a stable inner attitude of self-protection. Schafer (1960) points out that Freud considered protection and comfort of the ego an important superego function resulting from identification with the comforting, protecting, loving parent. In our children, it may be that identification with their mothers' aggression and devaluation contributes to the way they disregard and devalue themselves. In nursery school, it seems that a new attitude toward the self is taken over by the children through "identification" with the teacher. It is not clear whether these new self-attitudes will last. They may only be present in relation to the teacher, representing the use of a familiar pattern of adaptation.

Action vs. Words

Greenacre (1950b), in her classic contribution, points out that in the etiology of acting out "the common genetic situation . . . consists in a distortion in the relationship of action to speech and verbalized thought, arising most often from severe disturbances in the second year [of life]." She indicates that in the early histories of patients who chronically act out, speech is inhibited or delayed. More important, however, is the fact that language "is used for exhibitionistic purposes rather than communication." Michaels (1959), in his description of the impulsive psychopathic character, also stresses language retardation and a disproportion between verbalization and action. In relation to our observations of infantile and retarded speech, and the children's tendency to express and communicate through body movement and action, several considerations seem relevant. The parents of these children are geared to action rather than talking, and the words they use may not have reliable, consistent meaning, and often should not be repeated. For the children, action provides a dominant means of immediate tension release, and gross body movement appears to be the only source of spontaneous pleasure. Although action inside the home is restricted by their parents, gross motor activity outside the home is by and large permissible and probably tends to remain free of conflict. The verbalization-action imbalance noted in our children would also seem to reflect the influence of environment on the children's intellectual development as already discussed. They remain to an extent tied to concrete thinking, understanding concepts which are shown and demonstrated physically rather than explained verbally.

We turn now to the use of language for exhibitionistic rather than communicative purposes. Greenacre (1950b) suggests the possible etiologic significance of visual sensitization in relation to the exhibitionistic and scoptophilic trends in habitual acting-out patients. There is no doubt that our children have been, and continue to be, exposed to many instinctually stimulating events. Looking and being looked at, however, also have considerable importance to our children in terms of their hyperalertness to protect themselves against danger and their need for attention.

The place in the mother-child relationship of Carol's mimicking words she does not know the meaning of in order to please and meet her mother's needs has been discussed earlier. This mimicry undoubtedly serves as an attention-getting, exhibitionistic device. Her recent language improvement and increased readiness to learn indicate a shift in the meaning of words to her. The changes appear to be connected with the sensitive and careful work of her teacher, Mrs. Ilse Mattick. In the setting of her relationship to her teacher, Carol has repeatedly carried into action, dramatically played out, and talked about the issue of separation and loss. This child, who initially used massive denial (oblivion) and seemed totally unaware of any aspect of separation, brought out her anxiety, confusion, and conflict in full force. Aggression, at first possibly expressed in her hyperactivity and reckless motoric discharge, appeared repeatedly in her play in the form of identification with the aggressor, and was expressed in anger toward her teacher. Then, on several appropriate occasions, it was directed affectually and in words toward her mother. Although Carol continues to focus on separation and loss, it appears that energy has been freed and can be used, if only temporarily, for progressive ego growth. Language which in part seemed to be tied to the maintenance of her most gratifying contact with her mother, thereby giving some assurance against dreaded abandonment, can now to an extent be used for communication and learning purposes. It is as though the multiple traumata of separation, inconstancy, and inconsistency of Carol's early life were walled off by massive denial (splitting of the ego). With the emergence of this buried area of Carol's life, it can be brought into contact with her reality-oriented ego, and her ego development is assisted by the release of energy (previously used for defense) and by some integration of her past with her present life.

SUMMARY

The recent hopeful signs in Carol raise the question of the future of these children. Will Carol's mother be able to respond to her daughter's expressions of anxiety and anger about separation and insistence on security? Or as Bobby increasingly communicates to his mother that he needs her rather than struggling to portray a maturity he does not feel and cannot maintain, will his mother respond or will she intensify her punishments? Although trust develops in the children, distrust lingers. In a sense, at the heart of the South End Family Project is the question, "How much can be accomplished by attempts to make restitution to these children for their deprivation by providing *corrective object relation-ships*?"[4] These questions remain for future work.

The emphasis in this paper has been on one trend that needs to be reversed, namely, the tendency to act upon impulse, which, combined with the model of their impulsive parents and the asocial quality of their environment, may predispose the children to future impulse disorder. This tendency has been viewed as an outgrowth of certain developmental deficiencies arising from disturbances in the mother-child relationship. The areas of developmental lag stressed were the dominant use of action rather than words for expression, delays in certain aspects of cognitive development, and the children's difficulties in forming integrated identifications and a firm sense of identity.

DISCUSSION

Dr. Samuel Kaplan:

Dr. Malone has presented us with some striking clinical illustrations of the types of children dealt with in this very much needed, pioneering, and courageous project designed to explore the development of services to a group of highly pathologic families. It is a very rich paper, he touches on many important theoretical issues, and I should imagine and hope that other members of this panel will take up some of the issues that he raises. In initiating the discussion, I am going to focus on one aspect of the paper having to do with diagnosis, since of course the issue of diagnosis must be the important prelude to the issue of prognosis and to the question as to what might be the future of children.

One would expect that children brought up in an

---

[4] Many writers have described this basic therapeutic approach to the young. The work of B. Rank (1949b) and her associates introduced the concept. Alpert (1957) applies it to less disturbed children in a nursery-school setting.

environment described by Dr. Malone would reveal the effect of poor object relationships, that they would show a tendency to act upon impulse, and would thus be predisposed to future impulse disorders. This assumption is in keeping with the large body of psychoanalytic literature, going back to the original work of Aichhorn with his emphasis on the importance of faulty ego and superego development in the pathology of social maladjustment. Such faulty ego development acts as a hindrance to the primary adaptation to reality.

Aichhorn stresses that the impact of internal and external factors which hinder the emotional development of the child prevent him from attaching his feelings to permanent love objects. This then interferes with the second step in the child's social development, that is, the adaptation to the cultural standards of the group. The child is unable to build up the identifications which should help him erect a barrier against the instinctual forces and eventually guide his behavior in accordance with social standards. The gross characteristics of the emotional climate surrounding these South End children in their infancy might lead one to anticipate a major fixation in the stage of primary narcissism, so that there would be a most inadequate transformation of narcissistic libido into object libido. Not only would there be an emphasis on autoerotic pleasures, but there would be an inadequate binding of destructive urges. In such a situation, destructive urges remain isolated and reveal themselves in excessive aggressiveness and wanton destructiveness, attitudes which obviously can be the basis of future delinquency and criminality.

I briefly review these basic psychoanalytic propositions which stress the existence of a variety of social maladjustments which are based on very early disturbances in the development of object love with consequent weakening of ego and superego functionings. However, as has been stressed by Anna Freud (1949), we are also familiar with other forms of social maladjustment with similar symptomatology which have not been based on the early stunting of object love, and are nearer to the neuroses. I am harking back to Dr. Rexford's paper emphasizing the concept of the continuum, and doing so specifically with the thought in mind that this panel is devoted to preschool children where there is a real problem in diagnosis. The symptomatic manifestations in this other group of children consist of eruptions of more or less undisturbed libidinal and aggressive impulses, seriously interfering with the child's effort to adapt to his real environment.

As I read Dr. Malone's description of these three children, and especially the descriptions of Carol and Bobby, I was left with some questions, some doubt as to where they should be classified. Should they indeed be classified under such a heading as "severe impulse disorder" or even "acting upon impulse"? One might even question the applicability to Bobby, perhaps even to Carol, of summary descriptions by Dr. Malone which are indeed, I am sure, applicable to most children in his group; i.e., he says that these children represent "a primitive, poorly differentiated personality dominated by primary process with a narcissistic, need-satisfying orientation toward objects and ego weakness." Carol repeats, in her experience with the children in the nursery school, the essentials of a sadomasochistic relationship set by her mother, does not demonstrate impulsivity except in her great enjoyment of gross motor activity. Furthermore, we note that she demonstrates rather marked compliance in her relationship with the teacher and extraordinary sensitivity to the moods and desires of those around her. She is indeed very pathetic as she makes an ever-constant and often successful appeal for acceptance. During the course of the year, Carol shows substantial growth in various ego functions including a dramatic display of the defense mechanism of "identification with the aggressor," broadening of her interests and of her self-directed play activity. This is a good deal of improvement to see in a relatively short period of time, about a year, in a child who is presumed to be as deficient in her object relationships as we would be led to anticipate from the nature of the emotional climate in which she was reared.

There is, indeed, not too much evidence of impulsivity, except for the fact that she grabbed toys in a highly provocative manner and was continually in motion during her early days at the school. I suspect that this might be the result of her heightened anxiety in the new school situation, coupled with her obvious pleasure in larger motor activity. Her impulse to grab seems to be a direct function of the sadomasochistic orientation, leading her to become the object of attack.

There is a question that one might ask concerning the autoerotic activities of which one should see more evidence in these children and which is not demonstrated in their usual forms. I would here ask the question whether the impulsive motor behavior is just this kind of manifestation of autoerotism.

To shift over for a moment to Bobby, he impresses me as a restricted, inhibited, anxiety-ridden child who openly and obviously displaces his fear of his mother to animals and to other adults. His restlessness is the counterpart of his controlled inactivity, that is, both are expressions of his extreme tension. Episodes of destructive aggression were real, were in response to frustration, and thus were appropriate in direction even if extreme in amplitude. He shows an active identification with his mother's devalued image of him, and initially relates to his teacher as he relates to his mother, that is, with fear and distrust. There again was little in the vignette to suggest impulsivity. Rather he demonstrates reaction formations, marked constriction, and, as Dr. Malone states, an empty and meaningless socialization. In the therapeutic atmosphere of this excellent nursery school, there was a lifting of some of the repressions leading to the defiant refusals and increased fearfulness. The core of his very difficult situation was expressed by Bobby in his feeling that compliance to mother's demands is indeed an absolute requirement for his survival.

How can we then classify the disturbances that these

children do manifest? Since this symposium is devoted to a developmental approach to problems of acting out, and especially since in the first section we were dealing with preschool children, it is germane to reflect on the deviations demonstrated by these children in the light of the period of normal social maladjustment. We are familiar with those emotional upsets in the life of the young child resulting from the impact of the environment, that is, the immediate family, friends, and neighbors. In so far as they are applied before there is a full development of the sense of reality and the capacity for understanding the environment and its rules, such behavior cannot be classified as asocial. While the child is still dominated or heavily influenced by the processes of primitive identification, projection, omnipotence, and fulfillment, he is unable to see the environment objectively. He reacts to what he *feels* exists in the outer world rather than to an actual reality; therefore he is unable to accept restrictions, to renounce or postpone wish fulfillment, and he suffers from an over-all overestimation of his own powers. As the ego and with it the sense of reality develops, this inherent social maladjustment gives way gradually to a social adjustment. When these infantile modes of mental functioning, referred to by Dr. Malone as residuals of the primary process, persist beyond their normal time, the behavior based on them is then classified as "dissocial." It is my impression that the children described by Dr. Malone, in so far as their behavior is in any sense asocial, might better be classified under this heading.

In his introductory section and in his final discussion Dr. Malone states: "This paper will focus on the developmental lag, especially the transition to the secondary process, seen in the children in our nursery school." I quite agree with this formulation that the clinical material in these children is more illustrative of, or demonstrative of, a developmental lag and the compensatory adaptive efforts made by these children. Carol, Bobby, and even Susan display a tendency to displace libidinal and aggressive attitudes from the family to the teacher and to the other children in the group. This displacement of emotions creates an unrealistic attitude to the environment and acts as a barrier to adjustment. It is significant that both Carol and Bobby do learn to differentiate between home and school, are able to make contacts with new people on their own merits and not as new editions of mother or grandmother, and thus to profit from this extension of their emotional lives.

What I have been doing in essence is elaborating on a point of view already expressed by Dr. Rexford in her beautiful and most lucid discussion of the range of psychological difficulties which may express themselves in antisocial behavior. It seems to me that Dr. Malone's children illustrate the diagnostic difficulties confronting us in our efforts to evaluate maladaptive functioning of early childhood. Therefore, I will quote one passage from Dr. Rexford's paper, to highlight the problem as I see it. "The children of the two groups [she is here referring to the neurotic group and the asocial group], one with the presenting problems of fears, inhibitions, and learning blocks, and the other with the manifest antisocial problems, could be placed on a diagnostic continuum with well-defined neurosis at one extreme and antisocial character disorder at the other. Though the members of each group could be differentiated from each other, many of the antisocial children did not present the picture of a typical character disorder but rather an admixture in varying degrees of internalization and externalization of their conflicts. Within the antisocial group itself there were readily discernible differences in the pervasiveness of motoric expression of impulses, in the impression of drivenness which they conveyed, in the variety and maturity of their defenses, and in their ways of relating to staff members. Similarly certain of the neurotic children displayed clear evidence of difficulty in controlling their impulses and of a tendency of erupting into action under stress."

Mrs. Beata Rank:

Dr. Malone modestly entitled his paper, "Some Observations on Children of Disorganized Families and Problems of Acting Out." His goal was to explore how much one could be of service to a small group of highly pathological families with only preschool children, living in a skid-row slum area, who never attempted constructively to use psychiatric or social work facilities. The therapeutic work was carried on with the families in their homes and in the therapeutic nursery school.

Dr. Malone's chief emphasis was that the children grow up in an environment in which impulses "are not merely fantasied" but are *real* because they are lived out. He stressed, however, with due perceptiveness, that although the paper focuses on pathology, it would be misleading to emphasize only this aspect of the families. On the contrary, he stressed, "The children are attractive, sturdy, well coordinated, and appealing. They orient themselves quickly to the externals of a situation by virtue of their skill in reading cues."

Dr. Malone aptly notes that the definitions of acting out which have arisen out of analytic practice refer to specific, complex, organized behavior, and are *not* identical with the behavior of the children in his project. He would rather describe them as "acting upon impulses." As formulated subsequently, he felt he was dealing with a primitive, poorly differentiated personality dominated by primary process with inadequate integration by the secondary process, strong pregenital fixation (mainly oral), with a narcissistic need-satisfying orientation to objects, and ego weakness, particularly with reference to the capacity for internalization.

As Dr. Kaplan mentioned previously, it may not be warranted to see in this behavior strong proof of pathology if we take into account that all the three children used as illustrations of this thesis were of preschool age. The children's boundless energy and use of gross motor activity are certainly more conspicuous than in the average child in a more secure environment geared to establishment of more meaningful, more secure object relationships without the anxious expectations of displeasing, of losing love and affection. The lack of trust, the uncertainty of the constancy, the fear of being left are obvious, but not to a degree that hope is lost altogether — and these children were able, with help, to acknowledge the anger and the disappointment of being left.

What has been most evident to me is not that the mothers were detached and "not there," but rather that the mothers' control over their own emotions was shaky and unstable, that the devaluation of the child fluctuated with the degree of her own self-esteem, that she thus transmitted her own worthlessness to the child. What seemed to me to differentiate these children from those who turned out to be "atypical" is that they have not given up "but are desperately trying to conserve mother love by meeting her expectations." (See the numerous examples of Bobby.)

The activities of these children have a driven quality, the main goal being a bid for attention; this attitude hampered them in performing tasks to completion and by the same token impaired the drive for mastery.

Dr. Malone's discussion of the psychoanalytic proposition of development is based primarily on David Rapaport's (1960) contributions, Peter Wolff's illuminating monograph (1960), and Piaget's observation of the development of secondary process. Dr. Malone also pays tribute to Hartmann's concept of the inborn autonomous ego apparatuses. These scholarly formulations are used by Dr. Malone to highlight the significance of the mother-child relationship and the influence of the disturbed mother-child relationships in the three interrelated areas of development: (1) transition from primary to secondary process; (2) process of internalization; and (3) the dominant use of action rather than words.

Dr. Malone has done a superb job of presenting the metapsychological concepts so clearly and succinctly. Still, I cannot suppress a feeling of regret that some of the propositions eluci-

dating his fascinating clinical material were condensed in a
way thay may present a challenge for many a reader to coor-
dinate the clinical and the theoretical.

Dr. Charles A. Malone:

I appreciate Dr. Kaplan's focusing on the question of diagnosis. This area is one of our particular interests. In our work
with these children, we have been trying to come to a better
understanding of what they are like and how they compare
with other disturbed preschool children. I would certainly
agree with Dr. Kaplan, and I attempted to emphasize this in
my paper, that these children do not belong in the category of
the hyperactive, extremely aggressive and destructive child.

In terms of the point about autoerotic behavior, it has been
my clinical impression that these children reveal little autoerotic behavior—less than we had anticipated. And, as Mrs.
Rank has pointed out, they do not tend to withdraw. As indicated parenthetically in my paper, our children do not set
themselves up as independent of people and attempt to gratify
their component instincts directly. Rather, what is striking
about them is that they are very attached to people; they can
never let people out of their sight. The children are very much
influenced by the very real external dangers in their lives—being left or brutally punished by their parents, plus the dangers
in their skid-row neighborhood. Consequently, the children
have this quality of hyperalertness and focus on the outside,
particularly on people. In spite of the fact that our children
apparently do not take in or respond to many external stimuli,
they watch the teacher with great care, and notice everything
she does.

Dr. Kaplan discussed briefly the therapeutic response of
the children in terms of what it indicates diagnostically and
prognostically. First of all, the improvement in Carol followed
a considerable period of careful and skilled work by her
teacher. Secondly, at times of stress, particularly the stress of a
possible separation or disappointment by their mothers, the

children's improved adjustments wash away rapidly. They regress readily and one sees them again relate in a superficial nonspecific way. So the question remains: how solidly can the relationship be built up and to what extent can the children make stable identifications? I did not intend to convey the impression that Carol or the other children are not capable of making identifications, I rather wished to emphasize the imitative quality of their identifications and some of their other difficulties in forming useful and lasting internalizations. Our children readily make identifications, but it is questionable whether these new identifications are enduring. Furthermore, I wonder whether the children are or will become capable of synthesizing their various identifications into a consistent unity or identity. We are hopeful because we feel that the children are very responsive and we observe encouraging improvements.

One final comment: because this paper deals with the children, I have not stressed the obviously vital role of the work with the parents. Here again we have seen hopeful signs, but are uncertain about the extent and stability of the changes. We are particularly concerned, as we provide the children with such unique experiences, whether we can assist the families and the community to provide continuing support for the children's development after they leave our therapeutic nursery school.

OBSERVATIONS OF

DELINQUENT BEHAVIOR

IN VERY YOUNG CHILDREN

David E. Reiser, M.D.

This paper will present some of the findings and impressions derived from clinical evaluation and treatment of a group of fifteen children who were referred to the James Jackson Putnam Children's Center because they were hyperactive, impulsive, aggressive, destructive to an extreme degree. These children were between the ages of three and a half and five years at the time of referral. We speculate that their disturbed behavior reflects defects in ego development which may represent the precursors of delinquent behavior in later years.

The children in this series (thirteen boys, two girls) had been disruptive in home, neighborhood, and nursery school by running away, killing or hurting animals, frequent fighting, scratching, biting, stealing, fire setting, and vandalism. Beyond the potential significance their infantile dissocial behavior may have as an early form of delinquency, we believe that antisocial behavior in the nursery-school years can be distressing and destructive enough in its own right to warrant closer investigation.

Most of the psychoanalytic studies of delinquent children have been based upon experience with children of latency age or adolescence. Dynamic formulations and inferences about the infancy and early childhood years of these children have necessarily been reconstructions, occasionally supplemented by anamnestic material contributed by parents. At Children's Center, with our major focus on the psychological developmental disorders of preschool-age children, we are in a position to study and treat these children and their parents while these decisive developmental crises are actually in progress. Our findings are derived from the child's own verbalization and dramatization of his conflict, correlated with the parents' attitudes and reactions to the child's behavior.

We do not offer these findings as representative of the vast and complex realms of juvenile delinquency, but as a preliminary report of the early years of life of the predelinquent child within our economic, sociologic, cultural clinical sampling. By illuminating some facets of delinquency in the preschool years, our data may contribute to the fuller study of the ontogenetic development of the patterns of acting out in children of different ages, and under varying psychological circumstances.

At Children's Center we are able to observe in preschool children the myriad manifestations of the aggressive instinct as mediated by the ego under widely varying levels of maturation and integration. In our well-baby clinic, for example, we observe how the *newborn*, with his primitive ego structure, makes the imperious claim for direct, immediate, unconditional fulfillment of demands for gratification. Among the children of atypical development, characterized by *ego fragmentation*, we see aggressive drives expressed as a diffuse motor discharge; so low is their toleration for frustration, a constant state of tension and anxiety is created.

Any parent, teacher, or therapist who observes a group of normal preschool children knows there is nothing unique about the findings of impulsive, aggressive, hyperactive, and destructive behavior. Such behavior is anticipated as an aspect of normal development as the growing child struggles to bring his aggressive and libidinal energies under the aegis of his immature but steadily developing ego. Among children of "normal" nursery-school groups, one can observe toy-breaking, stealing, fighting, quarreling, running away, angry ourbursts as some of the manifestations of normal aggression. What distinguishes the aggressive behavior of the "normal" group from that of our "predelinquent" group is that in the former it is more often put to adaptive purposes; is more likely to be neutralized by an admixture of libidinal strivings; is less pervasive, and does not so invade and consume the ego as to leave little energy available for developing an ever-widening repertoire of ego defenses. At the Center it is further possible to trace the vicissitudes of the aggressive drive in children whose defensive system is patterned along neurotic lines, facilitating transformation of the aggression into internalized fantasy forms.

The following vignette will reveal how a dissocial nursery-age child appears at the Center, and how he is portrayed by his parents. We shall need to go beyond behavioral descriptions and seek a dynamic appraisal of the child, as we study his ego adequacy, his styles of handling libidinal and aggressive instincts, and his relationship to his parents.

Danny D. was three years and nine months old when he was referred to Children's Center for "taking off," which his mother specified as "a running away in search of something she cannot find." (Mrs. D.'s slip that Danny was searching for something that she could not find reflected the manner in which the child's acting out is often in behalf of an unconscious need in the parent.) The parents feared it would lead to more severe delinquency in later years, and perhaps problems in school.

Danny began running away as soon as he learned to walk at fifteen months. Mrs. D. tied him with a rope to the fence, but Danny easily freed himself. She feared he would wander into busy traffic nearby. Her routine was to wait twelve minutes for him to return, which he never did, then to call the police. When found, Danny would confront her as if she were the lost one, saying, "Where have you been?"

During the months preceding referral, Danny had been trying to jump out of the nursery-school bus; also he had caught and killed a squirrel. Threats, punishments, and strappings failed to alter Danny's behavior. Stubbornly, he insisted in having his own way.

Danny was the first of two boys born in the mother's second marriage. Pregnancy and delivery were not complicated; he was full term and bottle fed. When Danny was a month old, his father started a game of pulling the bottle out of Danny's mouth until he screamed loudly, whereupon the father would put the bottle back in. Danny's first words were, "No, no," uttered near the end of his second year. Toilet training was attempted at one year, but Danny rebelled. It was accomplished with the help of a baby-sitter during a ten-day period when his mother was absent from the home. The mother claimed that Danny was not affectionate; whatever she offered him, he spurned and went in the opposite direction.

The family lived on the outskirts of town; there were no playmates for Danny except once a week when his mother would import someone. Generally, Danny played alone. When he found some older playmates, he poked them until they sent him away. When he was very lonely, he would "break down and play with the girls," his mother said. Toy trucks were his special love. The father is a truck driver, and Danny tries to copy his mannerisms, his stride, his gestures.

Mrs. D. was an only child whose father died when she was five. Her mother went to work, leaving her to fend for herself, which she claimed was "fun." Her first marriage ended in divorce when Mrs. D.'s mother disapproved of the man because he had a chronic disease.

Danny's father was reluctant to be interviewed; uneasily, he said his life was a "closed book." Eventually, he disclosed that his own father died when he was four. His mother died when he was fifteen years old, which precipitated a series of petty thefts, for which he was adjudicated delinquent, and placed on probation. The father impressed the interviewer as secretive and suspicious about having his son come to the clinic. Quickly he confessed to the episodes of pulling the nursing bottle out of Danny's mouth, and thought that accounted for Danny's present misbehavior. He felt that Danny's lack of friends was no problem, for he himself had grown up alone.

Danny presented himself to his interviewer at Putnam Center by pointing out stitches on his face, and "bleeding on his heel," explaining he had been struck by a truck. Choosing cars to play with, he confused front and back. He discussed his father's anger when Danny throws blocks, and father takes them away and spanks Danny. He described African lions and tigers that bite and eat people, then enacted a series of crashes between large vehicles and small ones, leaving the "engineer" hurt, and the small car safe. He enacted a game of father visiting a playhouse, and Danny hiding the clocks from father. This was followed by a fire fantasy in the playhouse. When the therapist announced the end of the session, Danny pretended to burn the Center down; then he rushed out of the room and hid from the therapist. He impressed the examiner as a rigid, frightened little boy with a tendency to injure himself.

Psychological testing by Mrs. Grace Young revealed an I.Q. of 100 on the Revised Stanford Binet. Carrying a truck into the testing room, he patted it, "He's my good boy." He showed preoccupation with objects falling apart, and pieces pulling off. He tried to pull the tail off a toy cat, and tried to remove test objects stuck to the card. He was confused by the hidden objects test, and disturbed by the figure of the man with a missing leg. Of objects he would handle, he asked: "This can't break?" as he would twist them and bend them double. Of the Home Scene, he observed, "Her crying," and urged, "Let's go find the people," as if restless and anxious to end the test. The examiner felt he was attracted to objects fastened to the test cards, and wanted to set them free.

The parents interrupted therapy after a half year. Danny's behavior became worse; he killed a rabbit and bird, and tried to choke his younger brother with a rope. He slashed furniture with scissors and knife, leaving tiny holes in the upholstery. Not unlike circumstances in her own childhood, the mother absented herself from home, leaving her ten-year-old daughter home. The mother had great unconscious rage toward Danny, but resisted her therapist's efforts to convey it. She deflected attention to the father, who was missing appointments. She claimed he had an important secret, and tried to involve the team in prying it out of him. The team felt that the painful affects the parents would have to deal with carried over from their childhood experiences of death of parents and desertion and were more than they could bear. Choosing not to remember, the parents acted out, and broke treatment.

Even though our study of this child permitted us to observe him directly in the fourth year of his life, we believe that a comprehensive longitudinal study of the vicissitudes of aggression must ultimately go back to the neonatal period.

Our evaluation of Danny's behavior as an expression of feelings of helplessness and chronic anxiety and as an identification with his frustrating parents is more meaningful than the superficial descriptive label of "delinquent runaway." Killing animals was "delinquent," to be sure, but was an effort to do actively what he fantasied would be his fate (to be killed), as he revealed repeatedly during his few months at the Center.

Beata Rank (1949a) provides an orientation for understanding Danny's desperate "delinquent" behavior:

Observation of a group of seriously disturbed atypical young children at The James Jackson Putnam Children's Center . . . illustrate the great importance of the emotional climate of the mother-child relationship within which the infant experiences his early gratifications and, later, increasing deprivations and frustrations. Deprivation is necessary, we said—following the statement of Hartmann, Kris, and Loewenstein [1946]—for the development of the ego, for the differentiation of self and the outside world.

However, every transition from indulgence to deprivation brings tension, which is tolerated only when the child feels secure, confident that indulgence will again follow deprivation. As the child learns to distinguish between himself and the mother, he develops understanding for her communications. The detailed processes of this understanding are unknown; hence we speak of the quasi-mystical union of mother and child, of the dynamic unit that mother and child represent. When the mother herself is a poorly organized personality, narcissistic and immature, though not infrequently extremely conscientious and eager to become a mother, the child's ego has a very precarious existence. It remains largely undeveloped and hence is not capable of organizing and controlling drives (libidinal and aggressive). . . .

It is only when treatment has progressed sufficiently so that ego functioning and reality recognition are strengthened that the *diffuse* explosive motor discharge is gradually abandoned and the child reacts to fear and frustration with more or less goal-directed aggressive and destructive behavior. In other words, only when the child's relationships with others are sufficiently developed do such outbursts assume the form of hostility toward the frustrating person or object [pp. 43-44].

. . . we do not conceive of aggression as an *unmodifiable innate* force of destruction. We surmise that aggressive behavior means adaptation to the surrounding reality, hence is part of ego-organization. We have attempted to demonstrate that it is precisely the structure of the ego which defines the ways in which one expresses the reactions to inner or outer frustration [p. 47].

Although Danny was by no means a child of atypical development, Rank's remarks about the impact of the mother-child unit represent, in high magnification, what is characteristic of any human infant: that he develops the capacity to bear tension and deprivation within the setting of a constant secure relationship with the mother.

Among our series of fifteen children, several were physically separated from their mothers during the first months of life. One was premature, spending the first three months of life at the hospital and in an incubator; another was immobilized for several weeks in a hospital in an orthopedic cast; another spent the latter half of the first year hospitalized for extensive burns; two others were adopted children, living in an institution for several months until they were adopted.

In addition to the actual physical restraints described, there were indications that the mother-child relationship among the other ten children was tantamount to restraint. Mothers generally described these children as "monsters, gangsters—who should be caged." Danny's mother tied him with a rope, while another mother rigged a cage-like arrangement to confine her son, a year and a half old, in a crib. Though we have no objective tabulations to validate this factor, many of these mothers described precocious motor development.

According to Greenacre (1944), the psychological effect of restraint on the child is determined by several factors, especially the conscious and unconscious attitudes of the restraining person. Beres (1952) observes that extreme emotional deprivation in infancy is not only traumatic in terms of its effect upon ego development; it is also a frustrating experience which may set a pattern for the outbursts of aggression in such a deprived child when his demands are not immediately gratified in the later course of his life's experience.

When we speak of character structure evolving out of the interaction of internal forces and outer ones, we include in the designation of "outer reality" the influence of the parents and others who share in the upbringing; we refer to the physical, cultural, and emotional climate; and to adventitious life events as loss, death, separation, illness, injuries.

In reviewing the neonatal period, we found that most of

the mothers recalled that their dissocial child had been hyper-active and unmanageable since birth. Such a finding would not justify the assumption that the overactivity since birth was due to a "constitutional" factor alone free from the influences of interaction with parents. Aichhorn (1925), in his pioneering study *Wayward Youth*, stated that the genetic inheritance was not as decisive as the milieu created by the parents' conscious and unconscious attitudes, as they are evoked by the infant. Kate Friedlander (1945) calls attention to the unfavorable im-pact on ego development when a mother is unable to be consis-tent in the ways in which she gratifies or frustrates the child's instinctual urges during the first years of life. Some mothers of our series of fifteen preschool delinquents imposed bladder and bowel training before the child was a year old. Others showed the opposite extreme, of failing to encourage bladder and bowel mastery at an appropriate time. In some families both parents reacted toward the child as an intruder, a dan-gerous, destructive, and dirty monster.

The child's learning to postpone gratification is a necessary requisite for development from the pleasure principle to the reality principle. Aichhorn considered the main pernicious in-fluences on ego development to be: (1) too much libidinal in-dulgence; (2) too severe restrictions on libidinal indulgence; (3) inconsistencies and alternations between indulgence and re-strictions. He also designated, as early as 1925, the concept of the unconscious parental sanction for specific and general de-linquent acting out, later elaborated by Johnson and Szurek (1952) as "lacunae of the parental superego."

The dissocial children of our study have not reached the chronological or psychosexual level of development basic to resolution of the Oedipus complex; yet what is tantamount to parental sanction of dissocial acting out in our preschool group of children could be considered analogous to "ego lacunae" in the parent. Tenacious residues of their respective infantile neuroses, as unresolved developmental "arrests," seriously im-pair certain aspects of parental ego functioning. This impairment makes them particularly impotent to provide an ego model as a guide for their child in his efforts to master the correlated conflict. A parent who has found it difficult to postpone gratification, bear frustration, anxiety, and tension will find it difficult to help develop these faculties in his child.

Rexford and van Amerongen (1957) investigated the influence of unsolved oral conflicts in four mothers of impulsive, acting-out young children. These mothers' own unmet oral-dependent wishes handicapped them in giving love and affection to their children in a consistent fashion. Feeling that lack of gratification could lead only to intolerable tension and destructive retaliation upon the source of frustration (the parents), these mothers were unable to limit their children in a fashion of graded frustration to tolerate delay and to develop substitutive means for instinctual gratification. These parental problems did not represent active or unconscious sanctions of delinquent behavior, but the mothers' inability to demonstrate to a child other-than-delinquent means to bind tensions and achieve appropriate gratifications leaves the child lacking in a much-needed ego capacity.

The process which Rexford and van Amerongen demonstrated is a graphic model of how an unsolved conflict in the parent can work to the disadvantage of the young child. This process is by no means confined to the mother-child relationship: by the same process, unresolved conflicts in a father can impair his functioning with his child's attempts to master the related conflict. Danny's father was a trucker, having chosen an occupation which permitted him to be on the move continuously. He found it difficult to teach Danny other ways of containing anxiety besides running away. He confided that he considered Danny's climbing the fence and walking down the railroad tracks a great achievement because he himself had run away and rode the rails to a Midwestern city when he was eleven years old. When the therapeutic process generated anxiety in the father, he responded in his characteristic way — in flight from treatment.

In our group of fifteen dissocial preschool children, eight were still enuretic upon reaching age five. Michaels (1955) has called attention to persistent enuresis as the biopsychosocial paradigm for behavior that is characterized by lack of control due to deficiency in inhibition. As we trace the subsequent development of our fifteen children, the fate of enuresis may be a convenient index for delineating a form of psychopathic personality which Michaels describes as having an immature, relatively primitive and undifferentiated personality structure, poor object relationships, high degree of narcissism; guided by the pleasure principle; showing a disturbance in capacity to bind tension or tolerate anxiety; revealing little sublimation of impulses; impaired superego formation with little capacity for feelings of shame and guilt, and a pregenital libido organization.

Speech was relatively a late achievement, as the mothers recalled. This may reflect the mother's greater sensitivity to what her child *does* than to what he *says* and so may influence her recall. We are impressed that our dissocial acting-out preschool children do not find in *playing out* and *talking out* a substitutive alternative to acting out, in comparison to neurotic children treated at the Center. Play for the dissocial children seems to be more serious, and lacking in the libidinal aspects experienced by normal and neurotic children. Greenacre (1950b) attributed the tendency to act out to a distortion in the relation of action to speech and verbalized thought, arising most often from severe disturbances in the second year. Carroll (1954) observes that a child and his mother communicate at first in body language; this is followed by imitative behavior and playful mimicry. Much later, the child expresses himself in group motor play, and then group play with greater emphasis on language. In all play and fantasy, the normal child knows that this is just "make believe." The child does not use language to sample and test reality and action, but acts out complete dramatic sequences, rather than select some detail for symbolic representation. In our nursery-school groups, playing alone is not a manifestation specific to the dissocial child. However, many investigators have reported on the incapacity of latency-age and adolescent delinquents for group play such as participation in sports.

In his review of underlying causes of delinquency, Aichhorn reiterated throughout his case illustrations the role of trauma, usually in the form of the death of a parent. His clinical vignettes reveal how perceptive he was to the young child's feeling of helplessness, of being overwhelmed by the shocking news, and being unable (by virtue of incompletely mature ego equipment) to respond with appropriate affects. This stasis of emotional responses further impairs the experiencing of grief, and prevents the "work of mourning" from proceeding, leaving the beleaguered individual vulnerable to a variety of grief equivalents later in life. In our series of dissocial children, we commonly observe their substitution of hyperactivity and motor discharge in situations where it would be appropriate to feel badly and cry. It was still another of Aichhorn's sensitive clinical observations that acting out was a standard substitution for experiencing painful emotion.

In many of the case illustrations presented by Aichhorn (1925), the death of a parent was a significant if not a precipitating factor of delinquent acting out. His therapeutic strategy in each of these cases was to create a positive transference relationship in which the dissocial youth could feel secure enough to turn the static grief process into an active affective one, to therapeutic advantage.

Among the parents of our predelinquents, we are most impressed by their incapacity for bearing anxiety, grief, and sadness in relationship to their deceased parents. They deny the affect, or manifest its opposite. We feel that they very young child might well be confused by such duplicity. More important, the parental difficulty in bearing painful affects impairs their ability to help develop corresponding capacities in their children, leaving them thus predisposed to acting out *in lieu* of affective discharge.

Kate Friedlander (1945) refers to another factor, somewhat the opposite of the overinhibited emotional response just cited. She considers the adults' display of unrestrained emotions in the form of rages, violence, open sexual scenes as having the same impact as seduction, its significance intensified because the usual pattern in such families strictly prohibits the children from acting out their aggressive and sexual tendencies within the family. Thus, the ego of the very young child is flooded with excitation he cannot discharge, except by acting out.

To summarize the parental influences on the acting out of our young dissocial children, we find that the parents do not fall into any one diagnostic category. Their individual make-up ranges from chaotic borderline personalities with severe ego disorganization to those who, socially and professionally effective, exert their influence in a more subtle and unconscious fashion.

External circumstances. The parents of our dissocial children live in "respectable" neighborhoods. Low- to middle-income groups were represented in our series of fifteen, but none came from families where antisocial behavior was considered a cultural norm.

Although consultation and treatment in our Clinic is available to persons of marginal income, relatively few families from this group sought our help. There is, perhaps, an artifact in our sample, to the extent that our series of fifteen dissocial children belong to parents sufficiently sophisticated to show concern, to seek consultation, and to regard their child's dissocial behavior as something treatable, if not understandable. These parents have, as a rule, a stable working history and generally are law-abiding citizens. We have noted that the only clinic patients who consistently park in a well-marked area restricted for staff physicians (out-of-bounds for parents) are the fathers of our dissocial children.

Internal characteristics. Clinical interviews with these parents reveal again and again the leitmotifs of the infantile neuroses, of which they are unaware, and the recognition of which they resist strenuously as long as their child is acting out some part of it. Several fathers in our group reacted to news of serious fire setting by their sons with an offhanded, "Oh, boys will be boys!" as if to dismiss critical clinical understanding of it.

In general, these parents have difficulty promoting in their dissocial child allegiance to the reality principle. They vacillate between indulgence and severe restriction, finding it difficult to appreciate that a certain amount of instinctual deprivation, properly graded and timed, is necessary for social adaptation.

FOLLOW-UP STUDY

In an effort to answer the question of whether there exists a relationship between dissocial behavior of the preschool years and delinquency of latency and adolescence, we conducted a follow-up study early in 1962. From our clinical experience in evaluating antisocial behavior in all three age groups, we developed criteria for selecting from our records those children whose behavior at the time of referral to Children's Center, when they were of preschool age, suggested the potential for later delinquency.

Our criteria were simply descriptive behavioral items which characterize latency-age and adolescent delinquents: running away, killing or hurting animals, setting fires, stealing, frequent fighting, hitting, hurting (scratching and biting), rock throwing, lying. In addition to these *specific* behavioral items, we looked for the presence of one or more of the *general* behavior patterns of hyperactivity, and the description of the child as unmanageable and defiant. Finally, we checked for indications whether the child was disruptive in the community and elicited complaints from neighbors or teachers.

We used these criteria to select from our records a series of thirty-seven children evaluated but not treated at the Putnam Center between 1948 and 1958. (This is a different series from the group of fifteen dissocial children, presently or recently in treatment at Children's Center, referred to throughout this paper.)

Using the same criteria, we chose a similar number of control cases of children in whom antisocial behavior was not *manifested* and for whom we therefore would predict no subsequent delinquency in latency or adolescent years, on the basis of their preschool-age behavior at the time of their diagnostic evaluation at Children's Center. We excluded all cases of childhood psychosis, retardation, and organic brain damage from both groups. Cases were selected by a person not connected with the Center, strictly on the basis of the criteria.

We carried out our follow-up survey to trace the later history of the children in both groups, canvassing the files of those public and private agencies in Metropolitan Boston most likely to be involved with children who "get into trouble." The purpose of this rough screening was to discover how many children had committed acts of such magnitude and repetition which would have caused them to be adjudicated delinquent, or would have warranted such designation had their behavior been known to authorities.

Our prediction was that the children found to have committed offenses in later years would be those from the group which manifested antisocial (dissocial) behavior during early childhood as observed at Children's Center.

For the "delinquency-predicted" group and the control (neurotic) group, the follow-up information permitted classification of each case in one of three categories: (a) delinquent behavior, (b) no finding of delinquent behavior, and (c) family no longer traceable in the metropolitan area. Those classified under (a) were children in residential institutions (having been adjudicated delinquent), committed to the Youth Service Board, listed with the Probation Department (Juvenile Court), or known to clinics and other agencies treating them for delinquent behavior. Category (b) included the children for whom, on the basis of our gross criteria, there was no conclusive evidence of delinquent behavior, which is not to say that all of these children were not delinquent. In group (c) the family was no longer traceable by letter or telephone, leading to the assumption that the family had moved away.

TABLE 1

	Study Delinquency Predicted	Control Neurotic
(a) Delinquent behavior	9	0
(b) No finding of delinquent behavior	17	25
(c) Family no longer listed in area	9	10
Total	35	35

Eliminating the third category, we arrived at the following totals: representing those children in the two groups who were reached by our follow-up techniques	26 $x^2 = 11.2$ $p = .01$	25

The finding that *nine* out of twenty-six in the study group have already committed delinquent acts, as compared to *none* of the twenty-five of the control group, is thus statistically significant.

The following vignettes illustrate some of our findings:

Ronald P. was referred at three years, ten months of age by his private nursery-school teacher, who found his teasing, fighting, and excessive open masturbation a problem. At the time of our follow-up, he was thirteen years old, and, according to a child guidance agency, he was currently creating serious problems through fire setting and sexual play with his sister.

Mark D. was referred to Children's Center when he was three and a half years old by the Family Service Society on mother's behalf, because he was stubborn, had violent rages, and had to be expelled from the neighborhood nursery school. Our next record of him, at age thirteen, revealed that he had assaulted children on many occasions, breaking the arm of one and the leg of another; had maliciously destroyed automobile headlights and tires. At fourteen, he was apprehended for larceny, and at the present time, age fifteen and a half, he is in a custodial institution for incorrigible delinquent boys.

Paul P. was four and three quarter years old when his nursery-school director asked us to evaluate his problem behavior at school. At that time he was starting fights, destroying toys, and disrupting games. At age fifteen, he was committed to the Youth Service Board for repeated bomb scares telephoned in to public gathering places (schools, theaters, restaurants); he is currently placed in a residential center.

DISCUSSION

A logical question arises: what happened to the seventeen children (mostly boys) in the "delinquency-predicted" group in whom subsequently no delinquency was found. The gross nature of our follow-up study did not give us the data we would need in order to give a meaningful evaluation. Our prediction of subsequent delinquency was made on data assembled before any of these children had reached their fifth birthday. We are aware that many modifications may occur during latency and adolescent years. The influence of the school in providing channels for the child's energies and experience was available, as well as a wider range of substitutive, sublimatory activities such as organized sports. Our follow-up data did reveal that among the group of seventeen who did not show the predicted delinquency were various gradations of learning disability as reflected in being held back up to three grades. It will be illuminating to trace in greater detail the ego modifications that came to the rescue of these seventeen children, as well as the variety of environmental factors such as new home, neighborhood, and school which were mentioned by the parents as important therapeutic factors. However, in wondering about the fate of the seventeen wayward preschool children who apparently did not become wayward youths, we should not overlook the striking fact that in nine of twenty-six boys the prediction of later-age delinquent behavior could be made before their fifth birthday, on the basis of a few gross criteria.

This brief excursion into a quantitive follow-up study is an exception, and not typical of our projected future systematic study of precursors of antisocial character in preschool-age children. In conclusion we once again stress Aichhorn's ideas, according to which only a psychodynamic formulation about the dissocial child — with attention given to the balance of the libidinal and aggressive drives, appraisal of ego functioning and object relationships — can give us the understanding of the child as an individual, and provide the starting point for psychotherapeutic ego "re-education." This presumes mobilizing the multitude of developmental "arrests" which will forever remain in the dissocial child as crippling ego defects until treated in the security of a positive therapeutic alliance.

DISCUSSION

Dr. Theodore Lidz:

It is not clear to me if Dr. Reiser is suggesting that a large proportion of future delinquents will come out of this group who have this particular type of disturbed childhood behavior. He made it clear that the converse is not true — not all children showing the particular early disturbances will become delinquent. I ask, because in our work with a series of young adult delinquents who come from upper-middle-class and upper-class families, only one or two patients have had this type of childhood disturbance. I tend to believe that more of our schizophrenic than delinquent patients have had a childhood pattern resembling the one described. I am quite certain that most of the delinquent patients in our particular group, perhaps because of the social class pattern, have not been disturbed in this way during early childhood.

There is at least one type of delinquent who becomes antisocial in adolescence, but who had been a very good child in many respects, perhaps even overly conforming. Then, during adolescence or with the onset of puberty, they become quite disillusioned in their parents as objects of identification, and clearly state that, early in adolescence, they stopped being "dopey" — "dopey" or some similar term meaning "being taken in by their parents." They found out that their parents could not be trusted; there was a marked discrepancy between their parents' words and deeds; the parents were utilizing the child; they were acting out themselves, and perhaps really wanted the child to act out. At this time, the youths suffer the object loss that we have been talking about. It is not a tangible loss of the object, but they feel terribly disillusioned and must renounce the parental objects; in this sense, they suffer great deprivation and may develop a nuclear depression which is often masked by the acting out. They may seek to preserve the parental image in one way or another. We know that one superficial pattern of this type is to say, "How can I criticize my mother for being promiscuous or my father for being dishonest in his business when I am worse than they?"

I also was not quite sure if Dr. Reiser was describing a child who was a monster, or presenting the parents' description of the child as a monster. I wondered if Dr. Reiser was describing a myth — a retrospective falsification of the child's earliest years that serves either to reassure the parents that they could not have done better with this abnormal creature, or to express a belief that their child could not be normal, and pathological behavior had been anticipated from birth.

I would also like to ask Dr. Blos who in his paper speaks of precocious ego development, whether he means that this is an innate precocious ego development, or more in line with something Dr. Malone was describing earlier; that is, the children were expected to exert ego controls of a type that they could not possibly carry out at their actual developmental level.

Dr. Gregory Rochlin:

In recent years, increasing attention has been paid to a group of hyperactive children, in the hope that such studies may provide some information on tendencies toward delinquent behavior. Children of this type, although more common than is generally recognized, have been virtually neglected in the past as subjects for study or treatment; as a result, there is little in the professional literature on the subject of hyperactivity. While there are many explanations for the lack of research interest which these children have received, perhaps among the most important is that motor activity in the young child, even if excessive, is more favorably regarded than its opposite. Although the child who is hyperactive may be as emotionally disturbed as the shy inhibited child, the latter is apt to receive more attention than the former. This clinical finding has its parallel in adults. An outgoing, overly vivacious, or even hypomanic adult gets less clinical attention than the withdrawn isolated person.

I shall not review the psychodynamics here since I have done it previously in a paper entitled "The Loss Complex" (1959). My comments then were based upon a study begun in 1945 at the James Jackson Putnam Children's Center in Roxbury. At that time, a group of hyperactive children were collected from among the clinic population. Those children were all under four years of age. The parents complained that the child was incorrigible, overactive, excessively restless, destructive, and not to be influenced by discipline or indulgence. The overactivity dated from the earliest months, and is clearly evident as a rule by two years of age. Such cases are similar to those which Dr. Reiser has presented. There are considerations which suggest that the difficulty which these children show is not in the nature of their conflicts; the conflicts are the result of their problems, not the cause. The causes, I believe, will be found in the character structure of these children.

If we take the hyperactive child as an example of psychopathy, we see that his relationship to people and things as they are related to people shows a serious fault in development. Since the disorder begins early, the fault is best seen as a rudimentary one. Typically, the hyperactive child seems not to have gone beyond the sadomasochistic relationship with people. This characterizes the fault, the conflict, and the behavior. What early superego there is in the young child seems to become arrested in these children. Their narcissistic needs are excessive and seem to be the sole aim of the child's existence. He denies both the needs of other people (parents) and an interest therefore in fulfilling his relationship to them. The hedonism is so great that postponing or delaying gratification seems not to have taken place to an appreciable degree. Yet the narcissism is distinctly different from that encountered in other serious disorders as in autism or the atypical child. There seems to be more movement from the narcissistic libido to the object libido than in the atypical child, but these children do not resemble the autistic ones. One great difference seems to be in their intense sadomasochistic character. To make matters even more interesting, these hyperactive children characteristically have no trouble eating or sleeping. They do not have difficulty in mastering bowel- or bladder-control functions which notoriously become the basis for great masochistic struggles. It is only too evident that aggression is to an inordinate degree involved in the troubles of the hyperactive child. In these cases, it seems that aggression does not become modified or channelized. Whereas in the usual course of development, the eating, sleeping, or bowel habits often are the areas around which there is so much conflict in the disturbed child and are often a basis for an understanding of the difficulties, the hyperactive children seem free of difficulties in these areas. The hyperactive child suffers from a further aberration not typical of any other group of children that I know.

He cannot play consistently, let alone constructively. His sole preoccupation seems to be with destruction. But in his play and in his fantasies he is so distracted — I suggest, by the enormity of his aggression — that he does not develop or work through a fantasy or any way in which he can achieve a mastery over what it is that he may express in fantasy. He flits from one bit of play to another seemingly bent on one object — to fulfill his destructive and self-destructive impulses or wishes. It is evident from this why treatment of such a child is very difficult and hinges upon developing a very hard-to-come-by relationship. These clinical facts point to an early superego fault in which the instinctual wishes are invariably gratified far more than the superego is. These children show the early forms of behavior resembling those of the "psychopath." That such children are asocial is to be expected, and that they should develop into early delinquent behavior would be no surprise. But much more study needs to be done on this group of children whose way of life is hyperactivity: they have no episodes or periods of hyperactivity; on the contrary, this is the way they live. Other children who may have periods or episodes of hyperactivity are therefore not truly hyperactive children in this sense. It is important that the hyperactive child be included in the studies discussed here in this symposium. Some new considerations of asocial behavior may be learned from them.

Dr. Peter Blos:

A wealth of clinical data in relation to acting out has been put before us and each speaker has brought some conceptual order into his material. It seems appropriate at this point to return to Dr. Rexford's paper in which she has clearly outlined the four roots in which acting-out behavior is anchored: (1) oral conflict, (2) heightened narcissism, (3) intolerance of frustration, and (4) inadequate grasp of reality. These characteristics, in gradations of essential preponderance, to be sure, could certainly be observed in all the cases of the children presented in the various papers today.

One striking feature of these cases is the responsiveness and relatedness with which these children react to a benign environment and to a benign human contact. All this was well documented in Dr. Malone's paper. In the acting-out behavior of young children, we recognize the principle of multiple function; Dr. Kaplan has referred to the polarity of active-passive. We must remember that the children described here were subjected from the beginning of their lives to autocratic and inconsistent controls often enforced by neglect, violence, and brutality. The proclivity to action represents partly a protective shield to safeguard psychic and physical integrity and autonomy. Therefore, in acting out, we can recognize various functions: defensive, restitutive, compensatory, and adaptive.

Regardless of the diagnostic categories, the wide range of which has been so well demonstrated by Dr. Malone and Dr. Reiser, another feature of general significance deserves emphasis. I refer to the precocious ego development which was so impressively demonstrated by the clinical material. The ego development of these children progresses out of step with and rather independently of the normal schedule of psychosexual development. We might say that in these cases of young children the epigenetic sequence of mental development is seriously upset. Consequently, the psychic structure shows pathognomic signs of malformation. The ego is forced to take over satiatory and protective functions at a time when they actually still are functions of the young child's environment — the function of the mother. Thus, the child's ego is prematurely forced to develop rapidly in specific and selective aspects. In order to pinpoint the fatal deviation from the developmental timetable, one might say that the ego takes over the self-protective function before object constancy is established and before the internalization of maternal function has taken place. The ego developing precociously in a situation of extreme stress and deprivation remains impoverished in terms of internalized objects and identificatory defenses. Such an ego serves simply and directly the discharge of tension through motoric channels.

The actions of these children preserve a quality of archaic motoric discharge which precedes the symbolic expression of language.

Language development comes after object constancy has been achieved, and after the identification with primary love objects has taken place. If this epigenetic sequence is upset, we encounter malformations of the ego which are clinically observable as unstable, highly ambivalent identifications and as a failure of the ego in its adaptive functions. The form which this ego malformation will take in terms of social development is colored by the particulars of each family situation, which, of course, are legion.

Our effort throughout the papers today has been to single out certain focal aspects which in the majority of acting-out phenomena are of typical significance. The one I shall describe later should be considered along these lines as an ego malformation typical of acting out and anchored in the four characteristics of acting out which Dr. Rexford has presented earlier.

Dr. Lidz and, later during the intermission, Dr. Pavenstedt asked about my use of the term "precocious ego development." I was inaccurate and I think I should share this correction with you. It is this: through Anna Freud's work, we have become acquainted with the pathogenic aspect of precocious ego development. We ordinarily think of it as a precondition for a compulsive-obsessional disturbance in childhood. Of course, this is not what I meant to imply by my remarks.

Children who present a typical precocious ego development master certain social and intellectual skills at an early age, while other ego functons and libidinal positions are in no way commensurately advanced. The selective precocity is usually due to the fact that the environment has given emphasis to them as premium achievements. This condition does *not* prevail in the acting-out child of our discussion. I should therefore not have spoken of "precocious ego development" but rather of a particular pattern of ego development which is clinically demonstrable and has been described in Dr. Malone's paper. His clinical description of the children under study alerted my attention. I was struck by the facility these children develop very early to read cues, to manipulate the environment, to know well what other people like, dislike or fear, how to present themselves endearingly if need be, how to get adults into rages in order to effect a response on the level of sadomasochistic object relations. This is the particular kind of precocious ego development I was talking about. It concerns an aspect, a very particular aspect, of the ego. It would be better to use Fritz Redl's term: he speaks of a "hypertrophic ego development" as characteristic of the acting-out child.

THE CLINICAL PROCESS AND
RESEARCH METHODOLOGY

Maxwell J. Schleifer, Ph.D.

The clinical interview has made available data for exploratory and descriptive case studies. Such studies have provided the basis for insights into and theories of human behavior which have attracted students from a wide range of professional fields. Several of these professional groups have adapted aspects of the clinical interview as one of their major research devices. However, when the clinician attempts to use the data derived from the clinical process for more systematic examination of clinical hypotheses, he is apt to be seriously questioned. Professional persons most experienced in work with the experimental research model often indicate that the clinician either cannot understand or does not respect the requirements of rigorous scientific design. The clinician, having demonstrated his ability to think logically and consistently in the process of carrying out his studies, in turn, is mystified by the demands upon him as he turns to systematic research.

His interviewing methods and theoretical understanding, major skills and undoubted assets for the clinical process activities are considered unreliable as research devices and as most subject to bias and distortion. To meet the requirements of rigorous design, he may be asked to alter greatly his usual style of interviewing and dealing with patients. He then concludes that the subtlety and sophistication of his methods are not understood or comprehended by researchers committed to the experimental model, and he reminds himself that better understanding of human beings and progress in helping people have taken place and will continue to take place without experimental studies.

This lack of fruitful communication between "clinician" and "researcher" has handicapped many serious efforts to examine the clinical process by means of rigorous research designs and obscured the potential contribution of the clinical process as part of an experimental research model.

The main purpose of this paper is to illustrate an approach to integrating the clinical process into an experimental model while preserving the valuable skills and insights of the experienced clinician and to portray the advantages that accrue to this approach.

PROBLEM FORMULATION

A series of clinical exploratory and descriptive studies at the Douglas A. Thom Clinic (Rexford, 1959) and a review of the literature (Johnson and Szurek, 1952) had indicated two specific areas critical in the evolution of antisocial behavior in young children: (1) the issues of gratification, frustration, and control of instinctual impulses; and (2) particular attitudes of the parents toward these issues.

We were interested in developing a research plan that would facilitate the use of data derived from the clinical interaction with families for the systematic examination of the contribution of parental attitudes to the development of antisocial behavior in young children.

To avoid the problems posed by the quantity of data obtained during the clinical treatment of families, we decided to restrict our initial interest to the diagnostic phase of contact with research families. Our usual clinic diagnostic studies had provided us with a great deal of information; they had been clinically relevant and enabled us to sketch the broad outlines of treatment approaches.

In reviewing our past experience, we noted the delays of families with antisocial children in coming to a clinic. Despite early and often prolonged complaints about the child, it had taken unusual efforts by many people to induce these families to call for any assistance. In these families there was a high incidence of discontinuing contact with the clinic shortly after it had been made. Once programs were undertaken, appointments were consistently broken and treatment often terminated prematurely. Thus, it seemed clinically relevant to study factors related to these families' early contacts, to enable us to understand better how to help them continue any constructive efforts they had finally begun.

Next, we attempted to formulate a hypothesis that could be illuminated by the data available from this phase of the contact. We approached this problem by asking what we as clinicians desired to understand about the family from the diagnostic process and tried to make explicit the methods by which we understood and organized our information. We reasoned that integrating these factors into a research plan would enhance our ability to gather, by our research methods, data that would lend themselves to a rigorous examination of a clinical hypothesis.

First, we examined the purpose for which families make contact with the clinic. Families come to a clinic for help with respect to the need for change in the maladaptive behavior of their child. We make no assumptions about the kinds of help or change that they desire or require, expecting that this will be illuminated through the diagnostic process. For example, families with antisocial children quite often want us to intervene with the school, so that they will no longer bring pressure to the family because of the child's antisocial acts in his classroom.

Then we reviewed the considerations that have led child psychiatric clinics to involve parents in studies or treatment.

This common practice derives not only from our need of information from them. We have learned repeatedly how the attitudes and behavior of the parents toward the clinic and the child are crucial in facilitating and maintaining any change in the child.

Our purpose for seeing a child in a diagnostic study is to assess his capacity to use an adult in the process of altering his current maladaptive behavior and rechannelizing his energy in a more constructive fashion. We believe that the ability of the parent to allow this to happen is related to the child's ability to alter his behavior. Thus, we derived a hypothesis relevant to the diagnostic phase: parental response to the need for change in the persistent, destructive, aggressive antisocial behavior patterns of the grade-school-age child is related to the child's readiness to change to more appropriate adaptive and socially acceptable behavior.

DATA COLLECTION

We then examined the nature of the data available to test this hypothesis. Our usual diagnostic sequence contained a joint application interview of approximately one and a half hours with both parents, three individual interviews of about fifty minutes each with the mother, one with the father, three interviews with the child, and usually psychological testing of the child. For the research study, we added three interviews with the father, psychological testing of both parents, a home-visit study, and a neurological study of the child.

We delineated the direct and the indirect observations we could make from such a family study. The clinic team directly observed the family's mode of action around the clinic's activities, e.g., the interviews, the tests, etc. From these reports, we obtained indirect observations about the family's actions and functioning outside of the clinic either in their present circumstances or in the past.

The family's activities within the context and confines of

the clinic gave us an index of the nature of their future activity with respect to the clinic team: such information is crucial to treatment planning.

The indirect observation gave us clues to why the families interacted as they did with the clinic team and an understanding of the circumstances that precipitated the maladaptive behavior in the child. These data were comprehended and interpreted within the context of the family's relationship to the clinic team members. Other researchers had problems in using genetic material because of their inability to integrate it in its proper context. Therefore we decided we would first deal with the family's direct relationship to the clinic team.

It was important to consider factors that would influence the reliability and comparability of data collected by these methods. We recognized that there could be great variations between the content of data collected by different interviewers as well as data collected by the same interviewer on different occasions. We did two things to manage this. First, we standardized the external characteristics of the data-collecting procedure: that is, the original instructions to the families regarding the nature of the diagnostic sequence and of the research project, the physical setting of the interview, the length of time provided for it, and the methods of recording it were the same for all the families. We also arranged that the separation entailed between parent and child in the clinic would occur in the same fashion with each family.

We then turned to the role of the interviewer. All clinic-team members working with these families needed and could use. All families would have to meet and deal with this attitude irrespective of the identity of the interviewer. Thus, we decided that the different ways in which these families react to the interviewer are dictated by their own psychodynamics. "Parental response" and "child's readiness to change" in the main hypothesis were defined in terms of the behavior and feeling toward the clinic team; these reactions then constituted the basic order of research data.

Each of the interviewing situations presented different difficulties in recording. We wished to reduce or eliminate the problems of selective recall and distortion in recording the data. For the interviews with the parent, we used tape recordings. The interviewer also was asked to describe the nature of the feeling and attitude and the covert responses of the family during the diagnostic sequence.

MEASUREMENT

To process the data, we needed a method that would measure interaction, the focus of the study, and also be flexible enough to deal with interaction between two or more individuals so that it could comprehend situations ranging from the individual interview to the multiple situation in our joint application and the home visit.

Measurement methods are particularly prone to misunderstanding by clinician and research methodologist. Measurement methods are intended to organize behavior into categories which are defined so that they can be consistently applied. The labels assigned to the category often have meaning of another sort in specific dynamic theories. In such a case, the data then may be incorrectly interpreted according to the theory, and hence the findings misunderstood.

We adapted the Leary Scale for Interaction (1957) and modified it for our own research purposes. The Leary Scale characterizes interaction in two major dimensions; first, ranging from positive to negative; and second, ranging from active to passive. The two dimensions of active to passive and positive to negative are interrelated and ultimately comprise four categories: Positive active, positive passive, negative active, negative passive.

In our study, these categories identified the adequacy with which the patient's response fulfilled the interviewer's immediate request, and thus characterized the patient's approach and attitude toward the interviewer. These categories do not have direct dynamic or clinical meaning. They may ultimately be comprehended in a clinical framework, but only after the clinical meaning for each category has emerged from application of the scaling to a variety of clinical groups.

1. *Positive-active*, which contained content that was overtly helpful to the interviewer in the understanding of the cases, provided pertinent information and suggested interpretation or opinions in order to further joint understanding of the problem.

2. *Positive-passive*, content which returned to the question asked in an attempt to answer adequately; comments which overtly sought help and which were followed with a demonstration of the use of the help or the help sought; expressions of the agreement which were elaborated, or spontaneous comments that were of respect or admiration for the therapist or things or people associated with the therapist.

3. *Negative-active*, expressions of unalterable principles and opposition to changing opinions, boasting and exhibiting achievements of knowledge, attempts to control the interview situation, to direct discussion away from the therapist's aim.

4. *Negative-passive*, anxiety, guilt, defensive behavior such as withholding, doing and undoing, and defending one's self from blame, masochistic, self-depreciating comments, complaints and expressions of inability to cope with problems.

SAMPLE

For the research study, we selected families in which extraneous factors would not interfere with our aim to focus clearly on the parental role. The families had to be of average intelligence, native-born, to have had the major responsibility for rearing the child, and no specific constitutional handicap. The children had to be of average intelligence, have no major constitutional deficit, and to have shown antisocial, aggressive, or destructive acts refractory to usual disciplinary methods for at least two years.

To delineate the uniqueness of their parental role, we selected for a comparison families with neurotic, inhibited children. The latter group was chosen because these families have handled the problems of aggression and instinctual gratification in a way antithetical to that of our experimental group; moreover, previous studies indicated that the neurotic, inhibited child showed greater response to treatment by child psychiatric methods than the child with antisocial behavior patterns.

To summarize, we had integrated the clinical process within a total research plan. A clinically relevant hypothesis had evolved from examining a clinically explored area, the clinical assumptions of the diagnostic process and the nature of available data. A method of measurement, appropriate to the data and relevant to the hypothesis, had been selected and adapted. Criteria for the selection of groups of patients who would enhance the investigators' ability to test the hypothesis were determined.

To illustrate the contribution of this approach, a segment of data, the parental interview, about one aspect of the total hypothesis will be presented. This sector does not deal with the material about the children or other types of data about the parents. The specific hypothesis for these data was that the parents of the antisocial children would utilize fewer positive-passive interactions with the clinic-team members than the parents of neurotic, inhibited children.

Three sets of findings will be presented: (1) the characteristic of the parents' mode and method of interacting with the therapist; (2) the topics of communication in the various interview situations; and (3) the relationships of patterns of interactions to the areas in which communication takes place. The data will be presented around the four interview aspects of the diagnostic sequence.

Mothers

In the patterns of interaction, although there were specific significant differences in the various categories between the two groups of mothers, there was no consistent differentiation for any category throughout all the interview situations (see Figure 1). There was a tendency for the positive-passive category to begin to develop differentiations over the sequence of the three interviews and in the third interview, for the parents of the antisocial children to show statistically significantly fewer of such reactions. We considered that this might be due to the development of positive relationships to the interviewer on the part of the mothers with neurotic children.

The absence of a specific finding of clear differentiation might have been due to the fact that the topic around which communication took place could influence the way the parent interacted with the therapist. Therefore, the topic of communication was examined. The content of the interview was divided into three topics: the content about the child in the present and the past; the content about the family's present circumstances, excluding the child; and content about the family's past circumstances, excluding the child.

The topic of communication shifted throughout the interview sequence (Figure 2). In the application interview, communication tends to revolve around the child. In the first and second interviews, communication about present circumstances excluding the child became the dominant focus. In the third interview, concern about the child again returned to the most prominant position. Although there were statistically significant differences in the amount of communications between these two groups of mothers, the patterns of the dominant foci were quite similar for both groups.

We next examined the patterns of interaction with respect to the topics of communication. The relationship between style of interaction and the topic of communication differentiated the two groups of mothers. The mothers of the antisocial

FIGURE 1

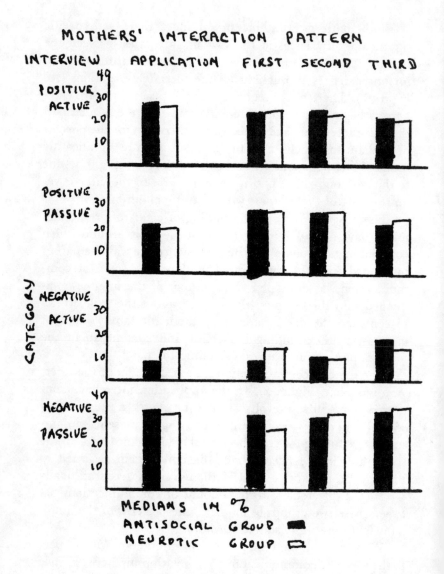

FIGURE 2

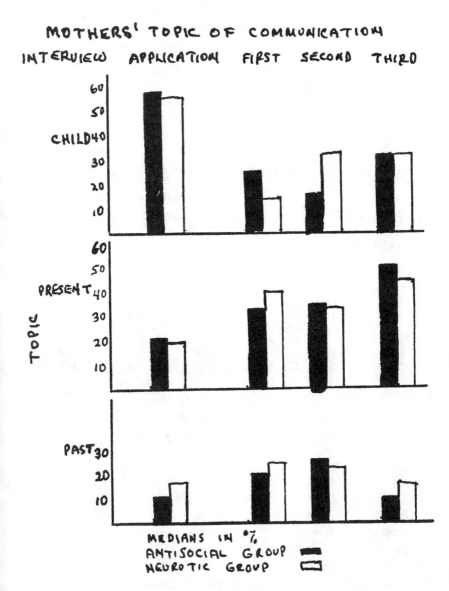

MOTHERS' TOPIC OF COMMUNICATION

children gave fewer responses in the positive-passive category
with respect to the dominant focus of communication of any
given interview (Figure 3). As the focus of the interview
shifted, the positive-passive interactions of the mothers in the
antisocial group revolved around less important areas of communication. This finding indicated their lesser ability to work
with the nature of tasks that the clinic team poses.

FIGURE 3

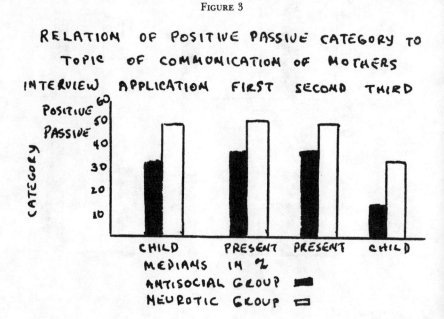

RELATION OF POSITIVE PASSIVE CATEGORY TO
TOPIC OF COMMUNICATION OF MOTHERS

Fathers

Half the fathers in the antisocial group did not have a third
interview, thus making it difficult to assess the meaning of the
findings as part of the sequence and particularly shifted the
potential interpretations of the third interviews.

As with the mothers, no single category consistently differentiated the fathers in all of the interview situations (Figure 4).
The appearance of some trends in the second interview could

FIGURE 4

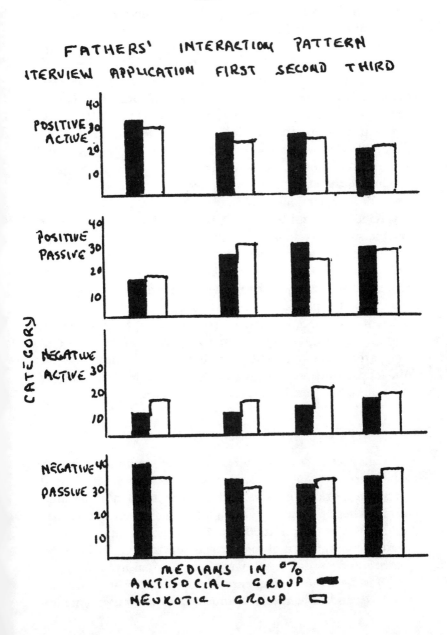

FATHERS' INTERACTION PATTERN
ITERVIEW APPLICATION FIRST SECOND THIRD

MEDIANS IN %
ANTISOCIAL GROUP ▬
NEUROTIC GROUP ▢

not be confirmed due to the large number of fathers of antisocial children who did not have a third interview.

Again we turned to the topic of communication. The communication about single topics did not consistently differentiate the two groups of fathers (Figure 5). Single areas about
the interview situation did differentiate them. The third interview was difficult to interpret because it may have been that
only the most motivated fathers of the antisocial children had
this interview and the least motivated did not. In the first and
second interviews, it was quite striking that the fathers of the
antisocial children talked significantly more about the past,
excluding the child, than did fathers of neurotic children.

The interrelationship of interaction and topic of communication did not consistently differentiate the fathers as it did the
mothers. This again may have been due to the lack of a third
interview with many fathers of the antisocial children. We saw
in the fathers of the antisocial children more eagerness to talk
about the past. Only in the third interview did they show great
interest in the present, and this finding may have been somewhat of an artifact due to the large number of fathers who did
not attend a third individual interview. An examination of all
the parental responses indicated that the role of fathers in the
diagnostic sequence was different from the role of the mothers
and probably must be understood differently.

Discussion

An approach to developing a research methodology which
deals with the problems of using clinical interview data and
preserves the skills, insights, and flexible approach of the clinician has been presented. Findings from a segment of the data,
i.e., interview data of mother and father, were used to illustrate the application of the methodology. These findings described and substantiated part of our original hypothesis.

However, the experimental model did not preclude descriptive and exploratory approaches to the data. Further-

FIGURE 5

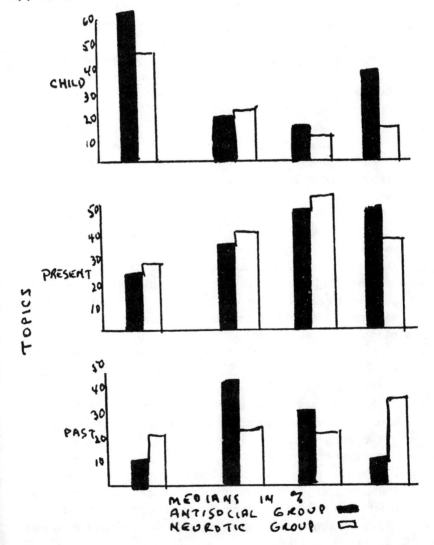

FATHERS' TOPIC OF COMMUNICATION
ITERVIEW APPLICATION FIRST SECOND THIRD

MEDIANS IN %
ANTISOCIAL GROUP
NEUROTIC GROUP

more, a research model must ultimately be evaluated in terms of its contribution to practice, theory, and avenues for further research.

The clinician is usually concerned about the impact of a research plan on the effectiveness of his clinical approach to patients. Early in our study, having previously observed the difficulty that families with antisocial children had in maintaining a contact, we wondered about the effect of an expanded diagnostic sequence. Contrary to our expectation, although eleven fathers with an antisocial young child did not have a third interview, only one family discontinued all attendance after an initial contact.

We thus considered what factors in the research plan contributed to this unexpected but welcome finding. First, we believed the preparation of the family for participation in a research study indicated to the families our sincere interest in them. Second, we continuously reviewed, discussed, and planned each contact with the family; thus we could better anticipate difficulties which might arise and improve the level of coordination among team members. Third, by placing specific and clear limits on the contact and its purpose, we reduced the pressures felt by families with antisocial children and the clinicians who dealt with them. This circumstance increased the willingness of the clinic member to pursue a family if an aspect of the diagnostic plan was not fulfilled. Reducing the pressures on the clinic team and the family created a climate in which careful consideration could be given to a variety of treatment approaches.

Reaching a child-psychiatric clinic is a highly selective phenomenon. We did not assume that these families would react in the same fashion to staff members of other agencies with different functions and goals. We carefully considered conditions necessary for the optimal treatment of the family. We could then meaningfully alter our more usual treatment plans for these families and observe the potential effect of different treatment approaches. These exploratory treatment ventures

enabled us to consider more effectively the particular contribution a variety of agencies could make in dealing with these
families.

Since the diagnostic sequence was our data-gathering
focus, we constantly were examining the purpose and function
of this phase. These considerations directly influenced the
work done by staff members with regular clinic families. The
discussions of the research, moreover, enhanced the ability of
trainees to see diagnosis as a purposeful, active process rather
than as a passive, data-gathering device. In this investigation,
we started with global assumptions about the diagnostic sequence. Our first description of the data forced us to re-
examine these assumptions. This, in turn, enabled us to describe more effectively the groups compared.

The families in our study did not differ in over-all patterns
of interaction in the diagnostic process or in the topics of communication. An examination of the topics for communication
began to circumscribe particular tasks that the clinician posed
for the family. That is, in the joint application interview, the
family was requested to describe what led them to come for
help for their child. In the first individual interview, one attempted to discover something about the parent as an individual; in the second, to examine some of his past functioning
that would help us understand his present action; and in the
final interview, to see whether the parent could organize this
understanding in terms of making effective plans with respect
to the child.

In examining our data, we noted that often our
experienced interviewers elicited interaction patterns in the
third interview which the less experienced interviewer did not
elicit until the family conference. The experienced interviewer
seemed to have more deeply ingrained the particular tasks or
functions to be accomplished and the less experienced interviewer did not. The latter had to organize all his material before he could confront the family with the nature of the tasks
with which they would have to deal. This lag often had a

detrimental effect on the family which may be related to the number of fathers who did not come for a third interview. The observation raised questions about the nature and skills of clinical personnel required to deal with and make treatment plans for families with severely disturbed children.

Integrating the clinical process into the experimental model enhanced the functioning of the clinician. Contributing directly to the research tasks by using his skilled clinical approach, he was also provided with an opportunity to subject the clinical process to careful scrutiny. Freed by the tape recording of the interviews, he could concentrate on the ongoing process. The requirements for his dictation were to focus on his own reactions to the families, the nonverbal aspects of the patient's behavior, and the implications of each interview for treatment planning for the family. He was also able to contrast his own reactions with those of several other clinical people who dealt with these people under other circumstances, i.e., psychological testing and home visit. Thus the interview data, still available for clinical case and descriptive study, were enriched for clinical as well as research purposes.

As clinicians we were interested not only in behavior typical of a group and in statistically verifiable patterns but in the behavior of those members of the group whose patterns were atypical. It is clear that all families in the antisocial group did not react in an identical manner and that the pattern for some was typical of families with a neurotic inhibited child. This was true at times for mother or father or child or combinations of these three family members.

We identified four basic continua relating to: (1) family, (2) mothers, (3) fathers, and (4) children. Examining the range of antisocial families, we identified two well-defined groups. First, a group of well-organized families, in which the parents seemed specifically to provoke the nature of the antisocial acts. The mother often played the role of detective and systematically tracked down the criminal deed while "educating the child" in potential future disruptive activity. This group more nearly resembled the families usually described in the child-psychiatric literature. The second is the group of chaotically organized families. The poor control these parents had developed about their own instinctual activity provided a climate in which instinctual activity in the child flourished. In her paper, "Permission, Promotion and Provocation of Antisocial Behavior," (see below) Dr. van Amerongen further elaborates upon these two groups.

For quantification purposes, we have the most specific data on the individual members of the family. We are faced with the problem of statistically integrating data from different sources about any individual member, and then integrating the data from each individual to draw a picture of a family. At present, from the experimental data, we have a segmental picture of the family. We hope to make further headway with this problem by examining the methods which the clinician uses in accomplishing this task. All researchers in human behavior are faced with the fact that at present an understanding of functioning and interaction is derived from data about individual members of the family rather than from direct observation of family interaction. If one tries to get the most comprehensive picture of an individual, one requires data from many different sources under many different conditions. If one aims for comprehensiveness, he risks losing sight of more precise factors and indeed of the uniqueness of the individual. Becoming too precise leads to the danger of losing an understanding of the context which makes the specific factors vital. Further delineation of methods of integrating the data from various individuals into a picture of the family unit would make a great contribution to the work of all professions studying human behavior. It would also enhance our ability to comprehend the data and findings of researchers who focus on different aspects of human behavior using different data sources and conditions of data collection.

To return to our own studies, we feel we can now systematically work with the genetic data from the clinical interview.

Initially, we had decided that a description of the relationship of the parents to the clinic team was necessary to provide the context for comprehending the genetic data. The later success in relating the pattern of interaction to topic of communication was a promising beginning dealing with the content of interaction. By again using clinical understanding to guide the development of methods for processing the content data, we are in a position to determine the relevance of genetic data to particular styles of relating in the diagnostic process and to the development of antisocial behavior in children.

Descriptions of the diagnostic sequence provide a baseline for applying similar methods to the treatment process. Such a step would facilitate not only the examination of problems in developing treatment approaches to individuals with particular clinical entities but also a searching examination of the general concept of "treatability." For example, in a family with an antisocial child, during the diagnostic sequence, the mother included the child in the communication significantly less than all other mothers. Further, only a small percentage of her positive-passive communication centered upon the topic of the child. She concentrated on the past and the present, with a high percentage of positive-passive interaction. After two years of treatment, she has done very well, she looks and feels better, and has taken a new job outside of the home in which she finds great pleasure. However, she wonders if she should remain in the marriage and has done little to alter her relationship to her son or her husband.

Summary and Conclusions

Studies of the clinical process have made and will continue to make important contributions to our understanding of human behavior. Though there are many problems, efforts to make better use of the clinical process in rigorous research can only enhance its contribution. Such a goal will require improving the collaboration between the research methodologist and the clinician. An important basis for such collaboration is the mutual understanding that there is no specific or ideal experimental model for research about human behavior in which the data include material from the clinical interview. There are many styles of dealing with the problems of a research design; the selection of an approach should be dictated by the skills, functions, and nature of the data with which a given professional group has the most experience.

One approach to integrating the clinicians' interests and activities into a research plan has been presented. A decision was made to examine more systematically an area in which the research group had carried out extensive clinical work, i.e., families with antisocial young children. A decision was then made to focus on the diagnostic sequence. By examining and making explicit clinical assumptions about this phase of clinic contact, we developed a relevant, feasible hypothesis. It was then possible to complete an experimental research plan. One aspect of the efforts at measurement was presented to indicate the possibility and importance of developing adequate measurement techniques. It was indicated how the clinical descriptive and exploratory aspects of the research plan were enhanced by being related to an experimental approach. By describing the interrelatedness of the total research plan, we hope that we will encourage other clinicians to enter into research activity with the expectation that their skills will be crucial to the total research design, rather than to a selected phase.

DISCUSSION

Dr. D. Wells Goodrich:

Broadly speaking, Dr. Schleifer has presented us with two related discussions. He has illustrated the feasibility of interdisciplinary research carried out within an intensive treatment outpatient clinic and has stressed the mutual advantages to the clinical process and to the investigative process which derive from such collaboration. His work illustrates the observation that, to be most meaningful, such collaborative research focuses upon problems which are real to the clinician. To this part of the paper, I have nothing to add.

Secondly, Dr. Schleifer has presented us with some data from a carefully designed study which compares the interactional behavior profiles of mothers and fathers of antisocial children in the clinic intake process with behavior profiles of parents of neurotic children in the same situation. Unfortunately, there was insufficient time for Dr. Schleifer to present all of the findings from the large amount of data which has been collected, but enough has been given us to see the kind of contribution which this research represents. To the clinician used to integrating the qualitatively complex totality of information available through the clinical process, such quantitative profiles which take into account only a very limited set of behavioral dimensions are bound to appear disappointing at first. I hope that my discussion — which will refer to other similar studies — using the same general methodological approach in clinical settings — will illustrate the long-range potentials of such research.

Before commenting on Dr. Schleifer's paper, I should like to underscore the shift in theoretical context which has occurred in the program today between the papers which preceded Dr. Schleifer's presentation and his own paper. The earlier papers considered acting-out behavior within the context of the special clinical theory of psychoanalysis. With Dr. Schleifer's quantitative exploratory study, we are now operating within the context of the general psychoanalytic theory of behavior. Whereas the special clinical theory draws upon experience from therapeutic work built up on the basis of observations over the past seventy years since Freud's earliest clinical explorations, the general psychoanalytic theory of behavior — which draws also upon social science, biology, and mathematics—is at present much less clearly formulated and less differentiated. One of the reasons for this is that it has been difficult to discover methods for studying human behavior which would satisfy social scientists, other behavioral scientists, and psychoanalysts as well. Dr. Schleifer's approach illustrates a step in the right direction, although it is well to admit that we are here dealing with only a few global aspects of the ego's interpersonal adaptive functioning. While the clinician inevitably feels impatience with such a crude category of communication as "positive-passive" or "negative-active," the language of the special clinical theory, at least for many years to come, must differ from the language of the general psychoanalytic theory of behavior; the latter must meld with the languages of social science, of mathematics, and ultimately of biology. Actually, of course, if we consult the publications of Timothy Leary (1956) and his coworkers, who devised the behavioral classification system employed by Dr. Schleifer, we see that the term "positive-passive" refers to overt behaviors or statements which indicate commonly understood modes of relating: interpersonal *cooperation, seeking help, asking advice, passive acceptance and submission.*

Dr. Schleifer's research considers the nature of the lack of fit between the traditional clinic intake process and the interpersonal behavior patterns of the parents of antisocial children. For years, clinics have been concerned with the problem of reaching these families and maintaining a therapeutic relationship with them. The finding that the parents of antisocial children do not conform to the expectations inherent in the clinic intake process, the expected response pattern being that of Dr. Schleifer's control group of parents of neurotic children, provides evidence that technical modifications of the intake process are required for parents of antisocial children. Whether such technical modifications can consist merely of altering the form of the clinic intake process for these families, or whether a more radical alteration of traditional ways of initiating treatment would be appropriate has, of course, been the subject of some research in recent years, for example, by social agencies in New York City.

The finding that the average neurotic patient shows during contacts with the clinic an increase in positive-passive inter-personal behavior toward the interviewer is consistent with findings by Erika Chance (1959). She studied a representative sample of the families attending a psychiatric clinic in Phila-delphia using methods somewhat similar to Schleifer's. She demonstrated over the course of the clinic's contact a steady measureable increase in the mother's help-seeking (positive-passive) behavior toward the interviewer. Incidentally, she observed that those mothers who were most extreme in this re-gard, that is, who exhibited the greatest preponderance of such positive-dependent behaviors, had children who were the most inhibited at the outset of treatment in the expression of positive-passive behavior. These children of the mothers who were very high in expressing positive-passive behavior also took longer than the other children before beginning to express such behavior toward the interviewer. A conclusion which can be drawn here is that there was competition between the mother and the child for positive-passive roles in these families and that the child lost out in this competition. One may as-sume also that one of the beneficial effects of the traditional clinic approach for the patient or family with neurotic defenses is the full acceptance of passive needs. To us as clinicians, this is pedestrian everyday experience; to have such information, however, in a reliable quantitative form is a definite contribu-tion to a general interdisciplinary understanding of behavior.

Dr. Schleifer's results seem to me to support the many clini-cal observations that the dependent, positive-passive position for the families of acting-out children is quite intolerable (al-though latently much needed) because of their high degree of insatiability and distrust. The importance of maintaining a reasonable degree of complementarity between the expecta-tions of the clinic and the conscious or unconscious expecta-tions of the patient, in order that the treatment relationship be maintained, was illustrated also by Chance's data on the mutual expectations of therapists and patients in the Philadelphia clinic. She assessed expectations as to whether the patient and the therapist would be giving or taking, friendly or hostile, and what the direction of the shifts over time in therapy would be. She found that the most durable therapeutic relationships were those in which the mutual patient-therapist expectations were most complementary. In these relationships, both patient and therapist expected that initially the therapist would be giving and the patient taking, and that as time passed there would be a shift in the patient's behavior away from hostile expressions to the therapist and toward more friendly interchanges and away from passive behavior and toward more active expressions. An interesting question is whether incongruity in these aspects of role expectations about the therapeutic situation is in some way related to the findings of Hollingshead and Redlich (1958) who documented in New Haven several years ago the high dropout rate of working-class patients as compared to middle- or upper-class patients.

To return to Schleifer's data on the low amount of positive-passive behavior of mothers of antisocial children as the intake process develops, it is interesting that using the same Leary categories of overt interpersonal behavior, Rausch et al. (1959), Dittman and Goodrich (1961) have found a psychodynamically related process in hyperaggressive boys in residential treatment. We have shown with matched groups of normals studied in the same residential situation that normals are measureably different and that these quantitative differences are consistent with clinical understanding about the differences in ego structure of these two groups. For example, Raush et al. studied the interpersonal behavior patterns of hyperaggressive boys early in residential treatment and compared them with their behavior patterns eighteen months later after some clinical improvement had taken place. Whereas the earlier time, the hyperaggressive boys showed three times as much negative active behavior toward adults (boasting, rejecting, provoking, and attacking behaviors) as did the normals, there was a decrease of approximately fifty percent in this type of behavior after eighteen months of treatment. With regard to positive-passive behavior, initially there had been about half as much in response to adults as was observed with the well-adapted boys; after the eighteen-month period, the disturbed group showed a significant increase in positive-passive behaviors. These results support the clinical observation that the acting-out child is initially afraid to express toward parental figures his passive-dependent wishes, but that as the relationship toward the adult becomes more trustful and intense the passive wishes can be gradually tolerated and expressed more openly. As this occurs, of course, the defensive controlling aggressive behaviors (negative-active behaviors) are no longer needed and tend to decrease.

To summarize, the work of Schleifer taken together with that of Chance and of Raush and Dittmann supports the hypothesis that, while the expected patient role in most therapeutic relationships involves at least a tolerance for a positive-passive interpersonal position in the families of acting-out children, this position is experienced as dangerous, and is tolerated with difficulty.

I would like to turn now to another matter upon which Dr. Schleifer's research design and conclusions depend. This is the assumption that there is a substantial degree of similarity between the intake process as experienced by one patient as compared to the intake process as experienced by another patient. I raise this matter because, although we are accustomed to think of an individual as being substantially the same from one situation to the next, we are sometimes a bit skeptical that similar social situations evoke similar responses. Actually there is a small literature which supports such an idea. For example, in an extensive observational study of average children in a Midwestern town, Barker and Wright (1954) also found similar behavior patterns evoked by similar ecological settings. Neubauer and Beller (1958) have reported that different attributes of preschool behavior appear systematically in the nursery school as compared with the interview situation. And in the research cited earlier Raush et al (1959), by means of information transmission analysis, were able to identify statistically which aspects of each boy's behavior profile were more an expression of his individual personality and which aspects of the behavior profile were more an expression of the expectable demand qualities of the social situation. To select three examples at random from this work, Raush et al. found that (a) during mealtimes with a group of hyperaggressive latency aged boys, there was predictably less negative-passive behavior (complaints, accusations, etc.) than was observed in other situations; (b) during breakfast time, the boys showed the greatest amount of friendliness; and (c) during structured competitive games, more hostile behavior was evoked. In the light of these studies, therefore, I feel it is a tenable assumption that the various intake procedures used with these subjects of Schleifer's research in all probability did have a substantial degree of similar influence on both the families of antisocial and the families of neurotic children.

Now I would like to introduce an observation from our study comparing normal and hyperaggressive boys at the National Institute of Mental Health because it raises a question which Dr. Schleifer is in a position to explore further. This is the observation that, using the Leary categories of behavior, the hyperaggressive boys show a much more stereotyped and limited set of interpersonal responses than do well-adapted boys of the same age. One of Raush's most interesting findings was that, after eighteen months in residential treatment, the behavior profiles of the hyperaggressive boys came to resemble more those of the normal boys and also showed less stereotypy and more meaningful specificity of response to social situations. I would think it an interesting question to investigate whether the parents of antisocial children, in Dr. Schleifer's study, will not also show more stereotyped behavior than his control group if he should compare their behavior during the home visit with their behavior during the intake process, the therapeutic situation, and the psychological test situation.

Despite the fact that these very general categories of interpersonal behavior do have some usefulness for comparing widely different situations and widely contrasting groups of families, it is important to recognize the limitations of this methodology. To capture the nuances and subtleties of behavior, which from a technical therapeutic point of view are fundamental, this method is inadequate. What we require in the years ahead for this type of observational research to become more applicable to clinical work are more sensitive classification systems. Typologies of therapeutic interventions and of patient responses are required which are developed specificially for a particular type of patient and for a particular type of therapeutic setting. Edward Bibring's paper (1954) on types of psychoanalytic intervention and K. Eissler's paper (1953) on parameters in psychoanalytic work indicate the direction here. As for attempts to begin phenomenological classification of certain aspects of acting-out behavior, I would refer to the interesting papers by Brenman (1952) and by S. J. Sperling (1953) on teasing.

Several years ago, Goodrich and D. S. Boomer (1958) wrote a paper aiming at classification of therapeutic interventions with hyperaggressive boys which were used by members of the child care staff trained by Fritz Redl. I hope that someday, when such systems as these can be applied with the rigor that has been used by investigators using the Leary method, we will then begin to realize more clearly the potential contribution of behavior research to clinical work.

The quantification of activity patterns as they exist in the clinical situation tends to support or call into question clinical hypotheses. Dr. Schleifer's paper brings into focus technical problems related to the intake process to wrestle with as clinicians; the paper suggests as well some theoretical problems for behavioral scientists. I believe that students of human behavior have intended to avoid taxonomic, detailed, descriptive classifications. We have often been seduced too soon into the experimental model before we really knew enough about the natural situations to create meaningful experiments. Greater concern with the richness and detail of clinical phenomena collected in the manner of the naturalist is required. Therefore, I congratulate Dr. Schleifer, Dr. Rexford, and the Thom Clinic for taking steps toward precise analysis of the behavior patterns which are the warp and woof of our clinical work.

Dr. George E. Gardner:

I am very much interested, Dr. Schleifer, in the problem presented in securing the cooperation of families in research of this sort and I would like to ask a few questions relative to it.

First of all, I am interested in your comparison group. Could you describe in more detail your neurotic and inhibited children? Then the question arises, when we are trying to do research, what can we give to these people in return for their continued presence as "research subjects"? To put it more directly, did you promise them a treatment service of some type or only a diagnostic study and evaluation of their difficulties? If only the latter, did you promise them as a clinic that you would try to do something for them or try to get further help elsewhere? I am also interested in the problem of selection, or more specifically, in the communications to them in reference to your research plan and their participation in it.

Dr. Maxwell J. Schleifer:

With respect to the question of what we promised them, it has become almost my third principle of research that if you are going to study people, you must give them something and this "something" is what keeps them being studied. We promised them only a diagnostic study, but I think, whether consciously they perceived it or not, we ourselves felt an ongoing concern for them. But we promised them overtly no more than a diagnostic study. I think that this helped rather than hindered the work, because many of these families with anti-social children were enabled to feel that they were not trapped in a never-ending process whereby they would just stay in the clinic forever, but that once the task was mastered, it was over.

Dr. Gardner:

May I talk to this point. My concern is still that we have difficulty getting these beginning clients to cooperate in a purely research-oriented affair. There is another point: if you are working in research in a child guidance clinic and you do a diagnostic study through interviews such as you have outlined, this, in our clinic, is known as the "kiss of death" because we never can get them into any *other* clinic for needed treatment. We can never get any other agency to accept them. If you have an inpatient department, you can never get anybody in one of the placement agencies to place them, even though your inpatient service is full (plus a waiting list), merely because you have already done the diagnostic study. So I am just wondering if you are really able to do much for them after they get through the diagnostic study, and about the degree of guilt that staff members may carry in such a situation.

Dr. Schleifer:

We offered all these people some kind of treatment contract based on what we felt they could best use at that time, and based on our observations of them in the different situations in which we saw them. For example, some of them did well through a home visit and no other approach, so we constructed a treatment program along these lines. Others showed an ability to work with one kind of person rather than another, and so we constructed a treatment offer to them which took this observation into account. What has always interested me about this frequently mentioned research dilemma is that in my experience with this research project as well as others, groups who are ordinarily unavailable in maintaining contact, or unavailable after a contract has been made, are usually *excessively* available to the research approach.

As an illustration, I think of the Judge Baker work on the school phobias. Ordinarily when you get a child back in school, the family leaves the clinic. With your own research project, you did not lose very many. So this is another illustration of how something about the conditions of the research study itself facilitated the maintaining of a contact, and did not lead to the distruption that the clinic team would expect. I cannot give a specific reason for this phenomenon. I have come to believe that it involves the investment which they feel we have in them that makes for cooperation in research studies.

PERMISSION, PROMOTION, AND PROVOCATION OF ANTISOCIAL BEHAVIOR

Suzanne Taets van Amerongen, M.D.

The parents of the children from whom our clinical observations stem belong to a group of approximately twenty-five families which were selected for study at the Thom Clinic. The children referred were mostly boys between six and ten who had a history of persistent and repeated fire setting, stealing, wanton destruction of property, vicious attacks upon adults, siblings or peers, of at least two years' duration prior to clinic referral.

All were white, American born, of at least average intelligence, and in good physical health. They had lived from birth on with their own parents, who were also born in the United States, and who had assumed the major responsibility for the child's upbringing. These families were self-supporting and had their own living quarters, separate from relatives.

The stringency of our criteria for selection was based upon our wish to study and increase our understanding of the antisocial behavior pattern in young children who had not ostensibly suffered from life experiences generally regarded as especially detrimental to healthy character formation.

Through studying the relationships between both parents and their aggressive destructive child, we hoped to come closer to unraveling the role parental attitudes play in the emergence and maintenance of this behavior. It is more difficult to judge the importance of this aspect of the child's character formation when we deal with children who have been exposed to a host of disruptive or adverse external circumstances and traumatic events, or who are faced with developmental tasks which are apt to tax particularly their ability to control impulses.

In none of our families existed the gross economic, social, cultural, or racial factors that are commonly held responsible for antisocial development. Though they all met our research criteria according to the letter of the law, few, it turned out, met its spirit. For instance, our families had their own independent living quarters, but several of them spent most of their time taking care or being taken care of by mother's or father's parents. They were financially self-supporting, but we often found that the husband worked for his father and that the couple lived in a duplex house owned by the wife's parents who occupied the other half of the dwelling and charged our family a nominal rent.

In many families, the child had not been hospitalized for any length of time and had not had any serious operations or illnesses; however, he had repeatedly been rushed to the emergency ward because he had fallen out of his crib at age two, contracted a severe cut at three, or burned himself at five. He was never separated from one or both parents for any length of time, but father worked seven days a week, spent one evening at the lodge, another in the National Guard, a third visiting his relatives; in other words, he was seldom available to the child.

The child was taken care of since birth by his own parents, but mother made it clear that his management was carried out under the grandparents' remote (and often not so remote) control, or the landlord's insistence upon peace and quiet. One mother considered herself lucky in having a succession of ille-

gitimately pregnant living-in baby-sitters who took care of her
son from an early age, while she busied herself with his
younger siblings. It became rapidly clear to us that, in the majority of our cases, father and mother were still heavily
dependent upon their own parents and had strong though very
ambivalent attachments to them. Some had transferred their
attachments to other parent or sibling figures in their immediate surroundings. In many of our families, both parents
seemed to labor under considerable chronic emotional strain.
Due to their preoccupation with and strong emotional investment in childhood attachments, resentments, conflicts, and
disappointments, the marital relationship often impressed one
as singularly barren and void of mature mutual companion-
ship, participation, affection, respect, and love.

I shall now turn to some findings which those of us who
participated in this study have repeatedly encountered and
which we think are relevant to the questions of the genesis and
maintenance of antisocial activity.

Reviewing the circumstances under which these families
came to the clinic, it is impressive that almost all of them felt
forced, and ostensibly were forced, to come because parents
and child were confronted by a very specific crisis situation.
Several children were threatened by court action when their
repeated fire setting caused severe damage to community
property. Others were on the verge of expulsion from school
because the school prinicpal and teacher refused any longer to
tolerate their vicious attacks or because the parents of their
victimized schoolmates threatened to go to the school board to
demand the culprit's removal. In one way or another, the community had "moved in on" the family, had threatened its
status quo, and demanded that something be done about the
child. Despite the fact that the child's disturbed behavior had
been in evidence for at least two years and in many cases was
anteceded by other kinds of difficulties, none of these parents
had voluntarily sought or made any attempts to seek assistance
for either their child or themselves.

THE PARENTS' ATTITUDES

When we consider the first joint diagnostic interview of both parents, with the psychiatrist at the clinic, these parents behave in a remarkably similar fashion. Sitting side by side, father and mother rarely communicate together verbally. They do not interrupt, correct, or disagree with each other; they do not ask each other for support, corroboration, or clarification, except perhaps when it comes to pinpointing specific dates at which certain events in their own or the child's life took place. They passively wait for the interviewer to address the one or the other. While mother is usually visibly tense, father displays marked inertia, often withdrawal, and commonly seems uninterested and bored. The parents interact verbally in a parallel way with the interviewer, but not with each other. Nevertheless, we have the impression that they present him with a united front.

The content of this session centers around a repetitive, often minute description and enumeration of the child's destructive acts and of the various ways in which they, and particularly the mother, have tried to curb his actions. She has punished, slapped, and deprived him, burned his hand on the stove to teach him a lesson, made him return stolen goods to the drugstore. She has threatened to send him away and bribed him with material gifts to no avail. The sum and substance of her depressing, often complaining or indignant review is that she has "done everything and nothing works."

When the interviewer wonders what might motivate the child to behave as he does, both parents in turn blame the bad boys in the neighborhood, the intolerant school teacher, or the troublesome police officer who is "out to get" their child. When we press further for the why of the child's behavior, the parents' tone of voice becomes increasingly whining or defensive. They do not know, because the child says that *he* does not know—or they suspect that he deliberately defies his parents and with malice aforethought refuses to stop his behavior or to let them know the reason for his antisocial activity.

When the interviewer wonders how it is that the parents have not sought help for themselves or their child previously, differences between the ways in which each parent views the predicament begin to emerge. Frankly, father never thought there was much wrong with the boy anyway. Without exception, all fathers in our study have at some time during the diagnostic sequence used phrases such as "boys will be boys." Were it not for the outside pressures, the child would sooner or later have "outgrown" his troubles. "Time will take care of it." Many men feel that their wives nag the child too much. He is all right when alone with the father. As the father emphasizes how the child poses no problem when he is with him, it appears as if it were very important that someone else in the family or an outsider, not he himself, be the target of the child's aggressive impulses. The fathers identify with their child's antisocial behavior; they also played with matches when they were his age. Some speak admiringly about their boys' fearless exploits which they enviously contrast with their own grudging passive submission or outwardly conforming behavior. Many of our fathers are or feel continuously abused by their demanding employers, wives, in-laws, or own parents. They seem to receive gratification from their child's defiance of authorities which they themselves dare not fight openly.

The interviewer increasingly gets the impression that in subtle (and often not so subtle) ways these men permit, even aid and abet, their sons' aggressive destructive activity. One father glowingly reported how he and his son, who set fire to the attic, have been able to improve their living quarters considerably with the money collected from the insurance company, improvements which the family otherwise could never have afforded. Another provided his son with a fancy bee-bee gun knowing full well that the law does not permit children to possess, let alone use, such a toy in the city.

These men are more perturbed about their sons' regressive

behavior or poor schoolwork, but generally show a lack of concern for the antisocial behavior except for its now acute nuisance value.

When, in the course of subsequent diagnostic sessions, we voice our desire to help the child and family and wonder about their wish for continued participation in a treatment plan, the fathers use their jobs and evening commitments as insurmountable obstacles to any form of sustained contact with us. Most of them were able to conform only to minimal and temporary diagnostic demands. Those whose wives and children went on with treatment after completion of the study have stayed away as much as possible. When summoned by us, some have appeared in body, but very few were able to reconsider their attitudes, and others categorically refused to come in, withdrawing increasingly from the family as work with mother and child progressed.

I have already mentioned the mothers' defensive self-justification or negativistic passive helplessness in the first joint session. I shall now discuss some of their responses to the subsequent diagnostic sequence and illustrate our findings with clinical material.

One group of mothers clearly could not tolerate any, even temporary, inroads upon their defensive organization. They had to cling to projection, denial, or passive resistance, and made it increasingly clear that the Clinic should manipulate the community authorities to refrain from interference or intervention since the child presented no problem whatsoever to them at home; or provide them with magical devices which would curb the child's behavior instantaneously.

In the course of three individual sessions with the psychiatrist, they repeatedly complain that things are no better and indicate that, since the child's behavior has not markedly changed since last week's visit, the Clinic is not doing anything for them or to him.

To deny him and themselves certain gratifications, or to have to reflect upon the causes, meaning, and implications of his aggressive destructive acts, proved to be an unbearable task. The community's attempt to block these outlets seriously threatens the family equilibrium. Consequently, the clinic contact represents a further threat against which these women desperately defend themselves by means of massive denial, projection, and stubborn passive resistance.

Prompted by immediate community pressures, the seriousness of the child's misdemeanor, or the parents' resistance against recognition of the emergency of the situation, we resorted in desperation to active intervention in some of the families. In two instances, the repercussions made us uncomfortably aware of the drastic consequences which such manipulations can have upon the tenuous family balance.

One mother came to us with an eight-year-old boy who already was under the jurisdiction of the juvenile court which had requested our recommendations. At first she wanted the court to place her child, but her husband was "dead set" against it. In the course of the study, the child's father reversed his decision when it became obvious to him and to us that his wife was becoming increasingly negativistic at the prospect of having to alter her extremely masochistic and indulgent attitudes toward her son. The mother then became totally unwilling to consider placement which was finally recommended by us and implemented by the juvenile court. A few months later, we heard that her bouts of drinking, which had only been sporadic, had assumed alarming proportions and that she was indulging in blatant adultery in her home practically under her husband's eyes.

To a second family, we suggested as a first step that the parents not delegate the major responsibility for their truanting, stealing, and fire-setting boy to an illegitimately pregnant baby-sitter whom the family had taken into their home. We also intimated that the mother should try to refrain from allowing her son to sleep with her routinely. Shortly thereafter, the child's father called us to help him find a housekeeper since his wife had run off with another man.

A second group of women seem to defend themselves more specifically against awareness of aggression and guilt. They rely heavily upon continuous, slavish, and often ineffectual activity with menial housework or sick relatives in order to maintain their feelings of self-esteem, to assure themselves of their virtue and usefulness in order to counteract passive-dependent wishes and chronic depression. Their dealings with their antisocial child are characterized by inconsistent attitudes and practices. They indulge and infantilize him, but also leave him to his own devices. After things have gone out of hand, they mobilize a variety of drastic countermeasures. It is as if they see his delinquent acts as magically inflicted evil spells, unrelated to their own or the child's feelings or relationships.

When, in the course of their diagnostic experience, we attempt to help them build bridges between feelings, thoughts, and acts, when we try to bring home to them that the boy is driven by his own inner impulses rather than besieged by the devil, characteristic changes in their assessment often take place. They now try to convince the psychiatrist that the child willfully chooses to act the way he does, that he wants to spite them for no good reason, and they substantiate their view by proudly enumerating how they have paid him back in kind in order to teach him a lesson or right from wrong. We have already referred to measures such as burning the child's hand on the stove, sending him all alone back to the drugstore to return what he stole, or depriving him of any and all outside activities.

When we now question their view of the child's cold-blooded evilness, his conscious awareness, and free choice of delinquent behavior, and wonder about the presence of helpless feelings, resentment, jealousy, wish for attention and the like, the picture they paint becomes inconsistent in a very specific way. One moment he is the unfeeling, fearless, and uncontrollable monster, the next the most sensitive, helpless, and lovable human being. Since they have done everything for him and to him, his behavior is probably all their fault.

The recognition that feelings and thoughts motivate one's actions, that love and hatred can exist side by side, cannot but lead to the awareness that this counts for them as well. This painful awareness during the diagnostic study tempted many mothers to discontinue further contact. The rapid transition from massive denial and isolation of affect to overwhelming guilt poses a great problem for the interviewer. Preparation for treatment requires considerable skillful maneuvering. In some cases, the seriousness and persistence of the child's antisocial behavior did not allow for enough time or leeway to establish a supportive therapeutic relationship with either mother or child.

Lastly we have encountered some mothers who present their child's difficulties to us in a peculiarly seductive and enticing way. Since I conducted the diagnostic study and subsequently treated two of these women, I shall illustrate our findings.

CASE ILLUSTRATIONS

Mrs. B. was a shapeless, cross-eyed plain Jane. In the first joint diagnostic session, she settled down with her meek and mousy-looking husband for a lengthy, elaborate rendition of her son's misdeeds. At first, she gave a general description of Jay, eight years old, who for several years has been stealing from stores, the church, schoolmates, and his mother's pocketbook. Also, he repeatedly wandered away from home. He did very poorly in school and was a behavior problem there as well as at home.

As she started talking about his interactions with her, she vividly pictured an intensely sadomasochistic relationship which gradually evolved over the past years between her and her son. Amid gales of laughter, she described how Jay defecated in the living room, and smeared the walls with feces. He hurled obscenities at his mother, while she chased him from room to room brandishing a stick. When he tried to get

out of the house, she locked the doors, whereupon Jay leaped
out of the window. When she refused to let him back in, he
screamed that she carried on with the milkman, so that the
mother rapidly allowed him to re-enter the house because,
though his accusations were false, "what would the neighbors
think?"

The interviewer suddenly became aware of a strong temp-
tation to join in Mrs. B.'s merriment and registered the regressive and seductive quality of this mother's way of presenting
and dealing with her son's alarmingly disturbed behavior. As
the physician maintained a contained pensive and puzzled
countenance, Mrs. B.'s laughter gradually subsided.

Feelings of guilt, shame, loneliness, and insecurity now
came to the fore. In subsequent interviews, she spontaneously
criticized her management of Jay and volunteered that,
probably due to lack of support from her husband and the
absence of her mother, she had been increasingly lonely and
had not been able to be a good mother to him. Mrs. B. defended herself against loss of self-esteem due to rising anger and
guilt as well as increasing anxiety about Jay's aggressive,
destructive, and provocative behavior with denial and regression.

During the diagnostic study, she was able to give up her
denial, to tolerate awareness of depression and guilt, and to respond with a genuine wish for continued help in order to re-
capture a more mature mode of functioning.

Mrs. B. was a somewhat infantile hysterical woman whose
gradual regression and decompensation began when Jay was
about four years old. At this time, shortly after delivery of her
second child, she had to return to the hospital for a complicated gall-bladder operation. A few months after her return
home, her parents who had stayed with the family for one year
and had been a considerable support for her as well as her husband left the country, and ever since then Mrs. B. "has not felt
the same." Jay's hyperactivity seemed to set off complex and
ambivalent responses in Mrs. B. and helped to revive her own

childhood struggles with dependence and independence, control or indulgence, and her conflicting feelings toward both her parents.

Her own history revealed that as a child she had felt that her mother, a substantial woman devoted to the care of her home and children, preferred her older sister to her. She was her father's favorite. Her father, though a good provider, was given to drinking bouts much to his wife's and oldest daughter's anger and scorn. Mrs. B., so she told me, used to look for her father in the local cafés in order to alert him to her mother's ire and help him return to the house unobserved by the backdoor while she distracted her mother's attention.

Mrs. D. and her husband had an eight-year-old son who, after several years of markedly aggressive destructive behavior, set fire to one of the community buildings.

In the application interview, Mrs. D., without much encouragement, monopolized the session. She was an attractive, well-groomed woman, impeccably dressed in clothes more fitting for a cocktail party than a morning appointment at a child-psychiatric clinic. Mr. D. sat by like an obedient schoolboy.

Mrs. D. stated how she has felt for a long time that her son Steven "was doing a lot of things which were of great concern." At the age of four, he had a passion for knives with which he used to make gashes in his mattress, damage the walls in his bedroom, or chase smaller children in the neighborhood. Mrs. D. tried to hide these knives but Steven would always find them. "Steven is not the type of child who will tell you, you have to tell him. You have to know and tell him what he did and then he'll admit it, but he won't just come out and tell you what happened to him, or what he is doing, you have to almost figure it out and then say, 'You did this,' and he'll say 'Yes.' "

To know or not to, to act or not, were recurrent themes in Mrs. D.'s dealings with Steven. She never knew what he was going to do next, but she always expected trouble. These ex-

pectations and suspicions, however, did not lead her to want to
find out the causes of the child's difficulties, or to take adequate preventive measures. Mrs. D. had considered seeking
professional assistance during the knife episodes, but her husband's conviction that Steven would get over his destructive
behavior, which subsequently changed into stealing and fire
setting, was enough to deter her from further action.

As she described her detectivelike dealings with her boy, I
was aware of its compelling, disquieting fascination, as if I
were a spellbound spectator of a mystery play or reading a
thrilling detective story.

In talking about the day of the fire, Mrs. D. said, "That
evening Steven came home late for supper, all excited telling
me about this fire. I don't know, I suppose there was
something in me that made me question him. I called him over
and said, 'What is this on your hands? They look dirty to me.
Were you near the fire?' He said, 'Well, I picked up some of
the things they were throwing out of the building.' I said,
'You're sure you were not near the fire?' never dreaming that
he was or that I thought he was."

The sadistic, enticing, and provocative quality of Mrs. D.'s
interaction with Steven soon characterized her relationship
with the psychiatrist. Triumphantly, one day, she told me how
she had threatened Steven to dress him in girls' clothes if he
once more wandered away, despite her admonitions and implicit instructions to stay within a few blocks of their
house — and she breathlessly waited for my reaction. She
wondered whether to deprive Steven of Boy Scout meetings,
since she had noticed that he was apt to return from these with
money "he found," so he said, "on his way home." She added
that she did not intend to pick him up at the clubhouse though
she might follow Steven by car at a distance to see what he did
on his way home.

She tried to find out by leaving small change or matches
around the house whether he still stole or set fires or had
learned his lesson. In one interview, while intently looking at

my face, she told, beaming, in a challenging tone of voice, how at night she always lay down for a while with Steven because he liked "to be made of." Since maybe she did not give him enough when he was younger, she made up for this now.

Mrs. D. was one of the two youngest girls in her family. She described her mother as a self-centered woman in poor health, and her father as a fastidious, good-looking man who supported his family adequately but displayed little interest in his wife and children.

Mrs. D. had an older brother who was her mother's favorite and was spoiled and indulged by her. He turned into an alcoholic and a psychopath. She was quite close to her younger married sister. Both women conducted riding classes in order to increase the family income and got a great deal of enjoyment and satisfaction out of this activity.

Mrs. D. was quite scornful of her demanding mother but found it impossible to refuse her anything. She resented this woman's indulgence of her alcoholic son and her recurrent demands made at all hours of the day and night upon Mrs. D. in his behalf.

Mrs. D.'s father separated himself from the family at a time when his wife needed lengthy hospitalization. Mrs. D. repeatedly had "to blackmail my father in order to force him to pay" for his wife's support.

Mrs. D. also had a hysterical character structure, but her conflicts seemed to center around issues of control, recognition, and sexual identification. Her son's display of phallic aggression threatened and enticed her. She "egged him on" as he did her, only to "cut him down to size" and expose his helplessness and dependence upon her, which she mercilessly exploited by showing him that she knew more and had more power than he did.

Her husband, a minister, was "all wrapped up" in his church and parish activities. He was afraid to assert himself with his son because, so he said, he had a vicious temper and could kill the boy if he let himself go. As a child, Mr. D. had spent most of his time with older men, friends of his father's, evading his mother and younger sisters at home. We can infer that Mr. D. avoided standing up to his wife also, because he was frightened of her phallic, narcissistic, and castrating retaliation.

SUMMARY

This study did not reveal any simple, clear-cut relationships between the parents' specific individual psychopathology and the child's disturbed behavior. In some families, the mothers suffered from a character disorder, while their husbands presented a neurotic picture. In others, the reverse was true. However, despite the differences in their individual personality structure, the parents seemed united, each for his own reasons, in permitting, promoting, or provoking the child's antisocial activity.

In regard to the children, this study substantiated what many others who have described and discussed destructive, antisocial behavior in youngersters have pointed out. This behavior is not indicative of a specific form of psychopathology. Some of the children had pervasive character disturbances manifested by primitive ego defenses, paucity of object relationships with adults and peers, inability to concentrate, to stick to any sustained or constructive activity for any length of time, tenuous reality testing, and marked disorganization and lack of impulse control. Other boys, despite this behavior, showed a predominantly neurotic picture. But all youngsters, without exception, had manifested at an earlier age several of a variety of other symptoms such as marked hyperactivity, accident proneness, learning difficulties, immaturity, and a propensity for regression.

The community crisis which brought them and their parents to us brought to light that in some of these families acting out was a familial mode of instinct gratification, tension relief, and rebellious self-assertion. For other parents, action and

activity were signs of independence and health and represented their own defense against passivity, dependency, and depression. Its destructive result was to them a matter of bad luck
which in time would reverse itself by magic or would be
channeled into constructive powers through exhortations or
retaliatory counteractivity. In still other parents, the boys'
manifestations of dependent needs, of aggressive and sexual
drives strongly reactivated their own conflicts over instinct
gratification, frustration, and control. The parents' conflicts
and ambivalence prevented them or interfered with their ability to help the child attain age-appropriate and effective ways
of managing the aggressive and sexual impulses. The latter's
display of overt aggressive destructive behavior in turn further
eroded particularly the mothers' defenses, thus prompting regression in her and promoting an increasingly abrasive interaction between mother and child.

DISCUSSION

Dr. Elizabeth Makkay:

If I interpret Dr. van Amerongen's material correctly, her
research findings indicate (1) that the antisocial acting-out behavior of a child may be viewed as representing "a familial
mode of instinctual gratification, attention relief, and rebellious self-assertion" and is therefore not considered by the
family as a sign that there is anything really wrong with the
child; or (2) that the acting out of a child may be a response to
various parental needs, such as a need for vicarious instinctual
gratification of the parents and a channel for expression of
hostility toward the child. In the latter instance, the parents
may consciously desire that the clinic change the behavior of
the child. Unconsciously, however, the parents not only need
to promote and provoke this behavior, but they are unable to
tolerate the clinician's attempts to help them understand the
possible relationship between their attitudes, feelings, and actions toward the child and the way in which the child behaves.

In some studies of other types of childhood psychopathology, the focus has been on the function of the child's disturbance in maintaining the neurotic balance of the parents' marital relationship. Here I have in mind some published papers by Bessie Sperry et al. (1958) of the Judge Baker Guidance Center concerning the role that the learning inhibition of the son plays in the marital relationship of his parents. In addition, the meaning and function of the child's disturbance in maintaining the sibling interrelationships are well known. In child guidance clinics, it is so common as to be almost regularly expected that, if one recommends the removal of the disturbed child from the home, one is likely to precipitate a disturbance in the functioning of another child in the family. Usually, this phenomenon is viewed as evidence of the parents' need to find a new channel for expressing their own unconscious impulses and conflicts through one of their children. If this happens, and if we see this second child in treatment, it is equally obvious that the removal of the first child has in some way upset the psychic balance of the second child by threatening his defenses, producing a libidinal loss in that it deprived the second child of an object for his sadomasochistic aggressive and sexual impulses, or causing an ego loss by depriving him of a defensive displacement object.

The second concomitant and collaborative treatment of parents and children with a wide variety of emotional disturbances in child guidance clinic settings tends to highlight the past and the present, the conscious and the unconscious components of subtle parent-child interaction in which one provides the other with the impetus toward pathological modes of reaction. Indeed, much of the literature originating from the research and clinical work of child guidance settings tends to focus upon a delineation of the predisposing and precipitating factors of symptom formation which derive from the parent-child relationship. Defects in ego and superego development in a child have been studied in relation to defects in parental ego and superego functioning.

Our clinical observations leave little doubt that persistent, chronic antisocial behavior in young children is intimately related to, and interacts with, conscious and unconscious components of the parents' personalities, and that much of it may be in response to verbal and nonverbal modes of communication that have become established between them. Edward Glover (1954) reminds us, however, that our object as psychoanalysts doing research is "not simply to account for the symptoms but by the study of the symptoms to establish the disease process giving rise to them and to detect the deviations from normal functions which permit or stimulate the development of the disease." He also reminds us repeatedly in his writings not to neglect to take into account the constitutional as well as the predisposing and precipitating factors which involve interplay between environmental and constitutional factors. If we limit our study to the direct influence of the environment upon the constitutional condition of the individual child, we are apt to leave out of account the most important factor of all, namely, the organized unconscious disposition—the endopsychic (Glover's term) factors which lie between the constitution of the particular individual and the circumstances of his environment.

Because of the lack of data derived from the psychoanalysis of children—and particularly from the analysis of antisocial children—and the relatively few published studies which involve the concomitant analysis of both mother and child, we are forced to analyze the data we can get by other means, such as direct observation, play therapy, and parental and school reports. In the analysis and interpretation of such data, we make use of what psychoanalytic insight we have and thus attempt to make up for this lack. Excellent examples of this method of gathering and analyzing data and demonstrating it value as a research method have been presented in this symposium.

There is a question I would like at this point to put to the panel, and particularly to both Dr. Reiser and Dr. van

Amerongen. This question refers to the data they have collected in their follow-up studies, data which serve to highlight one
of our basic problems — the problem of diagnosis of antisocial
tendencies in young children. The two sets of follow-up data
with which we have been presented appear to contradict the
emphasis which has been placed upon the importance of the
parents' need to permit, promote, and provoke antisocial
acting-out behavior in their children. The follow-up study of
the Thom Clinic indicated that forty-seven out of fifty-seven
antisocial young children had therapy, that thirty-six of the
forty-seven children did not show evidence of delinquent
acting-out behavior in adolescence, and that six of the ten
children who did not receive treatment were also nondelinquent. The follow-up study of the James Jackson Putnam Children's Center showed very similar findings: only nine children
out of the twenty-six diagnosed in early childhood as antisocial
became delinquent; seventeen did not. In both studies the predisposing and precipitating factors in the child's antisocial behavior — at least the acting-out part of it — were strongly related to parental modes of interacting with the child, the
parents' immaturity and inconsistency, and their lack of appropriate child-rearing practices. Is it not reasonable to
assume that the parental personalities, especially the unconscious components, do not change very much in a few years'
time? If that is so, the question remains: how are we to account
for the disappearance of the antisocial acting out in the adolescent children of these parents? Are we to agree with the
fathers who say: "Boys will be boys and he'll grow out of it"? It
would seem that in some ways these boys did grow out of it.
The problem is that we do not understand how they managed
this. We still do not know enough about the symptom shifts
which can and do occur in these children who demonstrate
antisocial behavior in early childhood and latency. We are well
aware that many of the preschool and early latency children
who may be creating havoc in the clinic today will become very
passive and nonacting out in adolescence — right at the time

when one would expect, because of the normal adolescent processes, that the need for action and for acting out would become stronger rather than weaker. We do, however, notice that many of these boys are still prone to other kinds of symptomatology associated with antisocial tendencies, although passivity in many of them may now take the center of the stage. Instead of their earlier overt aggressive action orientation, they seem to become prone to alcoholism, to homosexuality, and to drug addiction. It seems, then, that one of the urgent needs for future study is to follow these children over a period of time so that we can study the varying symptom pictures over the developmental continuum from infancy to adulthood.

It appears to me that many of the problems with which we struggle in child guidance clinic research arise from and evolve around a problem basic to all work with children—i.e., the problems involved in the diagnosis of young children, whether they are of preschool age or in early latency. To discuss this problem here, even though it is a basic one, would be too time-consuming and would only reiterate well-known issues.

Of special importance to this symposium, however, is the question of whether or not, or in what instances, the antisocial behavior of young children should be interpreted or understood in terms of acting out as it is psychoanalytically defined. Perhaps, as Rudolf Ekstein has suggested, it may help us both descriptively and diagnostically if we also use the term "acting up" in relation to childhood behavioral disturbances. Such a term implies the concept of aggressive behavior as a response to frustration with its disorganizing effects upon psychic functioning and development. It does not, of course, eliminate entirely the possibility that some nucleus of acting out is contained within the impulsive antisocial behavior of the child.

I shall conclude my discussion by raising two questions for the panel: (1) the question of how we are to account for the lack of antisocial acting-out behavior during adolescence in a large number of these children; and (2) the question of whether or not we can define all antisocial behaviors of young children within the psychoanalytic concept of acting out.

Dr. Theodore Lidz:

First let me note that there is a similarity between the project at the Thom Clinic and ours at Yale, even though we are engaged in a study of adolescent and young adult sociopaths rather than young children. We, too, have focused primarily upon patients who come from good social and economic backgrounds in order to eliminate the complexities created by poor neighborhoods, poverty, etc. It is of interest that, despite the fact that our patients come from very good neighborhoods, primarily from good suburban settings, these adolescents manage to become members of delinquent gangs or groups, even though it might be somewhat difficult to uncover such delinquent groups in these environments. Conversely, Dr. Chien (1956) at New York University in his study of narcotic addiction among adolescents found that the large majority of addicts even in very bad neighborhoods came from the severely disturbed homes. I would also like to comment on one of the most consistent findings in our study. Although none of the seventeen schizophrenics whose families we studied intensively had parents affiliated with advertising and public relations, four of the seven delinquents have parents in this field. Of course, this may be happenstance, but it may also be significant. It is in these fields that what is said or written has minimal relationship to fact and in which surface display is more important than solidity. I shall not remark upon the standards of honesty in these fields.

The matter of parental "permissiveness" in these families requires careful study. We have been interested in the inability of some parents to set limits for their children, but also in the rigidity of demands for conformity in other areas. Some parents appear to feel that any restriction will provoke uncontrolled hostility or even suicide in their child. They are projecting or transferring their own feelings onto the child. The patients usually seek delimitation and regard the unbridled freedom permitted them as evidence of parental disinterest. While the patients resent demands for strict conformity concerning superficialities, they are puzzled by their parents' blindness to anything deeply destructive.

The problem is, however, complex and very perplexing, particularly the behavior of some parents. Let me tell you of an incident that occurred but a few days ago. We have a youth in the Yale Psychiatric Institute who had stolen a number of cars and had broken into several homes to steal money. He would be in jail if psychiatric hospitalization had not been arranged, or if the parents were not well-known citizens. We were perplexed when we learned that the boy had managed to have a girl sleep in his room in the suburban home for five or six nights, with his parents being completely unaware of it. Now, we tend to keep this type of patient closely confined in the hospital for several months to uncover the depression I have previously mentioned. After the depression is unmasked, the patient usually starts to work meaningfully at therapy. During this period, the boy appealed to his parents to take him out of the hospital, but they insisted that he must remain. On one occasion, the father said, "You'll have to steal something from Occupational Therapy and pick the locks." Well, that is precisely what the boy did. In actuality, it is not at all necessary to pick the locks, for there is ample opportunity to run away on most any day. This youth, however, wished to do things in a dramatic way. The father's advice may just have been a coincidence.

However, a few days ago, it seemed necessary to place this boy in the seclusion area because another patient had reported that the two of them had plotted to demand the keys from an attendant and, if he did not hand them over, they would hit him over the head with a billiard cue and take the keys. It is of special interest that the patient said that he would not have been responsible if the attendant were injured because it would be the attendant's fault for not handing over the keys when they were demanded. I have, however, not reached the point of the story. The boy was confined and, naturally, the patient and his parents were rather upset. The parents were informed of the reason for the boy's confinement, and they became even more disturbed to know that he had considered using violence and injuring an aide. Nevertheless, when they came on their next visit, they were stopped by a nurse who noted that they were carrying a rather large box to take to the patient. They explained that it was nothing of importance, their son had simply wanted the contents of his upper left-hand bureau drawer, so they had brought these things along for him. The box was opened and it was found to contain two heavy door springs, a knife, and several other potentially dangerous instruments. The parents insisted that they had not known just what was in the box; they had simply dumped the drawer contents into it, and expressed surprise on seeing what they had brought. Now, this is a family which we have been seeing weekly in family group therapy and they are unable to explain their behavior or even to think that it was important or had any potential significance. I could cite other examples of similar behavior by other parents and, in our naïve way, we still find it very puzzling.

Just one further item. The problem of defects in superego formation in sociopathic patients is obviously very important and the Johnson-Szurek concept of the superego lacunae in parents who utilize the patients to express their own acting-out impulses constitutes a highly significant contribution to our understanding of the pathology. However, the theory is neither complete nor pertinent to all patients. In our rather small sample of delinquent girls who are sexually promiscuous, the fathers are very weak men with very poor impulse control themselves, and the mothers do not simply have superego lacunae but rather serious superego defects themselves. Every one of these mothers has been notably promiscuous or has been involved in some overt scandle about a previous divorce or divorces, or some other type of sexual acting out. In general, when we scrutinize the family environments carefully, it becomes quite clear that the sociopathic traits of the patient have developed in fertile soil.

TOWARD UNDERSTANDING THE
FATHERS OF DELINQUENTS:
PSYCHODYNAMIC, MEDICAL AND
GENETIC PERSPECTIVES

Dorothy Otnow Lewis, M.D., F.A.C.P., Shelley S. Shanok, M.P.H., and David A. Balla, Ph.D.

While it is reasonable to assume that fathers play an important role in their children's development, surprisingly little is actually understood about the paternal role (Lamb, 1976). This lack of knowledge is especially true in regard to the fathers of delinquents.

There are several possible explanations for our lack of knowledge in this area. One reason may be the emphasis in the literature on the role of the mother. Lamb (1976, p. 1), in an extensive literature review, noted that "contemporary social developmental theorists reflecting, no doubt, traditional cultural emphases (e.g., Briffault, 1927; Demos, 1974; Gorer, 1948; Sunley, 1955; Williams, 1965), had increasingly stressed the role of the mother in the socialization of the child (Bowlby, 1969; Layman, 1961; Tallman, 1965; Williams, 1965)." The

This research was supported by Grant #755-0371 of the Ford Foundation.

mother-infant nurturing relationship was given great attention almost to the exclusion of other relationships in the infant's life.

Another explanation for the dearth of information about fathers of delinquents is that fathers of delinquents are often difficult to find. That delinquent children tend to come from broken homes has frequently been documented (Glueck and Glueck, 1950; Robins, 1966; Stephens, 1961; West, 1969). When separations occur, delinquent children tend to remain with their mothers (Gardner, 1959), making it especially difficult to study their fathers. Even when the father of a delinquent child remains in the home, he is less likely to come to an informal clinical or probation interview than to an official court hearing where a definitive judgment is to be made.

Yet another reason for our lack of information about fathers is a consequence of certain theoretical orientations of many investigators. For example, in "social learning theory . . . the father is not essential to moral development . . . that is, an appropriate model does not necessarily have to be the father" (Grief, 1976, p. 224). According to social learning theory, reinforcement of behaviors can be performed by either parent or by any perceived authority figure. Furthermore, "modeling" (i.e., behaviors learned through observation) is thought to be determined more by certain personality characteristics of the model, such as warmth and nurturance, than by the gender of the model (Mussen and Distler, 1960). Fathers, therefore, need not be studied as a separate group from other reinforcers or models.

Finally, another reason for the relatively meager information available about fathers of delinquents stems from the emphasis in American social sciences on the social environment in the etiology of delinquency (Cloward and Ohlin, 1960; Short and Nye, 1958). It would seem that American social scientists until recently have eschewed genetic studies, considering them basically undemocratic.

In the light of sociological studies, social learning theory, and recognition of the importance of the mother-child interaction, one might ask why it is necessary to study the fathers of delinquents at all. There are, we believe, important psychodynamic, medical, and perhaps even genetic reasons for studying the fathers of delinquents.

From a psychodynamic point of view, according to Freud, the presence of the father, or even the fantasied attributes of an absent father, have effects on the resolution of the oedipal conflict and thus on socialization. Furthermore, the development of conscience (i.e., superego) is considered dependent, in part, on the internalization of perceived parental values. Since, in Freud's (1925) view, men are considered to be of especially strong moral fiber compared to women, the role of the father in superego development is especially important. Also, according to psychodynamic theory, one of the defenses we employ to deal with fear of a forceful individual is an identification with him. Thus, the presence of an authoritarian father can be expected to affect the child's personality development in specific ways.

From a purely physical point of view, as we shall discuss later, the presence or absence of the father often has much to do with a child's health and well-being. The kind of nutrition, protection, and general health that the child experiences is often dependent on the father's presence. Also, the physical effects of an assaultive father on a child may be as important in determining that child's adjustment to society as the psychological effects of living with such a father.

Finally, one cannot ignore the genetic influences of fathers, since every child receives half of his genes from his father. Investigators have in recent years looked at the transmission of certain vulnerabilities from one generation to the next. Genetic studies focusing on the schizophrenic continuum of disorders (Heston, 1970; Rosenthal et al., 1968; Reider, 1973), the genetic transmission of certain kinds of central nervous system dysfunction (Wender, 1972; Cantwell, 1975), and on the heritability of alcoholism (El-Guebaly, 1977) may all be relevant to the study of delinquent children and their fathers.

THE LITERATURE

Probably the imprecise, bland adjectives used to describe fathers of delinquents reflects a well-founded reticence of investigators to describe individuals, most of whom they have never seen. The literature is filled with vague descriptions of disordered households. The Gluecks (1950) referred to chaotic "under-the-roof" (p. 92) conditions and to paternal inability to discipline their children appropriately (Glueck and Glueck, 1970). West (1969) called attention to "disharmonious and inconsistent parents," but asserted "having an unstable father bore no significant relationship to a boy's conduct rating," (p. 95). Nye (1958) stressed the unhappiness of the marriage and the delinquent child's perceived rejection by the parent. Delinquents, she reported, tended to be critical of their fathers' physical appearance. Andry (1960) reported "faulty paternal relationships rather than maternal relationships" (p. 26) to be characteristic of the lives of the delinquent children he studied. Based on a study of delinquents and their parents in which fathers were actually interviewed, Andry reported that poor communication and little love existed between parent and child and that fathers were more to blame for this situation than were mothers. M. J. Rosenthal and his colleagues (1962), in a statistical study of 3352 clinic-referred children, found children's antisocial behavior to be correlated with a variety of faulty father-child relationships including punitive fathers, controlling and rigid fathers, and fathers who imposed early excessive responsibility on their sons. Cohen (1955) regarded the physical and emotional absence of the father as an important influence on the lives of delinquent children. Similarly, Siegman (1966), in his study of medical students, found the absence of a father during early childhood to be an important factor in the etiology of their youthful antisocial behavior. In contrast to these findings, Douglas and Ross (1968) reported no excess of delinquency in homes in which the father had died. Parsons (1947) stressed the lack of adequate sex-role identification for the boy in the etiology of male delinquent behavior.

Others have attempted to delineate particular personality traits in fathers which contribute to their children's delinquent behaviors. Descriptions of fathers' personalities have ranged from their being called excessively passive to exceptionally authoritarian (Duncan, 1971; McCord and McCord, 1959; Milebamane, 1975; Rosenthal et al., 1962). Jenkins (1966, 1968) related different parental personality types to different kinds of delinquent behaviors. These kinds of descriptions have in common a nebulous quality, that of groping to describe characteristics that are hard to document or quantify.

Attempts to collect "harder" data have often resulted in restricting inquiry to certain circumscribed areas of paternal behavior and functioning. Jenkins (1966, 1968), Robins (1966), Jonsson (1967), the Gluecks (1950), and others have called attention to the high prevalence of alcoholism in the fathers of delinquents. Similarly, Guze and his colleagues (1967) found alcoholism to be especially prevalent in the histories of fathers of convicted criminals.

One of the more common "hard data" approaches to the gathering of information about the fathers of delinquents is the study of the prevalence of paternal criminality. This kind of study springs from two different premises: First, that delinquent behavior is a learned response to parental influences; second, that the tendency toward criminality may be inherited from generation to generation. Another explanation for the relative abundance of such studies is that criminality is one of the few phenomena that lend themselves to quantification by virtue of official, publicly available arrest and conviction records. For this kind of study, fathers themselves need not be seen!

West (1969) reported that 38 percent of boys with serious

antisocial behavior had a father with a criminal record. Jonsson (1967) reported that 29 percent of the fathers of delinquents studied had criminal records. In our own studies (Lewis and Balla, 1976; Lewis et al., 1976), 19.7 percent of a random sample of delinquent children had a father with a known criminal record in the state police files. Robins and her colleagues (1975) reported that a father's arrest was the most common predictor of a child's delinquency. Taking into account considerations of heredity and environment, Hutchings and Mednick (1974) studied the prevalence of registered criminality in the biological and adoptive fathers of male criminal adoptees. They found that if the biological father was not criminal, criminality in the adopting father did not influence the child toward criminality. The combination of both a biologically and an adopting criminal father, however, associated with the child's criminality. Subsequently, Kirkegaard-Sorensen and Mednick (1975) reported the combination of a criminal father and a schizophrenic mother to be especially criminogenic for the child. The significance of this finding will be explored following the presentation of our own findings.

The great problem in studying paternal alcoholism and/or criminality is that both conditions cover not only a multitude of sins, but also a multitude of different kinds of behaviors, family interactions, and psychiatric disorders, only some aspects of which may have a bearing on the etiology of a child's delinquency. Clearly, most of the children of alcoholics do not become delinquent and, by anyone's statistics, most delinquents do not have a criminal father. If paternal alcoholism and/or criminality affects the development of a child's delinquent behavior, it is necessary to determine which psychological or biological aspects of alcoholism or criminality produce their deleterious effects and what other factors, environmental and/or biological, may interact with these particular paternal characteristics to produce antisocial behavior in a child. Until meticulous social, family, psychiatric, and neurological studies of the fathers of delinquents are undertaken, the significance of such factors as paternal criminality and alcoholism will remain elusive.

CLINICAL OBSERVATIONS

Our own clinical observations on delinquent children and their families referred to a psychiatrist suffer from some of the same problems we have described in the work of others. With a limited amount of professional time available, children and their mothers received most of our attention, while relatively few fathers were clinically evaluated. Furthermore, clinical observations were based on interviews with psychiatrically referred children and their parents, a sample not necessarily representative of the typical delinquent child and his parents. On the other hand, our observations were made on especially delinquent children and their families and are therefore of special interest (Lewis and Balla, 1976). In addition to interviews, information about fathers also came from court records of social investigations performed by probation staff.

Because so few fathers were actually personally interviewed and information from court records was not uniform, it would make no sense to try to quantify our clinical impressions. Nevertheless, certain kinds of clinical pictures emerged. First, many fathers were indeed out of the picture, having moved to other parts of the country, started new families, or wound up in prisons and/or hospitals.

Of the fathers remaining, only a few were described as well-functioning, competent individuals, supporting their families through steady employment. These individuals were definitely the exceptions. Far commoner was information clearly indicative of serious paternal psychopathology. While excessive alcohol ingestion was frequently mentioned, it was usually accompanied by descriptions of extreme violence, often toward the delinquent child. Several fathers were actually jailed for child abuse. One father, jailed for having severely beaten his son, a brain-damaged youngster, was also reported to have threatened his wife with a gun. Another father was so physically abusive to his wife and children that the children ran away from home and lived elsewhere when the father returned home drunk. Yet another father, known for his violence toward the family when under the influence of alcohol, had received a dishonorable discharge because he had nearly killed an officer. One father had beaten his son with a baseball bat; one father of a brain-damaged youngster had ground the child's head against the floor with his foot. Many of the children of such assaultive fathers were found to have signs and symptoms of various kinds of central nervous system dysfunction ranging from epilepsy to perceptual-motor disorders. By the time the child came to the court's attention as a delinquent, it was impossible to determine the role the violent father might have played in producing the child's neurological deficits. The significance of alcohol in relation to delinquency seemed frequently to be its effect on the release of aggression toward the delinquent child.

Many fathers who were physically abusive had histories of psychiatric disorders other than alcoholism. One such father, in addition to his brutality toward the family, was known to have tried to hang himself. Another father, who disciplined his children by locking them in their room and filling it with tear gas, was known to have been psychiatrically hospitalized as early as age twelve. Yet another father, discharged from a psychiatric hospital just prior to the birth of his son, was reported by the mother to have used the infant like a basketball, throwing him across the room into his crib, seriously injuring the boy. This father was known to burn his other children with cigarette butts at night when their mother was sleeping. Several fathers had been jailed for sexually molesting their children. The multiplicity of ways in which such paternal disorders and behaviors may contribute to the antisocial behavior of a child will be considered at the conclusion of this chapter. Suffice it to say, here, that such terms as "alcoholism" and "criminality" do not begin to convey the kinds of brutal, frightening experiences many delinquent children have endured at the hands of their fathers.

EPIDEMIOLOGICAL FINDINGS

Our epidemiological findings confirmed our clinical impression that many of the fathers of delinquents were seriously psychiatrically disturbed and that this disturbance manifested itself in antisocial behaviors. The epidemiological findings reported below are drawn from several studies regarding delinquency, parental psychopathology, parental criminality, and the medical histories of delinquent and nondelinquent children.

In one study of samples of 109 delinquent and 109 nondelinquent children from the same socioeconomic class matched for age, sex, and race, we found that 7.3 percent of the delinquent children had a father known to one of the two major psychiatric facilities serving the area, compared with 0.9 percent of nondelinquent children. The difference between these two proportions was significant ($X_y^2 = 5.795$, $p < .05$). Many treated fathers had been inpatients. Since outpatient therapy was available to this group, hospitalization can be seen as a measure of severity of psychopathology.

In another study of the parents of delinquents (Lewis and Balla, 1976; Lewis et al., 1976), we found that 19 percent of fathers of delinquents had criminal records in the central files of the state police, compared with 7 percent of the mothers, a significant difference ($X_y^2 = 25.91$, $p < .001$).

From the above data one could determine whether an association existed between paternal psychiatric treatment and paternal criminality. Indeed, we found that of the fathers of delinquents with criminal records, 22 percent also had received psychiatric treatment as compared with 6.47 percent of the noncriminal fathers of delinquents ($X_y^2 = 13.614$, $p < .001$). Clearly, an association existed within individuals between paternal criminality and paternal psychopathology as measured by treatment prevalence.

Up to this point, we might assume that paternal behaviors are transmitted to the child either in terms of a lack of judgment, poor reality testing, etc., or more directly in terms of role models for antisocial behavior. We wondered whether there was a less obvious linkage of paternal maladaptation and delinquency in children. In a previous study (Lewis and Shanok, 1977), we found that delinquent children had more serious and extensive medical histories than did a matched sample of nondelinquent children. Was it possible that paternal maladaptation might be related in some way to the physical well-being of delinquent children? In order to investigate this possibility, we compared the numbers of hospital visits of a sample of delinquent children with psychiatrically treated fathers and the numbers of visits of delinquent children with untreated fathers. We found that the delinquents with treated fathers averaged 18.11 hospital visits through age 16, contrasted with 9.55 visits for delinquents with nontreated fathers ($t = 1.678$, $p = .097$). Visits to hospital clinics were highly correlated with paternal psychiatric treatment, delinquents with treated fathers averaging 15 clinic visits compared with only 4.86 visits for delinquents with fathers untreated ($t = 2.655$, $p = .010$).

Of particular interest was the finding that there was no excess of hospital visits for delinquent children of psychiatrically treated mothers. Thus, paternal psychopathology was more closely associated with the physical well-being of the child than was maternal psychopathology.

We wondered whether paternal maladaptation as reflected by the fact of having a criminal record was related to a child's medical status. We found that delinquent children with criminal fathers averaged 21.4 hospital visits compared with 10.42 visits for delinquent children with noncriminal fathers. The difference between these numbers of visits was highly significant ($t = 2.519$, $p = .014$). Of special interest was the finding that 66.7 percent of delinquent children with criminal fathers had received a head or face injury before age twelve as recorded in the hospital record, whereas only 22.2 percent of delinquents without criminal fathers had experienced such injury. The difference between these proportions was also significant $(X_y^2 = 10.362, p = .002)$.

To our surprise, no significant association was found between maternal criminality and children's medical histories. Again, the maladaptation of the father seemed more closely related to the child's health problems than that of the mother.

We wondered whether the associations discovered between paternal maladaptation as measured by criminality or psychiatric treatment and children's medical histories was artifactual in that the fathers were only identified as criminal because they physically abused their children. In other words, the findings thus far might simply reduce to an association between paternal abuse and injuries to children. Indeed, there was some support for this hypothesis. There was a near-significant association between paternal psychiatric treatment and child abuse $(p = .143)$. No significant association, however, was found between paternal criminality and child abuse. Arguing against the view that the relationship of paternal maladaptation and children's poor health histories was merely a reflection of child abuse was the fact that only three of fifteen criminal fathers were identified in hospital records as having abused their children.

It might be assumed, from the above data, that paternal maladaptation in and of itself was sufficient to predispose a child to delinquency and/or a poor medical history. Such an explanation would be valid only if the wives of criminal and/or psychiatrically disturbed fathers were themselves well-functioning individuals. We found, however, that there was a significant association between paternal and maternal maladaptation. Specifically, in a previous study (Lewis et al., 1976), we found that of 63 fathers with criminal records, 20 (31.7 percent) had married women who had been psychiatrically treated, whereas of 283 noncriminal fathers, only 43 (15.2 percent) had married psychiatrically treated women. The difference between the patterns of marriage of the criminal and noncriminal fathers was significant ($X_y^2 = 8.4$, $p < .01$). Looking now at psychiatric treatment of fathers, of 35 psychiatrically treated fathers, 13 (37.1 percent) had married psychiatrically treated women, whereas of 311 nontreated fathers, 50 (16.1 percent) had married treated mothers ($X_y^2 = 8.03$, $p < .01$). Thus, there was a tendency for both criminal fathers and psychiatrically treated fathers to choose psychiatrically treated women as mates.

We wondered whether criminal parents of delinquents also tended to marry each other. To our surprise, we found there was no such tendency. Furthermore, although psychiatrically treated mothers tended to marry psychiatrically treated men, criminal mothers, unlike criminal fathers, did not tend to choose psychiatrically treated husbands.

Given our emphasis to this point on parental maladaptation and poor health histories in delinquent children, we wondered whether the combination of paternal and maternal maladaptation was especially associated with children's poor health histories. While the number of families with documented paternal and maternal maladaptation in this sample was too small to make statistical findings more than suggestive, one striking finding should be noted. Children with both criminal fathers and psychiatrically treated mothers averaged 13.00 visits to the hospital before age four, while the average number of visits before four for children without this parental combination was 2.95 visits ($t = 2.59$, $p = .011$). The same pattern of multiple early hospital visits was evident in the medical histories of delinquents with both psychiatrically treated fathers and mothers.

DISCUSSION

Our clinical observations coupled with our epidemiological findings suggest that many of the fathers of delinquents are seriously psychiatrically impaired and that this impairment may be even more closely associated with their children's delinquency than is maternal psychopathology. From our findings emerge certain reasonable hypotheses regarding the relationship of paternal psychopathology and children's delinquency.

The psychopathology of fathers of delinquents, while reflected to some extent in alcoholism and hospitalization statistics, often manifests itself in violent brutal behavior. This may explain why fathers of delinquents are more likely to go to jail than are mothers whose psychopathology shows itself in less violently aggressive ways.

What might be the effect of paternal brutality on the child? First the father sets an example of loss of impulse control and of violence with which the child may identify or model himself. Second, paternal brutality, particularly when directed against the child, may engender rage in the child and hatred not only toward the father but also toward other agents of authority such as teachers and counsellors who may remind the child of his father. Some support for this identification or role-modeling interpretation of the effect of the father was found in the association of paternal maladaptation and a child's early age of first offense (Lewis and Balla, 1976). (Many children in a correctional school who require securely closed settings because of assaultiveness toward staff were children who had been seriously battered by their fathers and expressed openly the wish to kill their fathers.)

We have learned from our epidemiological work that disturbed and/or criminal fathers tend to gravitate toward seriously disturbed women. These women are rarely emotionally strong enough to control their husbands' behavior and protect their children adequately. Frequently, the mothers of delinquents are themselves physically abusive to the children and are unable to counterbalance the effects of the fathers' impulsive violent behavior. A not uncommon family history of delinquents is that of a physically abusive father who after several years abandons the household, leaving the already battered children to the care of a distraught, emotionally disturbed, inadequate mother.

Unfortunately, the social milieu in which most delinquent children are raised, rather than bolstering the family by affording structure and nurturance, contributes further to the children's experience of violence and deprivation.

In addition to the psychodynamic problems engendered by a violent father, coupled with an inadequate or equally abusive mother, certain physical effects of life in such a household also may contribute to a child's antisocial behavior. Paternal rages often result in serious physical injury to the child. One need only recall the father who ground his son's head on the floor to appreciate the severity of injuries incurred by many delinquent children at the mercy of their fathers. Neglect by such parents, in the form of failure to protect young children from serious accidents or injuries, also takes its toll in multiple traumata to the central nervous system. That delinquent children as a group suffer more accidents and injuries during childhood than do their nondelinquent peers has been reported (Lewis and Shanok, 1977). Thus the frequent serious injuries incurred either at the hands of an assaultive parent or by virtue of parental inability to provide structure and protection contribute to a child's distractableness, impulsivity, and poor school performance. It is often impossible to distinguish which aspects of a delinquent child's behavior are attributable to the kind of psychological stress to which he is subject in the home and which aspects reflect actual injury to the central nervous system.

No discussion of fathers of delinquents would be complete without a consideration of possible genetic factors relating to delinquency. Studies from Lombroso in the ninteenth century to Mednick in the twentieth century have tried to explore the question of the inheritance of antisocial behavior. Our own clinical observations suggest that delinquency is a broad term applied to children whose behaviors and functioning range from adaptive to psychotic. We have been especially impressed by the numbers of delinquent children manifesting psychotic symptomatology and/or some form of central nervous system dysfunction (Lewis et al., 1973; Lewis and Balla, 1976). In many instances these symptoms of psychotic thinking and central nervous system disorder, which sometimes underlie and influence delinquent behavior, go unrecognized for years, and the child is considered merely obstreperous or sociopathic. We would suggest that if genetic factors play any role at all in delinquency, they are more likely to involve the inheritance of special vulnerabilities to maladaptive behavior in the nature of susceptibility to disorganized thought processes or to attentional and perceptual disorders. Only when such diverse kinds of vulnerabilities are environmentally influenced toward an antisocial set of behaviors may delinquency result. This kind of speculation is in keeping with the work of such investigators as Heston (1970) and Rosenthal et al. (1968) who hypothesized a schizophrenic spectrum of disorders, one manifestation of which was delinquent behavior.

Similarly, there is some evidence that certain forms of perceptual-motor and attentional disorders may in some cases be inherited. The work of Cantwell (1975) and Wender (1972) lend support to such hypotheses. Again, should specific central nervous system sensitivities be inherited, it must be stressed that this is not the same as the inheritance of potential criminality. Rather the vulnerable child may simply be more susceptible to malignant forces within his family or society than the child without such sensitivities. Our previous research suggests that delinquency per se is not heritable, but that the child of schizophrenic parents or the neurologically impaired child is more susceptible to the kinds of family and social stresses that engender antisocial behaviors than is the ordinary child of nonschizophrenic parents.

Conclusion

It would seem that many of the fathers of delinquent children are indeed a psychiatrically disturbed group whose frequent violence, when directed toward their children, has physical and psychological consequences relating to the etiology of delinquency. By setting an example of impulsivity and violence, by engendering chronic rage in the child, and sometimes by inflicting actual physical damage, such fathers contribute to their children's delinquent behaviors. Furthermore, they tend to marry inadequate equally disturbed partners who are unable to counterbalance their husbands' distructive behaviors through consistent mature love and protection. Clinically, many of the fathers of delinquents are as psychiatrically impaired as are many of the mothers. We would suggest that the expression of their psychopathology is more aggressive and socially unacceptable than is that of the mothers. Hence, they are more likely than mothers to be dismissed by society as alcoholics, sociopaths, or criminals, and to be incarcerated. This often leaves their children to the care of seriously disturbed mothers who are unequal to the task of giving their already traumatized children the kind of nurturance and structure they require to prevent antisocial behaviors.

THE CONCEPT OF ACTING OUT

IN RELATION TO THE

ADOLESCENT PROCESS

Peter Blos, Ph.D.

In clinical reports, the term "acting out" is bound to be in prominence. One has, in fact, come to recognize from experience that acting out during adolescence is as phase-specific as play is for childhood and direct language communication is for adulthood. We have come to consider acting out a typical adolescent phenomenon; indeed, the two have become almost synonymous.

Yet, on closer inspection, we realize that loose generalizations and a careless recourse to the concept of acting out are responsible for the extensive use of the term in relation to adolescence. There is no doubt that normal adolescents in our culture show a proclivity to action which is often of such intense and compelling nature that one is tempted to speak of an adolescent addiction to action. Whether the special condition of adolescence either favors acting out or merely gives a predisposition to acting out unbridled reins, this question will occupy us in this paper.

The theoretical distinction between action and acting out will not be elaborated at this point. The essential differences will gain in clarity through the delineation of acting out from the total phenomenology of action and through the investigation of the particular function which acting out assumes during the adolescent period. In clinical work, we must admit, these delineations are not always as easily established as we desire. Often we learn from fruitless efforts in dealing with play acting or uninhibited action discharge that what confronts us is an acting-out phenomenon; from the reverse, we learn a lesson equally well. What differentiates behavioral manifestations of similar appearance but of different structure will be explored in this paper. Such queries will lead to a search for the reasons why the adolescent process tends to promote and favor the mechanism of acting out as a homeostatic device. As a consequence of such explorations, the question will finally be asked whether the concept of acting out in its traditional formulation is too narrow to accommodate relevant adolescent phenomena, and whether it is necessary to expand the standard concept in order to enhance its clinical usefulness without violating its theoretical foundation.

The Concept of Acting Out: A Historical Review

In the concept of acting out we distinguish three aspects: one is related to the *predisposition* to acting out; the other to the *manifestation* of acting out in behavior; and the third is concerned with the *function* of the acting-out mechanism. All three aspects are by no means unconditionally interrelated. Acting out, for instance, can occur without an evidently strong predisposition, as dramatically exemplified during adolescence. Acting-out behavior, then , either can be due to a structural characteristic of the ego, or it might be stimulated and precipitated by an acute life circumstance such as a therapeutic experience or a maturational event such as puberty and adolescence. We can speak of a latent and a manifest aspect of acting out and, furthermore, of a transient and a habitual kind of acting out.

The predisposition to acting out has been formulated by Fenichel (1945), who speaks of an "alloplastic readiness," which appears as the unique involvement of the acting-out person with the outside world. The adversary in conflict as well as the source of stabilizing powers is experienced as external, which in turn keeps the individual in perpetual and excessive dependency on the outside world. Fenichel, furthermore, alludes to the oral modality of impetuousness and urgency and to the concomitant features of intense narcissistic needs and intolerance of tension. Last but not least, he mentions early trauma as a genetic prerequisite for acting out.

Early trauma is no doubt a prerequisite for acting out, but only through the lamination of this factor with other and specific predisposing components does acting out assume its unique quality. One gains the impression that acting out contains little of that special effort to master belatedly a trauma in small dosages by repetition. Acting out by its very nature has forfeited the capacity of mastery and turned it into an act of avoidance. There is a peculiar aspect to acting out which sets it apart from the repetition compulsion of the neurosis. This peculiar aspect lies in defective symbol formation by which normally action becomes replaced or delayed through trial action in thought and fantasy. If memory fails to become firmly and clearly structured through the acquisition of word symbols, then no workable organization of memory exists for an adaptive evaluation of current reality. Under such conditions, the preverbal modalities of problem solving and communication, namely, fantasy and action, remain the only available instrumentalities for coming to terms with a still pressing, i.e., unassimilated, past. In this sense, Fenichel speaks of acting out as a special form of remembering; we might refer to this as the function of acting out.

Greenacre (1950b), among others, has investigated more specifically the predisposing factors which render acting out the chosen mechanism for the reduction of tensions. Greenacre refers to three predisposing factors which have a specific

genetic link to acting out: "a special emphasis on visual sensitization producing a bent for dramatization"; "a largely unconscious belief in the magic of action"; "a distortion in the relation of action to speech and verbalized thought." The latter
disturbance occurs in the second year of life and has to be understood in terms of a defective fusion in word usage of the
thing it denotes and the emotion which is associated with it.
Under such conditions, the function of language has miscar-
ried and the action language of earlier stages continues to
operate side by side with it as a form of communication and
problem solving. Looking at acting out in these terms we recognize that this form of expression constitutes a highly organized and structured mechanism. This is in contrast to the more
primitive discharge process of impulsive behavior about which
we have to say more in the subsequent discussion.

It follows from the preceding summary that the sense of
reality in the acting-out individual is weak and vague; he easily
makes transient identifications and plays roles. Such facility in
changing the self is often remarkable. Carroll (1954) ascribes
this disposition to a rich fantasy life which exists isolated and
by itself, which allows no compromise with reality. Adolescents
of this type will tell you that their fantasies are more real than
anything in the outer world. They accept, consequently, the
outer world only so far as it gives credence to their inner reality; they attack it or they turn away from it as soon as the need
gratification it offers ceases to be in immediate and perfect
harmony with the need tension they experience. This
condition is typical for the adolescent user of drugs.

Let us make more explicit the distinction between the predisposing factors of acting out and the function of acting out
by turning our attention to the function of acting out as a separate topic. Freud (1905) originally used the term "acting out"
in the case report on the first adolescent to be analyzed, namely, Dora. In the Postscript to the Dora case, he referred to her
leaving the analysis with these words: "Thus she acted out an
essential part of her recollections and phantasies instead of re-

producing them in treatment." In other words, Dora took her revenge on the man who had deceived and deserted her. We recognize in this acting out the gratification of a hostile, retaliatory wish. Displacement is the mechanism of defense operative in the acting out which brought the Dora case to a premature termination.

Again, in 1914, Freud used the term acting out in a paper on technique, applying it to the analytic situation, especially to transference and resistance. He said: "We have learnt that the patient repeats instead of remembering, and repeats under the conditions of resistance. . . . We soon perceive that the transference is itself only a piece of repetition, and that the repetition is a transference of the forgotten past not only on to the doctor but also on to all the other aspects of the current situation." These concerns and formulations are intended to illuminate the analytic situation and they should, therefore, be treated separately from the acting out as a so-called symptom —or, rather, a symptom equivalent—which brings many adolescents to our attention.

Acting out within the therapeutic situation requires constant vigilance and scrutiny as to the extent it can and should be permitted to take its course or as to the urgency it has to be curbed lest it affect adversely the adolescent's life and defeat therapy itself. Generally, it can be stated that acting out in the transference or acting out in the service of resistance has to be interpreted or otherwise rendered innocuous. However, there exist other kinds of acting out, as we shall see, which do not require the same measures of interference because they serve different functions and are no threat to the therapeutic alliance.

One further function of acting out has been mentioned by Jacobson (1957). The resistance against remembering effected by acting out constitutes a form of denial. "Acting out," Jacobson says, "appears to be regularly linked up with a bent for denial." That this persistent denial goes hand in hand with a distortion of reality is borne out convincingly by patients of this kind. The function of acting out is denial through action; the magic of action and of gesture appears in such cases in great clarity. We touch here on a focal adolescent characteristic. The adolescent has a need to deny his helplessness through action, to affirm by exaggeration his independence from the archaic active mother, to counteract the regressive pull to passivity by denying his dependence on reality itself. Here, then, we encounter the megalomania of the adolescent who says: "Nobody can tell me," and we witness the adolescent's trust in the magic of action by which he hopes to control his destiny. If we succeed in penetrating the restitutive façade of such defiance, we are bound to discover fantasies barely kept apart from reality, since no stable boundary line between them exists. Individuals in whom these conditions prevail "equate reality of thought with external actuality, and wishes with their fulfillment — with the event . . . Hence also the difficulty of distinguishing unconscious phantasies from memories which have become unconscious" (Freud, 1911).

The sense of reality is disturbed in all acting-out individuals. However, it is the quality of this disturbance which arouses our attention. We soon discover that outer reality has never been relinquished as the source of direct satisfaction on the level of need fulfillment. The observation that to the acting-out individual the person in relation to whom acting out is effected plays only a small or no role at all, that one is easily exchanged for another, is one more proof of the primitive psychic organization in which acting out is anchored. We recognize in acting out an autoerotic use of the outer world which is always available for momentary and immediate gratification. This is contrary to object-oriented gratification. True object relation requires the recognition of a self-interest in the other person and can develop only within the boundaries of compromise and empathy. The acting-out individual, in contrast, turns to the outer world as a tension-relieving part object. Viewed in these terms, acting out constitutes an autoerotic equivalent. Anna Freud (1949) alluded to this by saying that

"The acting out of fantasies . . . is a derivative of phallic masturbation . . . its substitute and representative."

The mechanism of projection plays a prominent role in acting out and easily masks a psychotic process such as an incipient paranoid state; this is especially true for adolescent cases of acting out. Kanzer (1957b), who follows similar thinking, expresses an opinion which is exemplified in one of my clinical illustrations which will follow later. He says: "This regressive need for immediate object possession is probably more primary than the motor activity which serves it—relieving on the one hand castration anxiety and recapturing on a more primitive level the early sense of mastery resulting from the possession of the breast." In this sense, then, acting out has a restitutive function by denying the frustrating limitations of reality, declaring object and self to be intrinsically one and the same, and proving its concreteness by repeated affirmation through action. Consequently, acting out is always ego syntonic. In fact, whenever acting out yields to a recognition of an ego-alien aspect, then acting out has already passed over into the realm of symptom formation or has become a symptomatic act. This change goes hand in hand with a decline of narcissistic needs and an emergence of differentiated object relations.

One more function of acting out must be mentioned here because it plays a particularly important role in adolescence. I refer to the adolescent's need to establish a temporal continuity within the ego. This continuity can no longer be maintained by proxy, by the simple reliance on the parents' omniscience, a condition which we might paraphrase in saying: "Even if I do not understand or remember or know fully what really happened in the past, my parents do; therefore, nothing has been extinguished or lost as long as I continue to remain a part of them." We know that whenever parents falsify by word or action the reality of crucial events, the child experiences a disturbance in the sense of reality which may lead to a critical impasse during adolescence. In an attempt to restore the sense of reality we observe acting-out behavior of all kinds, frequently of an asocial or antisocial nature. Such cases respond often extremely well to a rediscovery of the undistorted past. I am inclined to give this fact a weighty significance by saying that acting out in the service of re-establishing temporal ego continuity, or, briefly, in the service of the ego, must be distinguished from those cases of acting out in which instinctual demands predominate, in which the re-establishment of a oneness with the object is sought through the magic control of the external world. Such a propensity will finally consolidate in the impulsive or narcissistic personality, while acting out in the service of the ego tends to become stabilized in the compulsive character. In clinical practice with adolescents, these two types of cases are often difficult to distinguish from each other; only through the systematic use of the therapeutic situation can a differentiation be established in time.

ACTING OUT: A PHASE-SPECIFIC MECHANISM OF ADOLESCENCE

The concept of acting out has been discussed in its various aspects: predisposing, manifest, and functional; its complexity has been made explicit. I shall now turn to the question: what are the unique characteristics of the adolescent process that facilitate acting out; or, in other words, is adolescent acting out determined by predisposing factors alone or can the adolescent process claim acting out as a phase-specific mechanism? Can we speak of an adolescent compliance in the sense of a developmental tendency toward meeting halfway certain predispositions which at other periods of development were dormant or less conspicuous? In any case, exprience tells us that the incidence of acting out rises sharply when the child enters puberty. This clinical fact alone clamors for an explanation.

As an avenue toward an understanding of the adolescent proclivity to acting out, I shall now explore those adolescent developmental characteristics which accompany psychic restructuring and which by previous definition have a special relatedness to acting out. This effort does not require that we retrace the long and intricate pathways of adolescence; I have told this story in great detail elsewhere (1962). Instead, I shall single out certain characteristics of adolescence which have a direct bearing on the subject of acting out.

In a broad sense, one can say that the adolescent process proceeds from a progressive decathexis of primary love objects, through a phase of increased narcissism and autoerotism, to heterosexual object finding. These changes in drive organization are paralleled by shifts in ego interests and attitudes which attain structural stability during the period of consolidation at late adolescence. The detachment of psychic institutions from the parental influence which brought them into being constitutes a major effort of the adolescent ego; conversely, this achievement facilitates the definitive formation of the self.

The disengagement from the internalized love and hate objects is accompanied by a profound sense of loss and isolation, by a severe ego impoverishment which accounts for the adolescent's frantic turn to the outside world, to sensory stimulation and to activity. The adolescent turns so frantically toward reality because he is in constant danger of losing it. The protracted process of object displacement opens the door to repeating essential facets of the past in relation to the current situation or the immediate environment. As long as these severance actions last, an astonishing impairment of reality testing—often only selective—is in evidence. The outside world appears to the adolescent, at least in certain aspects, like the mirror image of his internal reality, with its conflicts, threats, and comforts, which is summarily experienced as external. Reality testing, so flagrantly defective during this process, will be restored only after a turn to nonincestuous love objects has evolved and after pregenitality has been afforded its place as forepleasure. This differentiation of drives is accompanied by a hierarchical rearrangement of ego interests and attitudes.

The proclivity of adolescence to action is one of its most impressive characteristics. The confluence of several trends is recognizable in this phenomenon. One is the antithesis of passivity ("being done to") and activity ("doing to others") which in the early part of adolescence plays a dominant role when the regressive pull to the active phallic mother (preoedipal) and the identification with her give the drive organization of boy and girl its special countenance. Action and motion are valued as such, not necessarily as goal-directed behavior, but as means of resisting the regressive pull to the active mother and of averting the surrender to primal passivity. In this constellation, then, action assumes the quality of a magic gesture: it averts evil (castration), it denies passive wishes, and it affirms a delusional control over reality. This tendency in conjunction with a narcissistic isolation compounds the well-known megalomanic trend of the adolescent who uses the external world for his aggrandizement in the same way as the child used the parent for the gratification of his narcissistic needs. In both cases, a supply of inexhaustible riches — even if only imagined, namely, wished for — seems to lie outside; all that remains to be done is to keep the flow of these narcissistic supplies steadily flowing toward the self.

The picture of the adolescent process would not be complete without bringing to your attention one more general trend which is pertinent to our topic. The adolescent process, of course, evolves from preceding developmental stages which were never passed through without leaving imprints of trauma, arrestments by fixation, sensitizations as to selective gratificatory modalities, and lacunae in ego continuity. The adolescent process can be accomplished only through synthesizing the past with the present and the anticipated future. The integration of ego and drive organizations is the touchstone of this synthesis. Psychologically, then, the adolescent process is constantly striving to bring the past into harmony with the terminal stage of childhood, with adolescence. Is it surprising to find among the ways of remembering the one called acting out? In a very real sense, acting out can serve progressive development. We refer to this as adolescent experimentation, which dominates the scene before trial action in thought and play action in fantasy make it dispensable.

In the selective enumeration of adolescent characteristics, it has been my purpose to emphasize the fact that the adolescent process contains those psychological conditions which we have come to recognize as typical whenever acting out is to occur. We are not surprised, therefore, to observe acting out to be a more or less ubiquitous phenomenon of adolescence. Such typical acting-out behavior is usually transient, benign, and in the service of progressive development. However, any of the component aspects of the adolescent process which I have enumerated can lead to an impasse, a failure, an arrestment. In that case, the phase-adequate mechanism of acting out has turned into a permanent pathological condition. Whether this condition is marked by continued acting out or will turn into a neurotic or some other illness will depend on the predisposing factors. The transient ascendancy of acting out in adolescence can never by itself develop into a lasting acting-out disorder.

It seems to me that adolescence offers an opportune chance for the treatment of acting-out propensities, which to some extent always represent phase-specific measures in an effort to cope with the actualities of growing up. These actualities revolve around object losing and object finding which both intertwine in the process of establishing mature object relations; they revolve around—not necessarily conscious—remembering and forgetting, which intertwine in the process of ego synthesis. The dialectic tension between these opposites is resolved in late adolescence by the definite consolidation of the self. The writer James Baldwin (1956) has put this human condition, epitomized in adolescence, into these words: "Either, or: it takes strength to remember, it takes another kind of strength to forget, it takes a hero to do both. People who remember court madness through pain, the pain of the perpetually recurring death of their innocence; people who forget court another kind of madness, the madness of denial of pain and the hatred of innocence; and the world is mostly divided between madmen who remember and madmen who forget. Heroes are rare."

CLINICAL MATERIAL

The presentation of clinical material on certain acting-out adolescents serves two objectives. On the one hand, the material offers concrete evidence of acting out, while at the same time it demonstrates the intrinsic difficulty of comfortably subordinating the data to the standard concept of acting out. We are confronted with the dilemma of either broadening the concept or assigning some clinical facts to other categories. As a third possibility, we could consider acting out as a typical transient mechanism of the adolescent process which owes its prominence to the temporary weakening of inhibitory and repressive forces and, furthermore, to the ascendancy of regressive libido and ego positions.

Adolescent cases of acting out in the service of instinctual gratification are well known. Typical of this kind of acting out is the pseudo heterosexuality in the girl as either a return to the preoedipal mother via a substitute partner or as a revenge and spiteful action directed against the oedipal mother. I have described elsewhere (1957, see pp. 183-206, below) this kind of acting out which operates in the service of regressive instinctual gratification. We are furthermore well acquainted with those cases in which the adolescent acts out the unconscious wishes of the parent. I have selected clinical material which does not belong to any of these categories and which has received only scant attention in the literature. A paper by Augusta Bonnard (1961) marks the exception.

The following case material exemplifies adolescent acting out which operates in the service of progressive development or, more specifically, in the service of ego synthesis.

The Case of Frank, the Laborer

This late adolescent boy of nineteen had failed in college during his freshman year and found himself at a loss what to do with himself after his dismissal. Lethargy and aimlessness were prominent, as was a tendency to indulge in sentimental and fairy-storylike fantasies. He was plagued by indecision and confusion and was unable to make plans for his future.

Frank was an adopted child. Both his parents had achieved intellectual prominence and outstanding positions. The boy was brought up in the atmosphere of a cultured home; he had fitted well into this milieu. All through school, he proved himself able academically; he was socially competent and at ease; he was active in sports and in school life; he was liked by his teachers and peers. Due to this history, his failure in college assumed the dimensions of an inexplicable turn of events.

After Frank had left college, he started psychotherapy. First he held several jobs as a white-collar worker until he suddenly decided to become a laborer. I felt that his urgency to take a laborer's job was so elemental that I made myself a sympathetic partner in this radical departure from his accustomed life. I decided to wait and see. Frank felt extremely happy in his new job and he got along well with his fellow workers. Soon he decided to move away from the comfortable home of his family in order to live with one of the workers' family in the grimy section of a large city. He deeply enjoyed the simple pleasures and unsophisticated interests of his new milieu. The acting-out character in this boy's behavior was evident.

During the time Frank resided in the world of his fellow workers, it was possible to penetrate his childhood amnesia and bring crucial memories to consciousness. This was facilitated by the matter-of-fact familiarity with the new milieu and by associative links which related the present experience to his past. In having made a change of his milieu, he followed the relentless pull of the infantile object tie to foster parents: he had lived in a family of working-class people until he was adopted at the end of his second year. The early reality of his life became revived during late adolescence and was made conscious in therapy after it had become triggered off by remembering in action. Frank became able to recall memories of his early childhood as well as to re-experience the affection he had felt for his foster parents. The acting out as a special form of remembering was translated into the verbalized memories of his past. A gradual disengagement from his early love objects followed: he was now able to fall in love and experience the object finding of adolescence proper. As soon as the reliving of the past became dispensable, Frank returned to his adoptive family. Freed from the regressive pull to his original milieu, the abrupt separation from which had been traumatic, Frank returned to college, studied successfully for a doctorate, and became an equal in intellectual pre-eminence to his parents.

Frank's case invites some comments. First, it should be noted that no acting out had occurred during the time preceding or during eight years following his late adolescent crisis. While he had talked about his past earlier in therapy and while he knew the facts of his background and remembered some of the circumstances of his early life, the affective component of his memories came to consciousness only through the re-enactment of his early history. It seems that the consolidation process of late adolescence is hampered, delayed, or actually aborted whenever crucially significant unintegrated memories remain permanently dissociated and resist repression. This by itself prevents the formation of a temporal continuity in the ego. Without this psychic achievement of late adolescence, the separation from the parent can only be partial. The adolescent process, i.e., the second individuation process, if not proceeding normally, is often frantically simulated by either a restitution in fantasy or through a determined return to one's beginnings. These efforts bear the signs of acting out, as in the case of Frank. This adolescent could not go forward without first making contact with his unassimilated traumatic past in a desperate effort at integrating it. His acting out was in the service of progressive development. We are reminded of the giant Antaeus, the son of Poseidon and Gaea, the Earth. Antaeus proved to be invincible because each time he was thrown in combat, he rose with greater strength due to having touched the earth, his mother. Herakles defeated him by lifting him off the ground and holding him in midair. Thus disrupting the giant's contact with his origin, the source of his strength, he crushed Antaeus to death.

The Case of Carl, the Criminal

We are all familiar with adolescent cases in which acting out is related to a family myth. By this, I mean a willful distortion of facts concerning the family history. This type of case, in which identity confusion, imposterlike, or delinquent behavior often happen to be the major symptoms, differs radically in structure from those cases of delinquency in which the outside world becomes distorted through the projection of an intrapsychic conflict. In both instances, an intrapsychic event is experienced as external, but with the crucial difference that in one case the external world is distorted by authority figures in the environment who as the guardians of reality must interpret the world of facts to the child, while in the other case the child himself distorts reality for the sake of drive satisfaction. In one instance, adolescent deviancy operates in the service of the rectification of a myth or lie, while, in the other, a myth or a lie is to be created in order to fit reality to instinctual needs.

In order to illustrate these remarks, I shall present the case of Carl. This fifteen-year-old boy was brought to treatment by a relative who had become worried about Carl's criminal tendencies. Stealing, forgery, truancy, and lying were the presenting symptoms. All four kinds of infractions were usually executed in a manner that invited detection. The driving urgency in the boy's behavior, in conjunction with his sense of being fated for a criminal career, gave his delinquency the special countenance of acting out. The onset of puberty marked the onset of Carl's delinquent behavior.

The family myth, the willful distortion of the family history, became known through the information provided by the relative. Carl and his brother, his senior by three years, had been told by their mother that their father was dead. After a divorce when Carl was three and a half years old, the father was later convicted for embezzlement and sent to prison when the child was six. Before this event, the father had lost contact with his children who had not seen him for two years. According to the mother's story, the father had died in prison and she was a widow. The children, aged six and nine respectively, accepted the news about their father's death without a question, and they behaved as if it were true. Nobody spoke of the father at home except to compare Carl's "crooked little mind" with that of his dead father. Actually, the father had not died. A psychotic condition which rendered him intractable in prison and which proved to be chronic made his transfer to a hospital for the criminally insane necessary. At the time Carl started treatment, his father was an inmate of this prison hospital.

It did not appear strange at all to this boy that he knew no relations on his father's side, that he did not know the date or cause of his father's death or the place where he was buried, that he knew neither the circumstances of his crime nor the reasons for his parents' divorce. No wonder this boy complained about a strange incapacity to study history because he was unable to remember dates, names, and places. In order to dispose of an impenetrable confusion, Carl himself insisted that his father had died shortly after his birth and that he had never known him. Unconsciously, Carl had obeyed a gestured command which he remembered in treatment: "One day an uncle of mine came to the house and tore my father out of every family picture." The correctness of this memory was later confirmed.

The function of Carl's acting out can be stated as an attempt at keeping the memory of his father alive, as a vindication of the "good father," and as an extension of the temporal continuity of the ego into the dim regions of his early life. The father image was essential as a hold on reality and as a protection against depressive moods. Furthermore, the sense of reality could be sustained only by denying in action the mother's imputed unrealness of the child's perceptions and of their traces embedded in his memory. What Carl remembered about his early childhood were forbidden memories, especially in relation to affectionate and positive feelings toward the father. They had become extinguished as conscious memories by the same stroke of the mother's wrath and vindictiveness with which she had murdered the father. Carl's adolescence was fatally threatened by his submission to the archaic sorceress mother. This meant the abandonment of the father image with which he had to come to terms at adolescence, positively and negatively, through identification and counteridentification.

It was obvious that the dead father had to be unearthed and that the past history had to be revived and rectified before the delinquent aspect of acting out would subside. The proclivity to acting out proved only partly reversible; however, the employment of this tendency to bring about the inescapable fate of becoming a criminal was successfully averted by therapy. Carl's visit to his father at the prison hospital was followed by a compassionate concern about him. The boy wanted to send money to his father in order to ease his life and have him more respectably dressed. He conjectured that his father was mute because he was angry since nobody ever visited him or cared. He realized gradually how much he had missed his father and he became aware of his behaving to older men as if they were fathers who might take an interest in him. At such times, he became demanding and almost expected a restitution from the environment for having been denied the rightful possession of his own father.

A complicating factor in this case must be mentioned

because it contributed to the acting out, especially the stealing. Carl had an undescended testicle. This condition, which had been neglected, was operatively corrected early in treatment. The operation unfortunately served only a cosmetic purpose since the testicle had ceased to function. Carl, who made his own obervations on the comparative size and sensation of his testicles, was informed about the true state of affairs. Before the clarification of his genital status, Carl's stealing contained a kleptomanic component, namely, a magic attempt at bringing about genital intactness. Through stealing, then, he symbolically restored his masculinity and, conversely, defended himself against feminine strivings, namely, against homosexuality.

As always in cases wherein a family myth plays a pathogenic role, the rectification of the myth hardly comes as a surprise to the patient. So it was also with Carl: the parts of the puzzle which were always known to him in dissociated bits and pieces were gradually and laboriously fitted together into a coherent and meaningful whole. Carl recalled the "fancy apartment" he lived in when the family was once rich and he recognized in his desire for expensive living a lingering memory of those days. When he toppled on the verge of stealing again because he needed money in order to rent a chauffeur-driven Cadillac for an evening with his girl friend, he recalled that his father had actually driven a Cadillac in the company of strange women and girls. After his parents had separated, his father used to take him out in a big car. Carl's irrepressible desire to dress ostentatiously often drove him to stealing either money or merchandise, until he recognized in his own behavior the image of his father who was a fastidious dresser. After Carl had succumbed to another stealing episode, he explained to the therapist that he was hopelessly compelled to spend money on his girl friend. Fragments of memories and overheard conversations pieced themselves together into the recollection that his father was a lavish spender and entertainer of chorus girls. He began to notice at his home some expensive china, glassware, and bric-a-brac as the tangible remembrances of a past come to life and telling its story.

The acting out in Carl's case was repeatedly followed by remembering and experiencing particular affective and sensual states. The cumulative effect of this cyclic process became recognizable in the novel ability to employ trial action in thought and fantasy, as well as verbalized thought whenever the urge to act out arose. This alerting awareness attested to the ascendancy of the self-observing, i.e., introspective, ego which in turn strengthened both secondary-process thinking and reality testing. Acting out in terms of a maladaptive attempt at establishing temporal continuity in the ego gradually lost its genuine character and laid bare the fixation points of instinctual development. Symptom formation and the defensive nature of action now occupied the center of the clinical picture. Carl's passive tendencies intensified by his genital defectiveness were overcompensated by action. Action per se had become identical with an affirmation of masculinity. This second phase in the treatment of this acting-out case lies outside the scope of our special interest.[1]

The acting out and remembering in Carl's case invokes the image of Proust rediscovering "forgotten years, gardens, people in the taste of a sip of tea in which he found a piece of a madeleine" (From a letter by Proust to Antoine Bibesco, November 1912). Acting out, then, is the establishment of that particular experiential congruence by which present reality provides a link to a traumatic past; in this sense,

---

[1] A follow-up on Carl's case was fortuitously granted. Carl came to see me ten years later when some business and love affair confronted him with "big decisions." I saw him three times. Suffice it to say that (1) I could find no traces of acting out or delinquent behavior; (2) his vocational activities, after some drifting, had become focused and enterprising, showing ambition and reasonably good judgment; (3) his object relations were shallow, yet caring and responsible; he had formed relationships of some duration, if not of durability, with a few women; (4) he had kept in touch with his hospitalized father through the prison authorities and also personally; he continued to contribute what he thought would make his father's life more comfortable.

acting out is an alloplastic, maladaptive, restitutive process. The fact that acting out constitutes an organized psychic operation sets it off sharply from impulsive action, typical of the impulse disorders. Instead of an organized pattern, impulsive action is marked by a primitive mechanism of tension discharge to which Michaels (1959) has referred as "primary acting out."

Let us return once more to the adolescent condition. The adolescent's proclivity to action is obvious. It furthermore becomes apparent in the treatment of some acting-out adolescents that acting out is not an integral component of the personality and, once overcome, shows no further traces in the behavior of the adult. In other cases, it proves to remain a habitual reaction to tension and thus reveals its predispositional component. Acting out per se cannot be considered an insurmountable obstacle to treatment in adolescence, since it represents in its genuine adolescent form a phase-specific mechanism of the adolescent process.

DISCUSSION AND CONCLUSION

The adolescent's proclivity to action seems to me determined by two factors. First, we have to consider the fact that with the quantitative increase of instinctual pressure due to puberty, earlier drive and ego positions are regressively revived. The first and oldest antithesis in individual life, the one of active and passive, can be discerned again at adolescence. The early active position which came into existence through an identification with the preoedipal phallic (active) mother serves, especially during the beginning stages of adolescence, as a defensive bulwark against regression to primal passivity. This defensive measure against passivity becomes manifest during adolescence in unrestrained, inappropriate, and self-assertive actions. Second, the delibidinization of infantile love objects during the phase of adolescence proper, and the increase in narcissism during the phase of early adolescence, both result in an impoverishment of the ego. The threat of ego loss which accompanies this process is counteracted by a forceful turn to the outer world. Outer reality offers a restitutive anchorage before stable object relations are again established.

These two sources just described contribute to the dire need for action which is so typical of the adolescent process. Of course, we are equally familiar with the adolescent's inertia, lethargy, and aversion to action which only highlight the defensive quality of activity in the cyclic sequence of these states. In contrast to the typical adolescent break-through of instinctual drives, sexual and aggressive, and their random discharge in action, we come to realize that acting out represents a structured and organized mechanism.

Genuine adolescent acting out implies a fixation on either the phase of preadolescence or early adolescence. Both these phases are characterized by a strong regressive pull, by a revival of pregenitality, by an increase in narcissism, and by the maintenance of a bisexual identity. It goes without saying that these conditions affect adversely the ego's relation to reality. This latent predisposition will assume flagrant proportions under the impact of puberty whenever a defective sense of reality as well as a need for oneness with the object (i.e., with the outer world) existed before adolescence. The fact that both cases of acting out in the service of ego synthesis which I have reported have in common the loss of a significant object in early childhood suggests that similar cases might show a similar etiology.

Whenever acting out is in evidence we assume that an organized mechanism is in operation, not merely a discharge device of instinctual needs. This postulated organization appears in three distinctly different forms which are familiar to us from their clinical manifestations: (1) the repetition of an early object relation and of its gratificatory modality by displacement; (2) the activation of a fantasy and its articulation on the environment, in which case acting out appears as an autoerotic equivalent; (3) the effort at restoring the sense of reality by affirming memories in action which were denied, forbidden, or distorted by the environment during childhood. I refer to the latter as acting out in the service of ego synthesis.

While acting out is generally alloplastic and maladaptive, the distinctions which I suggest seem essential in terms of a differentiated treatment approach. In cases of adolescent acting out as an attempt at reviving partly abandoned object relations or drive gratifications by their displacement onto the outer world, treatment initially focuses on an increase in tension toleration, on internalization, and on a clearer differentiation between ego and reality, between self and object. This phase in treatment, then, aims at the establishment of an ego organization which is capable of integrating the second, namely, interpretative and reconstructive, phase of treatment. In the case of acting out in the service of ego synthesis, treatment initially focuses on the reconstruction of the dissociated, traumatic past, and secondarily assists the ego in the task of mastering anxiety and of integrating affects which follow in the wake of the confrontation with the historical truth. The various types of acting out can rarely be categorized as neatly as I have outlined them here for the sake of theoretical clarity but are usually mixed and require that therapy maneuver between a changing emphasis on one or the other.

Acting out as a tension regulator protects the psychic organism against conflictual anxiety: the conflict is exclusively between the ego and the outer world. On the other hand, acting out in the service of the ego, of ego synthesis, or of temporal ego continuity protects the psychic organism against anxiety deriving from structural defectiveness or disintegration. Structural anxiety arises as a consequence of ego lacunae or whenever the sense of reality is in danger of coming to ruin during adolescence. At this period, the borrowed strength or ego restitution through continued dependency on the parent is no longer desirable or tolerable lest progressive development be abandoned altogether. If this should occur, we witness the case of an abortive adolescence.

The problem of adolescent acting out—its genetic, dynamic, and structural distinctness, clarity, and differentiation—is obscured by several trends which are constituent parts of the adolescent process. We have seen that acting out at adolescence is the result of several confluent trends: predispositional, developmental, and functional. The nature of the adolescent process itself tends to blur the clear delineation of the concept within the clinical picture. This difficulty stems mainly from four adolescent characteristics: from the alternation between regressive and progressive movements, from the role of displacement in the process of disengagement from early love objects, from the frantic turn to the outside world in order to compensate for ego impoverishment, and from the efforts at ego synthesis which is the structural achievement of late adolescence. The relation of these adolescent factors to acting out has only partly been eludicated. However, their relevancy to our problem has become apparent; furthermore, a reconsideration of the standard concept of acting out has presented itself as desirable if the phenomena of adolescence are to be accommodated within its framework.

DISCUSSION

Dr. Henry Wermer:

In this symposium we have talked about acting out in children, adolescents, and adults. We regarded acting out as a particular phenomenon of mental conflict, and we discussed how such acting out might be not only ego-syntonic but also culture-syntonic. We all agreed that acting and behavior will have to be examined from various points of view.

As analysts and psychiatrists we can be experts on the individual dynamics of a given case, or maybe even a group of cases. These individual dynamics depending largely on intrapsychic conflicts are basically the same in all cultural settings. Nevertheless, acting out will have a different significance in different cultures and societies, and various social values may well influence both us and our patients. Some behavior we may regard as pathological acting out in one culture and as ego synthesis in a different milieu.

Let me briefly give you an example of what I have in mind. Some years ago I had the opportunity to analyze a young man from a country in the near East. When he came for treatment, he was a scientist at one of our universities. As a youth he had been a smuggler. He would cross the border of his country, acquire goods abroad, where they were more abundant, and then return home to sell them. He would carry as many as six suits of clothes on his body, sometimes women's dresses, and disguise his hair. He was a hero to his countrymen, something like your Robin Hood. He was, of course, a traitor to his country's authorities, who by the way let him get away with it anyway. In terms of our civilization, his behavior was terrible; in terms of his milieu, it was heroic — as heroic as the actions of our astronauts are to us. I shall mention the astronauts again later one. I remark on this only because, as an analyst, my concern was associated with the ego-id-superego conflicts. However, as an analyst applying our theoretic framework to the general issue of acting out, I cannot and should not refrain from adding to the ego-id-superego struggles the conflicts which the total psychic structure may be engaged in with external reality; this external reality includes culture, society, morality, and value judgment.

I will direct my remarks mainly to Dr. Blos's paper, but before doing so would like to say a few words about Dr. van Amerongen's paper. I think Dr. van Amerongen's paper is especially important because it contributes to our knowledge of the predisposition to acting out. I have in recent years had only little experience with the children that she describes and yet feel that I could confirm some of her observations. I have been impressed by the significance of the "absent father." It was mentioned earlier that the asocial overactivity syndrome is almost confined to male children. It is my impression that premature promiscuous sexual indulgences, petty thievery, and pseudologia fantastica are the female equivalent of the asocial overactivity syndrome of boys. A patient of this sort was shared by me and Dr. van Amerongen. She treated her as a child; I treated her as a late adolescent. There had been extreme sexual provocativeness in prepuberty which was used and abetted by her parents in a disguised form. They were actors and the patient became a front runner for her mother's highly erotic stage performances. It should be noted that this acting out was quite ego syntonic and readily accepted by the theatrical milieu in which the child lived. She came for treatment because her poor school performances injured other narcissistic needs of the parents. Another girl was the equivalent of the "asocial overactivity" syndrome and became pregnant at the age of twelve. She had been adopted when she was a few months old. Her adoptive mother probably had also been pregnant as an early adolescent. Also, the mother raved to me about the physical attractiveness of the thirteen-year-old boy who had impregnated her daughter. I do not regard the subtle promotion of acting out as a prime etiologic factor, but I do feel that it plays a role. This patient, by the way, did resemble the syndrome in boys when she conducted vandalistic acts around the ages of ten and eleven. She then destroyed thousands of dollars worth of furniture and art objects without significant provocation.

I find it difficult to discuss Dr. Blos's paper because I am almost in total agreement with him. It might raise more tensions, really, if I had to argue or be critical of Dr. Blos, but I personally would find it less of an effort to discuss disagreements than to talk about a presentation with which I can raise no issues.

When Dr. Blos, at the beginning of his paper, raises the point that (1) acting out and adolescence are almost synonymous, and then (2) proceeds to draw distinctions between play acting, action discharge, and acting out, he essentially outlined the beautiful paper that was to follow. I think he has also done something which has not been done before in such a clear and definite form, when he discusses acting out in terms of three factors: (1) predisposition, (2) manifestation, and (3) function. He then proceeded to illustrate it clinically and examine it more theoretically as a "phase-specific mechanism of adolescence." I would like to discuss, and focus on a few paragraphs in the paper rather than to attempt to discuss the paper as a whole. It is not only a paper on acting out, but it covers almost all of Dr. Blos's views on the process of adolescence. Dr. Blos's paper would have been a valuable contribution if he had done no more than remind us, first, that this acting out in the transference and acting out in some of our adolescents are not the same, dynamically, culturally, and genetically; they are probably also not the same economically. He says that everybody knows this, but I do not think so. Second, he states that "the transient ascendancy of acting out in adolescence can never in itself or by itself develop into an acting-out character disorder." This, I think, is of considerable significance for our clinical judgment and may also serve as an assurance to a good many concerned parents.

Dr. Blos has used the Dora case as an illustration of the function of acting out, and he quotes Freud: "We recognize in this acting out the gratification of a hostile retaliatory wish. Dora took revenge on the man who had deceived and deserted her." This is not going to be a belated defense of Miss Dora, who, I understand from Dr. Felix Deutsch's paper (1957), turned out to be a rather nasty woman who, according to what we know now, not only was deserted by two men, but who was really also deserted by a third man, and this was Freud. Freud at that time knew little about transference and how it might lead a person to regress to the point where actions rather than thinking and verbalization may again become the predominant mode of psychic function. Freud became the third deserter of this girl, being a scientist who had not yet dis-

covered what his patient expected him to know: Miss Dora was
the type of hysteric in whom we find thinking and action like
Siamese twins. Dora was also an adolescent who was struggling
with the very kind of phase-specific conflicts that Dr. Blos
describes and that Edith Jacobson (1961) has written about extensively. It is a conflict created by the "disengagement from
the internalized love object, is accompanied by a profound
sense of isolation, by ego impoverishment. This accounts for
the adolescent's frantic turn to the outside world, to sensory
stimulation and to activity." Dr. Blos concludes: "outer reality
offers restitutive anchorage before stable object relations are
again established." Further, Freud did not have to his advantage accumulated knowledge that is truly epitomized in Dr.
Blos's quotation of Baldwin about the heroic nature of remembering and the heroic nature of forgetting: "It takes strength to
remember; it takes another kind of strength to forget. It takes
a hero to do both. Heroes who remember court madness
through their pain. The world is divided between madmen
who remember and madmen who forget. Heroes are rare."
Freud did not know this, and thus he could not help his patient
on the level at which she was functioning. She was, let us face
facts, no hero. Freud, the creative genius never equalled in our
field, was a wonderful investigator of the psyche of the few
adolescents like Dora, or like the remarkable girl he analyzed
in a mountain hut. I think at this stage of his development he
was probably a flop as a therapist of these young people. The
Dora case was written sixty years ago, for its concept of the
predisposing factors such as syphilis in a parent has, of course,
been abandoned. The manifestations and functions of acting
out nonetheless are clear from the case. Dora relived by acting
rather than by remembering. Between the classic case of Dora
and the paper by Dr. Blos are the contributions by Dr. Greenacre as of today, by Eissler, Anna Freud, Spiegel, Bernfeld,
Josselyn, Adlai Johnson, Ernest Jones, and George Gardner, to
mention just a few. We, that is the members of this panel, the
audience who work with their "Dora cases of 1962," have an

advantage over Freud as technicians of the psychoanalytic therapy of adolescents.

It is to this aspect of Dr. Blos's paper that I would like to say a few more words. In reading Dr. Blos's paper and under- lining some paragraphs, I found myself compelled to triple underline some passages and to write in the margin, "This is where we come in," or "Freud didn't know what Blos knows now." Let me first stress what Blos knew in the case of Frank. I think the use of the Greek legend is a marvelous device to illustrate Dr. Blos's thinking. On the other hand, I believe that Dr. Blos's modesty prevents him from spelling out some of the crucial points in his management of this case. I would say his technique, intuitive and probably quite consciously perceived at the same time, permitted the boy to stay with Gaea, the Mother Earth, at least for a little while. Dr. Blos did not disrupt the boy's contact with his origin, the source of his strength. I would guess that Dr. Blos was so familiar with the concept of mother transference in this case that he did not even mention it. Freud partly lost his patient because he was unaware of "this complication."

Now, to my marginal notes, "This is where we come in." This was written on several pages where Dr. Blos states that the disengagement from the internalized love and hate objects is accompanied by a profound sense of loss and isolation and an impoverishment of the ego. There is no time to spell out all the technical implications this has for the treatment of an ado- lescent. Let me merely say that unless we, the therapists, caseworkers, or teachers, are prepared for a while to be the patient's external reality and are willing to be acted out on, and acted upon, we should retreat to the comfortable ivory tower of analyzing only well-compensated obsessional neurot- ics and never touch an adolescent. The therapist's narcissism will have to suffer, but, unless one can be the real god to the adolescent one day and remain modest in the face of such admiration, one should not treat adolescents. On the other hand, if one cannot tolerate having all one's middle-aged, or in the case of my younger colleagues, all of one's adult, clay feet thrown into one's face, one should not work with teenagers. I will never forget (and it was a good learning experience) how I felt when one of my young patients whom I had treated from preadolescence into adolescence suddenly and definitely, and with profound sarcasm and nastiness, beat me in chess in eight moves.

I would like to go to another comment that Dr. Blos made. Acting out per se cannot be considered an insurmountable obstacle to the treatment of adolescents, and it represents a genuine form of a phase-specific mechanism of the adolescent process. I think if we remember this—and again Dr. Blos said everybody knows it but I do not think so—we will deal with it as we deal with any developmental phenomenon or maturational crisis. I hope that as a result of this symposium the term "acting out" will lose some of its tendentious and derogatory implications and become as respectable as any other psychic mechanism. I think there has crept into our profession and population at large a tendency to use this term only in a derogatory way. We have the habit, if we want to think about somebody who is an awfully parsimonious fellow, to call him an anal personality. If somebody is terribly irresponsible, we say he is acting out, he is an acting-out character. Of course, this is true, but I think we ought to look upon it as we look upon any symptom. We should remember that Freud said at one time, "Transference will develop and will make a nuisance of itself." I think that is the correct quotation. And yet, what would we do in analysis, or as a matter of fact, in psychotherapy, without transference?

Let me now go to some of Dr. Blos's final comments about the three adolescent characteristics which tend to blur the concept of acting out. He mentions here first the alternation between regression and progression; second, the disengagement from early object relationships, the ego impoverishment, and the return to the outer world; and third, ego synthesis. Some years ago Dr. Berman, Dr. Zinberg, and others did some research on the development of professional identity in young student nurses. We tried to compare their development (they were chronologically adolescents) with the development of the professional identity of psychiatric residents (chronologically adults). We saw these people in groups in a form of group psychotherapy. With the student nurses we expected that there would be a lot of acting out during these sessions and we got even more than we had been inclined to foresee. With the supposedly mature young psychiatrists we were not prepared for their adolescent behavior. Dr. Elvin Semrad, the Clinical Director of the Massachusetts Mental Health Center, from which these experimental groups were drawn, on one occasion scolded these young doctors and said, "Acting out may be a lot of fun, but it never does anybody any good whatsoever." This may be correct for the young adult, but is this necessarily true for the still consolidating ego of the adolescent? How are we to decide whether the fast dragstrip racing of the teenager is a self-destructive, defiant, phallic, preoedipal acting out, or, on the other hand, by way of the care of the car, the interest in machines, a serious preparation for our contemporary concept of mental normality, maturity, and self-control, which currently seems to mark the idols of our civilization, namely, the astronauts. I do not know if even the intensive and individual study of a given adolescent can always clearly distinguish between pathological acting out and what constitutes a serious effort at ego synthesis. I personally feel that as a therapist, or as a parent, or as a teacher, we should be rather humble and keep an open mind about what is pathological acting out and what is ego synthesis through action or trial action.

As you can see, I enjoyed Dr. Blos's paper enormously. It enlarged my knowledge, not only on the topic of acting out, but on my understanding of adolescence. For this I feel — and I believe the whole group shares this feeling — very grateful to Dr. Blos.

PREOEDIPAL FACTORS IN THE ETIOLOGY OF FEMALE DELINQUENCY

Peter Blos, Ph.D.

In the study of delinquency we can distinguish two fronts of inquiry. I refer to the sociological determinants, on the one hand, and to the individual psychological processes, on the other. These two fronts of inquiry are essentially different; yet by the very fact that they study the same phenomena they become readily confused with each other, to the detriment of clarity and research. Both aspects are intrinsically and essentially interwoven in each case. However, our understanding of a case would be incomplete as long as we fail to distinguish between the "early unconscious predisposing factors (so-called endopsychic factors)" and the "constitutional and precipitating factors" (Glover, 1956); due to this differentiation it has become customary to speak of latent and manifest delinquency. In this communication I shall restrict myself to a discussion of some predisposing psychodynamic factors as they can be reconstructed from the overt delinquent behavior and supported by the historical data in the case.

Delinquency, by definition of the term, refers to a personality disturbance which manifests itself in open conflict with society. This fact alone has pushed the social aspect of the problem into the forefront, has stimulated sociological research which in turn has thrown light on those environmental conditions which are significantly related to delinquent behavior. My concentration in this paper on the individual process will not, I hope, be construed as an expression of my disregard for the contribution which sociological research has made. The study of delinquency has by necessity always been multidisciplinary and it should not be claimed by any one discipline as its exclusive domain of inquiry.

Delinquency statistics tell us that antisocial behavior has been on the rise for some time; this goes hand in hand with a general rise in adaptive breakdowns in the population as a whole. This rise in delinquency cannot be considered as an isolated phenomenon, but must be seen as part of a general trend. This view becomes even more convincing if we accept the opinion supported by Healy, Aichhorn, Alexander, Friedlander, and others, namely, "that the differences in the psychological make-up of the delinquent and the nondelinquent are of a quantitative rather than of a qualitative kind" (Friedlander, 1947). We have also become familiar with a change of symptom picture in the field of the neuroses; the classical conversion hysteria is less prevalent nowadays and has given way to other forms of personality disturbances, best summarized as pathology of the ego. Anxious parental gratification-readiness and even gratification-anticipation of children's instinctual needs seem to account for many cases of low frustration tolerance and dependency which we observe in children's clinics; contributing to this confusion is the parents' surrender of their own intuitive know-how to advertisement and extraneous controls. Under such conditions the child's ego is exposed to insufficient and inconsistent stimulation with the result that more or less permanent ego defects ensue; they become apparent in the malformation of delaying and inhibiting functions. The powerful drive toward immediate discharge of tension is typical of the delinquent, and the age of instinctual tension-rise is puberty. At this time the individual normally re-enacts his personal drama on the wider stage of society, and it is of course at this juncture of maturational stress that the inadequacy of the ego becomes apparent.

If I compare the cases of delinquency which come to our clinics today with those cases I remember from my work with Aichhorn in Vienna in the twenties, I am struck by the difference, namely, the predominance of poor ego integration and impulse disorders which we see today. Aichhorn's classical saying (1925) that the delinquent has to be turned into a neurotic in order to make him accessible to treatment, seems applicable today to only a small portion of the delinquent population.

The study of the psychodynamics of delinquency has always been prone to fall prey to general and over-all formulations. Prevalent ideas in the field of human behavior and its motivation have a tendency to provide the master plan for its solution. In fact, etiological determinants change with prevalent psychoanalytic research; the instinct-gratification theory as well as the theory of the missing superego have been left way behind; considerations of ego pathology have moved into the foreground. I do not question Kaufman's and Makkay's opinion (1956) when they say that an "infantile type of depression" due to "actual or emotional desertion" is found to be a "predisposing and necessary element in delinquency"; but it is equally correct to say that depressive elements are to be found in all types of emotional disturbances of children. What puzzles us most in the delinquent is his incapacity to internalize conflict, or rather his ingenious circumvention of symptom formation by experiencing an endopsychic tension as a conflict with the outside world. The exclusive use of alloplastic, antisocial solutions is a feature of delinquency which sets it apart from other forms of adaptive failures. It stands in clear contrast to the psychoneurotic or to the psychotic solution, the former representing an autoplastic and the latter an autistic adaptation.

Up to a certain point all cases of delinquency have psychodynamic similarities, but it seems to me more profitable to study their differences. Only by this method shall we penetrate into the more obscure aspects of the problem. In expressing a warning of this kind, Glover (1956) speaks of "etiological clichés" such as the "broken home" or "separation anxiety." He continues: "It requires no great mental effort to assume that traumatic separation in early infantile years must have a traumatic effect; but to convert this into a *direct* determining environmental factor in delinquency is to neglect the central proposition of psycho-analysis that these predisposing elements acquire their pathological force and form in accordance with the effect of their passage through the varying phases of the unconscious Oedipus situation" (p. 313). My clinical and theoretical remarks proceed from this point, especially as far as preoedipal fixations preclude the oedipal stage from consolidating and thereby prevent emotional maturation.

It has always been my opinion that male and female delinquency follow separate paths, indeed are essentially different. We are familiar with the different manifestations of both, but we would like to be better informed about the origin of the divergencies. Our thoughts immediately turn to the divergent psychosexual development of the boy and girl during early childhood. And, furthermore, it seems relevant to recall in this connection that the structure of the ego depends to a significant extent on the existing drive organization, which is subject to different vicissitudes in the male and female. The study of identifications and of the self-representation to which they lead in boy and girl explains the dissimilarities in ego development in the two sexes.

If we review the cases of male and female delinquency of which we have intimate knowledge, we gain the impression that female delinquency stands in close proximity to the perversions; the same cannot be said with regard to the boy. The girl's delinquency repertoire is far more limited in scope and variety than the boy's; it furthermore lacks significantly in destructive aggressive acts against persons and property, and also concedes to the boy the rich field of imposter-like adventuring. The girl's wayward behavior is restricted to stealing of the kleptomanic type; to vagrancy; to provocative, impudent behavior in public; and to frank sexual waywardness. Of course, these offenses are shared by the boy offender; they constitute, however, only a fraction of his transgressions. In the girl, it seems, delinquency is an overt sexual act or, to be more correct, a sexual acting out.

Let us look at the way this disparity comes about. In female delinquency the infantile instinctual organization which has never been abandoned breaks through with the onset of puberty and finds a bodily outlet in genital activity. The pregenital instinctual aims, which dominate the delinquent behavior of the girl, relate her delinquency to the perversion. An adolescent boy who, let us say, is caught in an ambivalence conflict with his father might defend himself against both castration fear and castration wish by getting drunk, by destroying property, or by stealing a car and wrecking it; his actions often are, even if abortive, nevertheless an attempt at a progressive development (Neavles and Winokur, 1957). The boy's typical delinquent activities contain elements of a keen interest in reality; we furthermore recognize his fascination with the struggle waged between himself and people, social institutions, and the world of nature. In contrast to this, an adolescent girl who possesses an equal propensity to acting out will, let us say, take revenge on her mother by whom she feels rejected by seeking sexual relations. Girls of this type have told me of persistent fantasies during sex play or coitus, such as: "If Mother knew, it would kill her" or "You see (Mother), I have somebody too." Aichhorn, in a paper on sex-delinquent girls (1949), considers the predisposing condition to outweigh any environmental factor. With reference to the rampant juvenile prostitution in Vienna after World War II, he states that his observations led him to believe that ". . . a specific instinctual constellation must be one of the determinant factors, but that environment and constitution can only be concomitant factors" (p. 440). Perhaps cases of delinquent girls which have been classified as psychopaths might be viewed as cases of perversion. Schmideberg (1956), in a recent paper, pursues similar trends of thought. She contrasts the neurotic and the perverse reaction or symptom, emphasizing the fact that the former represents an autoplastic and the latter an alloplastic adaptation. She continues: "In a certain sense the neurotic symptom is of a more social kind, while the perverse is more antisocial. Thus there is a rather close connection between the sexual perversions and delinquent behaviour, which is by definition antisocial" (p. 423). The impulsivity which is equally strong in acting-out behavior and in the perversions is well known. I hesitate to generalize as Schmideberg does, but would stress the point that the identity of delinquency and perversion outstandingly corresponds with the clinical picture of female delinquency, while it constitutes only one special variant of the diverse and far more heterogeneous etiology of male delinquency.

It is a justifiable request at this point to ask for those reasons which permit the view that male and female delinquency are differently structured. For this purpose it is necessary to turn our attention to the differences that distinguish the psychosexual development of the male and the female child. I do not intend to retell a well-known set of facts, but instead I shall highlight some relevant points of difference between the sexes by focusing on selective stations in the developmental schedule of early childhood. The developmental foci which will stand out in what follows also represent potential points of fixation which will lead the adolescent boy or girl into totally different crisis situations.

1. All infants perceive the mother in early life as the "active mother." The characteristic antithesis at this period of life is "active" and "passive" (Brunswick, 1940). The archaic mother is always active, the child is passive and receptive in relation to her. Normally an identification with the active mother brings the early phase of primal passivity to an end. It should be noted here that a bifurcation in the psychosexual development of boy and girl is already foreshadowed at this juncture. The

girl turns gradually toward passivity, while the boy's first turn toward activity becomes absorbed later in the identification which the boy normally forms with his father.

The early identification with the active mother leads the girl via the phallic phase into an initial active (negative) oedipal position as a typical step in her development. When the girl turns her love needs to the father, the danger always exists that her passive strivings toward him will reawaken early oral dependency; a return to this primal passivity will preclude the successful advancement to femininity. Whenever an unduly strong father attachment marks the girl's oedipal situation, we can always suspect behind it the precursor of an unduly deep and lasting attachment to the preoedipal mother. Only when it is possible for the girl to abandon her passive tie to the mother and to advance to a passive (positive) oedipal position can she be spared the fatal regression to the preoedipal mother.

2. The first love object of every child is the mother. The girl abandons at one point this first love object, and has to seek her sense of completeness as well as of fulfillment in her femininity by turning toward the father; this turn always follows a disappointment in the mother. Due to the fact that for the boy the sex of his love object never changes, his development is more direct and less complicated than that of the girl.

In contradistinction to the boy, the girl's oedipal situation is never brought to an abrupt decline. The following words by Freud (1933) are relevant: "Girls remain in [the oedipal situation] for an indeterminant length of time; they demolish it late and, even so, incompletely" (p. 129). Due to this fact the superego in the female is not as rigidly and harshly erected as it is in the male, it consolidates only gradually and remains less tyrannical and less absolute. In the girl the oedipal situation continues to be part of her emotional life throughout the latency period. Is perhaps this fact responsible for her ready turn to heterosexuality early in puberty? At any rate, we observe in female adolescence a regressive pull which exerts its influence in the direction of a return to the preoedipal mother. This regressive pull, determined in its strength by the existent fixation, is reacted against by the exercise of excessive independence, hyperactivity, and a forceful turn toward the other sex. The girl dramatically displays this impasse at adolescence in her frantic attachment to boys, in the attempt to resist regression. A regression will result for boy and girl alike in a passive dependency with an irrational overevaluation of the mother or mother representative.

3. The question has often been asked why preadolescence in boy and in girl is so markedly different; why the boy approaches his heterosexuality, which is ushered in by puberty, via a prolonged perseverance in preadolescence with a lengthy and often elaborate recapitulation of pregenital impulses; nothing of comparable scope can be observed in the preadolescent girl. There is no doubt that social milieu has an accelerating or retarding influence on adolescent development, and consequently a meaningful comparison of developmental patterns can only be made between boys and girls from a similar milieu.

Preadolescence as a phase marked by heterogeneous libidinal aims in boy and girl gives cause to severe tensions in children of this age. The girl approaches heterosexuality more directly and speedily than the boy. The relative value of masturbation as a bodily outlet of sexual tension for boy and girl may play a role in the girl's ready turn toward heterosexuality. However, I think that earlier events in the girl's life by far outweigh any such consideration. The observable difference in preadolescent behavior is foreshadowed by the massive repression of pregenitality which the girl has to establish before she can move into the oedipal phase; in fact, this repression is a prerequisite for the normal development of femininity. The girl turns away from the mother, or to be more precise, withdraws from her the narcissistic libido which was the basis for the comforting overevaluation of her and transfers this overevaluation to the father. All this is well known. I therefore hasten to make the point that the girl, in turning away from the mother, represses those instinctual drives which were intimately related to her care and bodily ministrations, namely, the total scope of pregenitality. The return to these modes of gratification at puberty constitutes the basis for correlating female delinquency and perversion; regression and fixation appear as always necessary and complementary conditions.

It seems, then, that the girl who in her adolescence cannot maintain the repression of her pregenitality will encounter difficulties in her progressive development. A fixation on the preoedipal mother and a return to the gratifications of this period often result in acting-out behavior which has as the central theme "baby and mother" and the re-creation of a union in which the mother and child are confused. Adolescent unmarried mothers and their attitudes toward their babies offer ample opportunity to study this problem.

In contrast to the condition which prevails in the girl I want to point briefly to the totally different situation of the boy. Since he preserves the same love object throughout his childhood, he is not confronted with the necessity to repress pregenitality equal in summary sweep to the girl. Ruth Mack Brunswick (1940), in her classical paper on the "Preoedipal Phase of Libido Development," states: "One of the greatest differences between the sexes is the enormous extent to which infantile sexuality is repressed in the girl. Except in profound neurotic states no man resorts to any similar repression of his infantile sexuality" (p. 276).

The adolescent boy who returns to pregenital drive satisfactions during transient regressive episodes finds himself still in relative consonance with his progressive sex-appropriate development or certainly not in any fatal opposition to it. Behavior disturbances due to these regressive movements are not necessarily as damaging to his emotional development as I consider them to be the case in the girl. "Paradoxically, the girl's mother relation is more persistent, and often more intense and dangerous than the boy's. The inhibition she encounters when she turns toward reality brings her back to her mother for a period marked by heightened and more infantile love demands" (Helene Deutsch, 1944).

4. It follows that there are basically two types of female delinquents: one has regressed to the preoedipal mother, and the other clings desperately to a foothold on the oedipal stage. The central relationship problem of both is the mother. These two types of adolescent delinquents will commit offenses which look alike and are equal before the law, but are essentially different in dynamics and structure. In one case we have a regressive solution, while in the other there prevails an oedipal struggle which, it is true, has never reached any degree of internalization or resolution.

Theoretical considerations tend to support the thesis that female delinquency is often precipitated by the strong regressive pull to the preoedipal mother and the panic which the surrender implies. As we can readily see, there are two solutions available to the girl who is faced with an oedipal failure or disappointment which she is unable to surmount. She either regresses in her object relationship to the mother or she maintains an illusory oedipal situation with the sole aim of resisting regression. This defensive struggle is manifested in the compulsive need to create in reality a relationship in which she is needed and wanted by a sexual partner. These constellations represent the paradigmatic precondition for female delinquency.

5. A few words about the latter type first. It is my impression that this type of delinquent girl did not only experience an oedipal defeat at the hands of a — literally or figuratively — distant, cruel, or absent father, but, in addition, she also has witnessed her mother's dissatisfaction with her husband; both mother and daughter share their disappointment. A strong and highly ambivalent bond continues to exist between them. Under these circumstances, no satisfactory identification with the mother can be achieved; instead, a hostile or negative identification forges a destructive and indestructible relationship between mother and daughter. Young adolescent girls of

this type quite consciously fantasy that if only they could be in the mother's place the father would show his true self, namely, be transfigured by their love into the man of their oedipal wishes. In real life such delinquent girls promiscuously choose sexual partners who possess glaring personality defects which the girls deny or tolerate with masochistic submissiveness.

In more general terms we might say that the delinquent behavior is motivated by the girl's need for the constant possession of a partner who serves her in surmounting in fantasy an oedipal impasse — but more important than this, to take revenge on the mother who had hated, rejected, or ridiculed the father. Furthermore, we observe the delinquent girl's desire to be sexually needed, wanted, and used. Spiteful and revengeful fantasies with reference to the mother abound; in fact, the sex act itself is dominated by such fantasies, with the result that no sexual pleasure is ever obtained. In these girls we look in vain for a wish for a baby; if pregnancy occurs, it is an act of revenge or competition which is reflected in the attitude to the infant: "It might just as well be given away."

6. In the case of female delinquency on the basis of regression to the preoedipal mother, we witness an entirely different dynamic picture. Helene Deutsch (1944) has called our attention to the girl's dissolution of passive dependency on the mother as a precondition for the normal development of femininity; these "severance actions" are typical for early adolescence. Deutsch continues: "A prepuberal attempt at liberation from the mother that has failed or was too weak can inhibit future psychologic growth and leave a definitely infantile imprint on the woman's entire personality" (p. 21).

The delinquent girl who has failed in her liberation from the mother protects herself against regression by a wild display of pseudoheterosexuality. She has no relationship to or interest in her sexual partner, in fact, her hostility to the male is severe. This is well illustrated by a dream of a thirteen-year-old girl who accused her mother of not loving her and spitefully engaged in sexual relations with teen-age boys; in the dream, she relates, she had 365 babies, one a day for a year from one boy whom she shot after this was accomplished. The male serves her only to gratify her insatiable oral needs. Consciously she is almost obsessed by the wish for a baby which, in its make-believe childishness, is so reminiscent of a little girl's wish for a doll.

Behavior, then, which at first sight seems to represent the recrudescence of oedipal wishes proves on careful scrutiny to be related to earlier fixation points lying in the pregenital phases of libidinal development; here, severe deprivation or overstimulation or both had been experienced.

The pseudoheterosexuality of these girls serves as a defense against the regressive pull to the preoedipal mother and, therefore, homosexuality. A fourteen-year-old girl, when asked why she needed ten boy friends at once, answered with righteous indignation: "I have to do this; if I wouldn't have so many boy friends they would say I am a lesbian." This same girl was preoccupied with the idea of getting married. She related these fantasies to the social worker in order to elicit her protective interference. When the worker showed indifference to her marriage plans, she burst into tears, accusing the worker with these words: "You push me! I don't want to get married!" Here we can see clearly how the heterosexual acting out receives its urgency or its decisive "push" from the frustrated need to be loved by the mother. This girl's preoccupation with marriage masked her longing for the preoedipal mother and found a substitute gratification in the guise of heterosexual pseudo love.

It is a well-known fact that an acute disappointment in the mother is frequently the decisive precipitating factor in illegitimacy. By proxy the mother-child unit becomes re-established, but under the most foreboding circumstances for the child. Such mothers can find satisfaction in motherhood only as long as the infant is dependent on them, but turn against the child as soon as independent strivings assert themselves; infantilization of the child is the well-known result.

7. One more possibility is open to the girl who is fixated on her mother, and that is identification with the father. This resolution of the oedipal conflict is often due to a painful rejection by the father. The girl who thus assumes the masculine role watches jealously over her mother and defies any man who aims at possessing her. We usually refer to this constellation as penis envy; in the etiology of female delinquency this factor does not deserve the overwhelming importance which was once awarded to it; of course its role in kleptomania cannot be denied, and the preponderance of this symptom in women testifies to its etiological significance; however, the dynamic factor of penis envy cannot be separated from the underlying accusation that the mother's seemingly willful withholding of expected gratification has prevented the child from overcoming his oral greed. ". . . in accord with the oral origin of the regulation of self-regard by external supplies—the penis or fecal symbol that was obtained by robbing, stealing, or trickery . . . is in the final analysis always thought of in all these forms as having been acquired orally by swallowing" (Fenichel, 1939, p. 149).

The theoretical considerations which have occupied our attention up to this point need now to be brought back to the individual case where they were studied originally. The case abstract which follows concerns Nancy, a young adolescent girl. The treatment aspect of the case is not made part of the record here; it is the language of behavior to which we shall lend our ear in order to discern a verification of the ideas voiced above.

When Nancy was thirteen years old she presented the family, the school authorities, and the court with a problem of sexual delinquency; her stealing was only known to her mother. At home Nancy was uncontrollable and loud-mouthed; she used obscene language, cursed her parents, and had her own way, disregarding any adult interference. "The names Nancy calls me are so sexy," were the mother's repeated complaints. Despite this seeming independence Nancy never failed to report her sexual exploits to her mother, or at least hinted at them sufficiently so they would rouse her mother's curiosity, anger, guilt, and solicitude. With glee she showed her mother stories she had written consisting mostly of obscene language. Nancy was an avid reader of "dirty sex books"; she stole money from her mother for their purchase. Nancy's mother was willing to give her the money, but Nancy explained to the social worker that this was not what she wanted; she explained: "I wanted to *take* the money and not have it *given* to me."

Nancy blamed her mother angrily for not having been firm with her when she was a little girl: "Mother should have known that I acted up in order to get her attention and to have adults fuss over me." She, Nancy, will never marry a husband who says only "dearie, dearie," but a man who slaps you when you are wrong. The criticism implied in this remark was obviously directed against her weak father. She did not blame him for being a man of no education who earned a modest income as a butcher, but for his indifference and his ineffectual role in the family. Nancy grew up in a small apartment located in a crowded city neighborhood. Nancy's family wanted for her the "finer things in life" and found ways and means to pay for them; thus Nancy had received lessons in dancing, acrobatics, and elocution. With puberty came the end of all these activities.

Nancy was preoccupied with sex to the exclusion of almost everything else. This interest reached abnormal proportions soon after menarche at age eleven. She boasted of her many boy friends, of having sexual relations, and asking her peers at school to join her "sex club." Nancy only liked "bad boys" who stole, lied, and had a criminal record, boys who "know how to get around a girl." She herself wanted to steal and smoke, but she did not accompany the boys on their delinquent excursions because she "might get caught." Nancy has been puzzled why she can always get a fellow if another girl is after him but not otherwise. She had established a position of respect among the girls because she would challenge them quickly to a fist fight: "I have to show them that I am not afraid of them."

Nancy admitted to the social worker that she desired sexual relations, but denied having ever given in to her desire; she said that she used her body only to attract boys and get their attention. She was, however, observed being intimate with several boys on a roof top and was found there dazed, disheveled, and wet. It was at this time that the case was taken to court; Nancy was put on probation under the condition that she receive treatment. In light of the evidence, Nancy no longer denied to the social worker that she had sexual relations, but she now expressed her hope to have a baby. She explained that she engaged in sexual relations to take revenge on her mother. She, Nancy, would keep the baby and marry the boy. Her mother, she was convinced, does not want her and, in fact, has never wanted her. At this time Nancy had a dream in which she had sexual relations with teen-age boys; in the dream, she relates, she had 365 babies, one a day for a year from one boy whom she shot after this was accomplished.

Nancy daydreamed a great deal; her fantasies concerned marriage, and she was consumed by the wish for a baby. She was afraid of not being attractive to boys and never getting married. Physically, Nancy was well developed for her age, but she was dissatisfied with her own body, especially her skin, hair, height, eyes (glasses), and ears (the lobes were attached to the sides of her face). At home she was extremely modest and never allowed her mother to see her in the nude. Nancy could think of only one reason for all her troubles, disappointments, and anxieties—namely, her mother; she was to be "blamed." She accused the mother of taking her friends—boys and girls— away from her, of begrudging her the happiness she finds in having friends, of putting a lock on the phone to cut her off from the world. Nancy said she needs girl friends, close friends, who will become her blood sisters; she and Sally scratched their initials into each other's arms with a razor blade as proof of their eternal friendship. The mother scolded

Nancy when she showed her the scars; this, to the daughter, was another demonstration of her mother's not wanting her to have any close girl friends. In disappointment she had tried to run away from home, but the tie to her mother proved to be too strong; before long she returned.

Despite the vehement rejection of her mother, Nancy nevertheless needed her presence at every turn. She would, for instance, insist that her mother accompany her on her visits to the social worker. Being at a loss about a summer job, Nancy thought that her mother should take a job as a camp counselor and she would assist her as junior counselor. Nancy was totally unaware of her mother's unfitness for such a job, nor was she able to assess reasonably her own abilities.

If mother, Nancy continued her accusations, had only had more babies, not just one child and a girl at that, Nancy was sure that her life would have taken a different turn. During the first interview with the social worker, who inquired sympathetically into Nancy's purpose for seeing her, she preserved a long sullen silence and suddenly began to cry. In her first words she expressed her overwhelming need to be loved; she said: "As an only child I have always been so lonesome." She always wanted a baby brother or sister and begged her mother to get one. She had a dream in which she was taking care of babies; they were really her girl friend's babies (see below) and Nancy's mother remarked in the dream: "It is a shame that such cute children have no proper mother to take care of them; let's adopt them." In the dream Nancy was overjoyed and ran to her social worker to tell her that they were adopting babies. The worker replied that it would cost a lot of money and Nancy answered: "But don't you know we are loaded?" Waking up from the dream Nancy asked her mother to take in a foster child. "The child," Nancy said, "will have to be a boy as I only know how to diaper boys." She fancied herself having a summer job taking care of children, in a family, way out in the country. When she was a little older, age fourteen, she actually took a summer job with children as a helper in the nursery school of a community center. There she was a child among children, an older sister who helped the little ones with their play. Nancy always liked to baby sit; she loved to hold a baby in her arms, especially if it was very young. When her cousin became pregnant Nancy looked forward to taking care of the baby, but added: "I will baby sit free for three months, that's fun, but later I shall get paid."

Nancy attached herself during these years of sexual preoccupation to a young pregnant woman of twenty who had married at the age of sixteen, had three children, and lived an erratic and promiscuous life. Nancy vicariously shared this woman's sex life and motherhood; she took care of the children during their mother's absence from her home. This necessitated staying overnight when this young woman did not return for a day or two; consequently, Nancy became a truant. Once she brought the three children to her own home to take care of them while her friend was engaged in her sexual escapades and not heard from for three days. Nancy emphatically sided with her girl friend against the husband with whom, Nancy said, she was once in love. She also protested violently her mother's accusations against her friend, commenting to the social worker: "My mother has a mind like a sewer." Nancy knew that she understood her girl friend; she knew that she was unhappy because her father had died early in her life and she never loved her mother. "It's no use," Nancy said, "arguing with Mother," and summed it up by saying: "My mother and I just don't understand each other." After such fights Nancy suddenly became afraid that the aggravation she had caused might kill her mother, who suffered from high blood pressure.

Nancy had found a temporary haven, indeed a dangerous one, in the home of her married girl friend. She felt safe in the close friendship with this pregnant mother who knew how to attract men and get many babies. Nancy also relished the jealous anger of her own mother who disapproved of this friendship. Now, Nancy felt, she possessed a girl-friend mother with whom she could share everything. During this time Nancy withdrew from the girls of her own age, feeling that they no longer had anything in common. An embarrassing testimony of the fact that she had outgrown her peers was her response to a group of girls discussing clothes; to the question, "What kind of clothes do you like best?" Nancy blurted out: "Maternity clothes." Such incidents drew Nancy more deeply into the make-believe family life with her girl friend. Nancy loved this woman and, as she said to the worker: "I can't get her out of my mind."

In her relationship to the social worker Nancy fluctuated between closeness and distance; this instability is well expressed by her own words: "When I think of coming to the office, I don't want to come; but when I am here, I am glad, and I feel like talking." She finally admitted that she would like to be confidential with the social worker, but gave her a warning by confessing that she really was a "compulsive liar." She made the suggestion to the worker that they both should reveal to each other the secrets of their lives; then they could learn from each other. The need for intimacy which exerted its emotional pull toward the social worker was conversely responsible for her repeated running away from her.

Nancy finally came to repudiate the "crude, rough stuff of the teen-agers" and her fancy moved into the direction of acting. Here she drew on interests and playful activities which belonged to her latency years. Wild and childish daydreams of meeting movie actors, fainting in front of them, and being discovered as the new star eventually gave way to a more sober approach to the study of acting. From acting Nancy expected to "become a lady"; by this she meant: to be gentle, to speak gently, to act gently; then, she was sure, people will like her. Nancy was given the following explanation by her mother when she started to menstruate: "Now you are a lady."

Nancy clung to her acting all through her adolescence; in fact, she achieved at the age of sixteen a modest degree of recognition in summer stock productions. The stage had become the legitimate territory where her impulsivity was allowed expression in many directions and where her exhibitionistic needs became slowly tamed by the aesthetic code of acting itself. By this time Nancy had become somewhat of a prude; she was a good mixer with her peers, but only to promote her self-interest in dramatic productions. As good a manipulator as her mother had always been, Nancy now became narcissistically related to her environment and learned how to exploit others. The interest in acting had become Nancy's identity around which her personality integration took shape. The core of this identity hails back to the "finer things in life" which Nancy's mother had always wanted for her daughter. In adolescence Nancy reverted to the imposed aspirations that were instilled in the child by lessons in the performing arts during the latency years. It was precisely this artistic endeavor which served in adolescence as an avenue for sublimation of the unresolved fixation to the mother. The vocational identity rescued Nancy from regression and delinquency, but it also prevented a progression to mature object finding; it was, after all, still the mother whose desire she continued to gratify by her artistic activity. When reminded once at the age of sixteen of her wish for babies, she snapped back with disgust: "Babies is kid stuff."

It seems hardly necessary to point out those aspects of the case which were to illustrate the etiological importance of the preoedipal mother fixation in Nancy's delinquent behavior. Her pseudoheterosexuality appears clearly as a defense against the return to the preoedipal mother and against homosexuality. The only safe relationship which Nancy found was a *folie à deux* with a pregnant mother-girl friend; this attachment and transitory identification rendered the sexual acting out temporarily expendable. However, an advance in her emotional development was precluded until a turn to a sublimated endeavor, namely, becoming an actress, had firmly taken possession of the girl. This ego ideal — adolescent and probably transitory — resulted in a relatively more stable self-representation, and opened the way to adolescent experimentation and to ego-integrative processes.

The delinquent behavior of Nancy can only be understood in conjunction with the personality disturbance of her mother. Upon closer inspection of the family pathology, we recognize —quoting Johnson and Szurek (1952)— "the unwitting employment of the child to act out for the parent his own poorly integrated and forbidden impulses." The diagnosis and treatment of this type of antisocial acting out has become a familiar one for those clinicians whose wits have been sharpened by the research which Johnson and Szurek have conducted over the last fifteen years. The "collaborative treatment" in Nancy's case followed the lines which were outlined by them.

My curiosity is aroused by another set of facts. From the analysis of adults who also happen to be parents, we know of their delinquent, perverse, and deviant unconscious fantasies, and we also know how often the parent is identified with his child and the instinctual life of his respective age. However, many children of such parents show no tendency toward acting out the delinquent, perverse, and deviant unconscious strivings of their parents; in fact, many demonstrate in this respect a resistivity which in the case of Nancy was totally lacking. Children normally seek in their environment compensatory experiences which will to some degree make up for the deficiencies which exist in the emotional diet of the family. This is especially true for children of the latency period, but also of younger children who establish meaningful relationships with older siblings, neighbors, relatives, family friends, teachers, and others. In contrast, children like Nancy are totally unable to supplement their emotional experiences in their broader environment, but continue to live their impoverished social life in the narrow confines of the family.

It seems, then, that a special kind of interaction between parent and child must be at work in order to prevent the child from establishing progressively his more or less independent life. This special quality of the parent-child relationship lies in a sadomasochistic pattern which has not only permeated the instinctual life of the child but has affected adversely his ego development as well. Primal ambivalence rooted in the biting stage of oral organization constitutes a nucleus from which a lasting pattern of interaction between mother and child emerges; this is carried like a *leitmotif* through all the stages of psychosexual development. The polarities of love-hate, giving-taking, submission-domination continue to exist in an ambivalent reciprocal dependency of mother and child. The sadomasochistic modality gradually inundates all interaction between child and environment; it eventually influences ego development via the introjection of an ambivalent object. As a consequence, inhibitory functions are poorly developed and tension tolerance is low. The stimulus hunger of these children represents the lasting expression of their oral greed. Does perhaps the impulsivity which we observe in the acting-out behavior of Nancy constitute an essential quality of an all-pervasive sadomasochistic drive organization? We should remember here, as Szurek (1954) has pointed out, that the "two factors, the libidinous fixations and the internalization of the parents' attitudes, determine which impulses of the child became ego-syntonic and which are repressed. To the extent that these factors interfere with the child's satisfactory experience in any developmental phase, the internalized attitudes are revengefully (i.e., sadistically) caricatured and the libidinous impulses are masochistically distorted, i.e., the libidinous energy of both the id and the superego is fused with the rage and anxiety consequent to the repeated thwarting" (p. 377).

The case of Nancy is of interest in the light of these considerations. Therefore, we shall now turn to her early life in search for those experiences which played a primary and predisposing role in terms of the sadomasochistic fixation on the preoedipal mother, and of the eventual adaptive failure at puberty. The transactional meaning of the delinquent behavior is not without consequence for therapeutic technique; however, this problem cannot be elaborated here.

Nancy was an only child, born two years after marriage. She was wanted by her mother who desired to have many children. The husband intended to wait ten years; his wife, unable to bear this delay, applied for a foster child but was turned down in her request. Soon after, she became pregnant.

Nancy was breast fed for six months; at four months the infant started to bite the nipple, causing the mother considerable pain. Despite the mother's protestations the doctor insisted that the mother continue to nurse; two months later when nursing had become an ordeal she was permitted to take the baby off the breast. For two months mother and child were engaged in a battle over sucking and biting, over offering and withholding the nipple. A lasting effect of this period can be recognized in Nancy's persistent refusal to drink milk. Thumb sucking started at the age of three months; it was forcibly suppressed by the use of gloves. We can assume that the infant obtained insufficient stimulation and gratification from nursing at an early age. The child started to talk at about one year and walked well at sixteen months.

Some events in the life of this child are of special interest. When Nancy entered kindergarten she vomited daily before school; this symptom disappeared after several weeks of enforced attendance. The teacher then noticed that the child ignored her presence in a way that suggested defective hearing. Tests, however, proved this assumption to be incorrect. When Nancy started the first grade she had temper tantrums in school and would try to run away. Her mother waylaid her and returned her forcibly to the classroom; after a few weeks her running away ceased for good. From this time on her conduct in school was a constant cause for complaints. All through her latency years Nancy was "stubborn, quick-tempered, a grumbler, and a complainer." Nancy slept in the parental bedroom until the age of eight. At that time she was given a room of her own. She then started to have nightmares and would come to her parents' bedroom. No disciplinary action kept her from disturbing her parents' sleep; when Nancy refused to return to her room, the mother made her sit up during one night on a chair in her parents' bedroom. After this ordeal the child surrendered, stayed in her own room and no longer complained about having nightmares. Nancy knew very few children and played with them but rarely; she preferred to stay in the company of her mother. She had "imaginary companions" all through her early childhood and very likely during her latency years; in her early adolescence she still used to talk to herself in bed and forbade the mother to listen in. The mother was just as curious about her daughter's private life as Nancy was about hers. With reference to Nancy's lack of friends the mother remarked: "Nancy wants too much love."

Two complementary factors in the early mother-child interaction seem to have predisposed Nancy and her mother to a lasting ambivalent attachment. The mother expected to have babies in order to gratify her own infantile needs, while Nancy—perhaps endowed with an unusually strong oral drive—made demands on the mother she in turn was not capable of fulfilling. This battle over self-interests which were not reciprocally tolerated was destined to continue without letup and without settlement up to Nancy's puberty. Her submissiveness to the mother's cruel discipline, her surrender of symptoms at the cost of masochistic gratification reveal the progressive integration of a sadomasochistic object relationship which precluded any successful individuation to develop; to the contrary, it resulted in the child's close, symbiotic entanglement with the archaic mother.

Nancy's attempts at separation in early childhood and puberty are apparent in her creation of "imaginary companions" and in her attachment to the mother-girl friend at the age of thirteen. These attempts at liberation were unsuccessful; pseudoheterosexuality was the only avenue open to this impulse-driven girl in order to gratify her oral greed, to take revenge on the "selfish" mother, and to protect herself against homosexuality. Having brought back Nancy's delinquent behavior to the predisposing antecedents residing in the second (sadistic) oral phase, the circle seems to be closed.

A typical personality configuration which led to delinquency in puberty was the subject of this genetic inquiry. The preceding theoretical discussion had alluded to other configurations which, however, were not illustrated by clinical material. The case of Nancy should be considered representative only of one type of female delinquency which permits the particular delineation as outlined in this paper.

POSTSCRIPT
1976

Peter Blos, Ph.D.

It is always a sobering exercise to re-examine a paper that one has written a score of years ago and scrutinize it in the light of present-day reality. Such a second look is particularly worthwhile when the original paper had proposed theoretical formulations concerning a certain type of female asocial behavior and had done so with the explicit purpose of giving the therapy of these adolescent girls a meaningful, i.e., clinically effective, focus. A reassessment of ideas related to female sexual delinquency seems especially urgent at the present time when the social scene of adolescence has undergone such radical changes in terms of mores, values, and their behavioral expressions, generally referred to as life styles.

Delinquency always contains a social reference, and consequently is contingent on the deviance from social norms or prevalent expectancies of behavior. The individual motivational system, or the dynamic configuration of delinquency is always influenced by social tradition and social change. This consideration only repeats the opening sentence of my original paper, namely, that in delinquent behavior we have to consider predisposing psychodynamic factors in correspondence with social norms of the intrinsic milieu. It is obvious that what we called sexual "acting out" in the nineteen-fifties cannot apply equally to the sexual behavior of the adolescent in 1976. Sexual (genital) activity of the young in the seventies has become the legitimate form of youthful behavior through the entire adolescent period, from the preadolescent to the late adolescent phase. We have witnessed over the years the almost total disappearance of privacy or secrecy in sexual matters. Indeed, it impresses the observer of adolescents that the openness of their heterosexual relations has the ring of a declaratory insistance that the parental generation be involved, positively or negatively, in the sexual behavior of the young. We can furthermore observe that the traditional ritualization of gender behavior has to a large extent faded away or has been progressively wiped out with a programmatic zeal by the girl. As a result, the openly seductive aggressiveness of the girl — especially the young adolescent girl — often exceeds the boy's proverbial sexual aggressiveness of old. The designation "sexual acting out" has lost much of its meaning when this kind of behavior has largely ceased to be in "open conflict with society." Whenever a so-called devious form of behavior acquires widespread acceptance within a significant segment of the population, the stigma of deviancy fades away and the behavioral expression — in this case, the genital activity of the young girl — becomes an increasingly fallible indication of abnormal development.

The question has often been asked in which way and to what extent the sexual behavior of the adolescent girl has been influenced by the contraceptive pill and the women's liberation movement. It is my opinion that the influence of these two innovations — one technological and one ideological — is far more conspicuous among the older adolescent girl, especially within the college population, but has an insignificant bearing on the young adolescent girl of — roughly speaking — junior and senior high school age. To be sexually active and to let it be known among peers as well as adults has become a symbol of status along the maturity scale. In the extreme — and this extreme has acquired the characteristics of a

movement—sexuality has become equated with mere action and experience. It has ceased, therefore, to be contingent on a personal and emotionally significant—i.e., intimate—relationship which transcends the sexual act and the
gratificatory dependency. The ease and seemingly conflictless
freedom with which the young girl consummates the sexual act
proclaims that to her the disapproving voice of the parents—
most often the mother's voice—is but a reflection of their old-
fashioned total ignorance of the importance of the sexual
experience. Enlightened middle-class mothers, realizing their
helplessness vis-à-vis the sexual revolution, turn their attention
to the prevention of pregnancy and suggest to the girl that she
take the pill or practice some form of contraception. Thus, the
pill has displaced old-fashioned "morality"; easy, safe contraceptive preparedness has made "judgment and inhibition" dis-
pensible in matters of sexual intercourse. Sexual experimentation without personal or romantic involvement has carried
away young adolescents since time immemorial. What we observe today is the practice of sexual experimentation as an aim
in itself and an extension of this stage of sexual behavior into
late adolescence under the security of the pill. Might we not
extrapolate at this point from developmental studies generally
and remind ourselves of the fact that the perseverance on any
developmental stage beyond its normative timing invites the
potential of a deviant or lopsided developmental progression?
We shall return to this issue.

One particular feature of the pill is entirely psychological;
it permits a temporary dissociation between swallowing a pill
and the sexual act itself. All other contraceptive devices
involve genital manipulation, whereas the pill is as innocuous
as a vitamin capsule. The fact that the pill is orally admin-
istered has subtly influenced not only the parental but also the
public attitude toward the sexual behavior of the adolescent
girl.

With the availability of the pill, boy and girl have become
equals in the unencumbered and safe attainment of the sexual

experience and the particular pleasure related to it. What has been said in the not-too-distant past about masturbation in adolescence, namely, that it represents (especially for the boy) a nonspecific voluntary regulator of tension generally, can be applied widely to the function of adolescent intercourse. The subject of sex, promoted by advertisement, screen, and the printed page, has become a kind of panacea, and its exercise per se the equivalent of emotional maturity. The peer group has come to endorse as mature the sexually active boy and girl. In other words, the peer group and its characteristic fostering of conformity has come to equate adolescent heterosexual behavior with independence, individualism, and adulthood. This behavioral mandate has replaced almost totally the initiation rites of old and is now imposed by adolescents themselves or by the so-called "peer culture" without adult participation or traditional ritualization. As in all standardized behavior it is not only a personal wish or desire that activates choice and form of emotional or sexual expression; the social persuasion of the significant milieu is an equally salient determinant of behavior.

Under the impact of pubescent urges, of the mass media's influence, and of peer-code pressures, many an adolescent girl goes "through the paces" of "making love" in accordance with social expectations, but without her being emotionally involved. The use of the sexual act as a means to attain a sense of fulfillment and group belongingness leads many girls into frustration and disappointment in their desperate search for happiness via promiscuous behavior. We might refer to this state as psychophysical dichotomization of the sexual act. This posture is normal enough as a temporary and experimental transition, but, if practiced as a "life style" during the entire adolescent period, it throws a shadow on the future sex life of the adult. This becomes apparent in a persistent difficulty or failure to integrate the physical sexual act with mature emotional responses. Having short-circuited the emotional adolescent development by a dependence and reliance on genital activity or, to say it differently, having sidestepped psychic restructuring by habitually using sexual satisfaction as a substitute for internal conflict resolution, leaves its mark on psychosexual development. Frigidity and emotional infantilism, both adumbrated earlier in life, often reach a definitive fixity in adolescent psychophysical dichotomization. Perhaps it is the incompleteness of the sexual experience that has afforded the "techniques of love making" such an influential and prominent place in present-day adolescent and adult sexual behavior.

It follows from all this that the contemporary trends in adolescent sexual behavior have made it meaningless to speak of "sexual delinquency." It has become extremely difficult for the clinician to assess the "normality" of the girl's heterosexual behavior when sexual intercourse has become "de rigueur" among an ever-growing segment of the female adolescent population, from early to late adolescence. Under these circumstances we have to reorient ourselves within a changed and ever-changing context of biological technology (contraceptive devices), adolescent mores, personal choices, developmental stages, and maturational givens.

In setting aside the outworn term of "female sexual delinquency" and "sexual acting out" as a typical adolescent syndrome of the girl, I propose using the following distinctions in the evaluation of phase-appropriateness in relation to the sexual behavior of the present-day adolescent girl. I shall describe three categories or types, which in actuality blend in various measures, but offer a framework for the purpose of assessment.

1. Sexual intercourse is predominantly the expression of an adolescent severance conflict in relation to childhood dependencies. One can detect in the adolescent an awareness, vague or poignant, of the ego-alien quality of the sexual behavior. In these cases, the impulsive sexual expression via intercourse usually declines or is spontaneously given up. Through the process of internalization, which constitutes an intrinsic aspect of the second individuation process of adoles-

cence, a psychic resolution of the severance conflict is gradually achieved. The girl must have some capacity for tolerating frustration or tension for these internal changes to take their course. In psychoanalytic parlance, these psychic mechanisms are referred to as repression, displacement, and sublimation. Girls who attempt this kind of resolution have to strike a balance between personal autonomy and the fierce social pressures of peer persuasion and dogmatism. Caught in this predicament, many girls resort to role-playing and pretend publicly to have an active sexual life until they have gained the inner strength to declare their personal choice of intimacy and their individualistic style of sexual conduct, independent of peer censorship.

2. Sexual intercourse is practiced in conformity with the social influence of the peer group and the mass media. As a collective severance ritual, it ought to establish the boundaries between the generations and lead to the relinquishment of adolescent sexual conformism. However, this form of (often promiscuous) sexual behavior loses, in the typical case, its developmental raison d'etre and acquires the permanence of a life style. As such, it extends throughout adolescence into early adulthood, essentially unchanged.

3. The girl practices sexual intercourse (often starting in early puberty): (a) as a defense against regression to the preoedipal mother; (b) as a gratification of infantile contact hunger ("cuddling") with genital anesthesia; (c) as an active caring for her partner by yielding to his physical needs in identification with the idealized mother of her preoedipal past. The emotional involvement is equivalent to the little girl's doll play, which has usually been perfunctory or nonexistent in her early life.

The adolescent representatives of these three categories show the same manifest sexual behavior. It remains the clinicians task to sort out the etiological and the dynamic factors in the girl's sexual behavior. To assess the manifest sexual behavior has become complicated by the normalization and increasing acceptance by society of intercourse from early puberty onward.

Differentiations in adolescent sexual behavior are of importance if we consider the consequences of adolescent psychosexual development for the sexual life of the adult woman and her competence as a future mother.

It seems to me that the girl whose sexual behavior is determined principally by the influences as described in the first two categories, has not abandoned her progressive psychosexual and psychosocial development, even though, for many a girl, induced or imposed forms of sexual behavior might endanger her advance to emotional maturity. The third category clearly represents a catastrophical arrest in emotional development. I have encountered in my clinical work of late the same constellation I described in my paper of 1957. Due to the public tolerance of early intercourse, the pathological aspect in the sexual behavior of these girls often remains obscured. However, there are indices in the over-all clinical picture that point to the abnormal character of the young adolescent girl's sexual activity. I have in mind signs of depression, so-called borderline features, extreme moodiness, and a florid infantile fantasy life.

Only a careful assessment singles out this girl from the other two categories. We ascertain in her sexual behavior an attempt to maintain her fixation on the tie to the preoedipal mother by using the environment as an infantile emotional "holding-on" position. It is common knowledge that with the advent of sexual maturation, the genital expression of libidinal and aggressive drives gains ascendancy and becomes—for a stretch of time—the focal avenue for the actualization of pregenitality as well. Should a developmental arrest, exacerbated by regressive trends, consolidate into a permanent condition, we encounter the type of girl who is sharply set off from the two other categories, regardless of the fact that they all share a sameness of sexual behavior. It is utterly senseless to call all of them "sexual delinquents"; yet we have to single out the regressed, immature girl as one in need of help and protection; she is a seriously endangered adolescent child, despite the universal clamor for universal sexual freedom as the unfailing road to emotional maturity.

We have to realize that intercourse for the emotionally arrested adolescent girl is not directly associated with genital pleasure, strictly speaking. The pleasure she seeks and experiences is of an infantile nature along the continuum of visceral satiation and contact-comfort; it is therefore dissociated from the biological reality of sexual functions, one being conception. Consequently, the pill has altered little or nothing in her sexual behavior or in her comprehension of the sexual act. If she wants a baby, this seemingly maternal wish is the expression of an infantile desire to re-establish the child-mother unity (merger), or she simply seeks the comforts of body contact without any genital sensation or arousal. In this context of immature emotional and physical neediness or in this mental state of infantile associations, it is no surprise that contraception in any form remains an extraneous and dissociated set of irrelevant and useless knowledge.

PROBLEMS OF ACTING OUT IN THE TRANSFERENCE RELATIONSHIP

Phyllis Greenacre, M.D.

This paper will describe and discuss a form of massive acting out in the transference relationship. An attempt will be made to explore its genetic basis and to suggest its significance in some acute psychopathological states as well as in more prolonged conditions. Questions of its amenability to treatment will not be dealt with except to a very limited extent. These comprise especially complicated aspects of the over-all subject, and require considerably more detailed and thorough study of the clinical situations and progress than is now available.

First of all, let us consider what we mean by *acting out*. It is a term used frequently in many different ways and sometimes with some degree of discouragement on the part of many young analysts. Unfortunately, it often carries an undertone of disparagement of the analysand who is not being a good and compliant patient bringing his dreams and his free associations to the daily hour. Instead he is misbehaving or even cutting up —in fact, causing trouble in the analysis by indulging in impulsive, unusual, and sometimes dramatic conduct elsewhere. He may tell in the hour some fragments of what has been going on, usually as though it were something which had just incidentally happened to him and not as though he had any initiative in producing it. Quite as frequently these events occur away from the analysis and remain unknown to the analyst for a long time (sometimes forever) unless he happens to hear of them from other patients or from some other incidental and unexpected source.

Every analyst knows that such acting out means that the patient is expressing in action old and as yet not thoroughly conscious conflictful memories instead of bringing them to the analyst in the tedious and fragmentary way in which such memories piece themselves together and are expressed in words in the analytic sessions. These old memories seem to have found their resting place in action tendencies in the patient, which are rearoused and claim precedence over—almost literally "get the jump on"—his capacity for reflection, introspection, and verbalization. We might define acting out, then, as memory expressed in active behavior without the usual sort of recall in verbal or visual imagery.

Because the patient is in one sense conscious of his actions, for generally he does not seem to be in a fugue or somnambulistic state, it is easy to slip into a feeling that he should know better than all this, that he is in fact being uncooperative; and to forget that he is not at all conscious of the significance of his behavior or of the underlying neurotic drives which bend outer reality to his needs in quite well-rationalized ways. Because of the acting out gratifies and discharges the rationalized drives, no insight is ordinarily attained and the analysis is stymied or delayed. Consequently, the patient who frequently acts out is at least a very difficult patient. One hears the statement occasionally even from quite experienced analysts that the patient must be forbidden to act out, if the acting out seems in danger of becoming habitual; or at least that the acting out *must* be stopped somehow, otherwise the analysis cannot go on. In my experience, prohibition or direct intervention are generally useless, increasing rather than ameliorating the tendency.

But there are patients with a habitual repetition of specifically patterned acting out, who continue with such episodes even after they have gained some insight into the conflict and become aware of the peculiar excitement which often initiates such a burst of acting out. Such stubbornly held-to patterns seem then to be expressing hostility of a deeply ambivalent nature. It is necessary to indicate to the analysand that the analysis cannot possibly continue as long as this kind of indulgence is accepted by the patient. In this way the expression of hostility can be forced into the analysis. This is the situation sometimes in the patients I shall describe.

Fortunately, however, most acting out in neurotic patients is sporadic, and the contents of the special episodes gradually find their way back into the analysis and can be interpreted in the various new forms in which they then appear.

It is almost an analytic truism that acting out may appear in the neurotic patient because of inadequate expression and interpretation of the transference relationship. And this makes sense, for if neurotic tensions and patterned unconscious memories are mobilized and are blocked or impeded in their communication one way or another to the analyst, then their expression will seek other outlets, i.e., away from the analysis and the analyst. I think that acting out is also increased if the analyst becomes too active and oversteps the boundaries of neutrality, gratifying the patient in benevolent or moralistic interventions.

In general, it seems to follow that as long as the material is brought into the transference relationship, even as a combination of words and action, the analytic sailing is fairly clear and the storms will not be too frequent or insurmountable. But there are other conditions, already referred to, in which acting out in the transference occurs readily, is not easily open to interpretation, and furnishes a strong barrier against therapeutic progress. I shall direct this paper to a consideration of these cases.

GENERAL CONDITIONS

We may first take a look at those developmental factors which contribute to all acting out and then attempt to distinguish which are most powerful in our special group of patients. The predisposition to be active, which is certainly based in some measure on constitutional build, probably plays some part, though a minor one, in the promotion of acting out. As an indication of the influence of body structure, one has only to recall the developmental differences between boys and girls. Boys begin to walk earlier and are definitely more active in the nursery years than are girls. The girls in turn talk earlier than boys do. But here we come to the two meanings of the verb *to act*, both of which have some significance in acting out: *act* in the sense of movement and activity, and *act* in the sense of dramatic behavior and impersonation. For at the same time that little boys show a predilection to more vigorous motor activity, little girls are definitely more precocious in play acting. The score seems fairly even.

It has been generally recognized that disturbances in the oral phase increase tendencies to impulsive activity and may be important influences in the matrix in which acting-out pressures develop. Urgencies of the oral phase which are not mastered in accordance with the appropriate maturational stage may then be perpetuated in the trait of impatience. Such urgencies may of course be due to a variety of interferences, among which are excessive indulgence or deprivation, and especially erratic alternations of the two, impeding the stabilization of a natural rhythm. Disturbances of mastery of toilet control may contribute their part, especially if these too are a continuation of erratic and contradictory attitudes in the behavior of adults who are part of the infant's milieu and responsible with him for the direction of his developmental prowess. Sometimes too early toilet training is genuinely combined with the oral phase, and the uncertainties and urgencies of toilet functioning then leave their imprint in augmenting the inability to wait.

Multiplicity of authoritative figures in childhood may contribute to later acting-out tendencies, especially if there is tension among these "parents." Common situations of tension are due to conflicting attitudes between the actual parents, or between mother and nurse, but other individuals may be readily drawn in. This situation favors acting out during later analytic treatment since it is reproduced in the splitting of the transference and the more than ordinary utilization of others than the analyst for transference projections. This complication is generally not difficult to handle through interpretation so long as any substantial part of it is brought into the analysis, even though the major acting out may be away from the analysis. An exception to this is encountered in those cases in which one or another of the contending early parental figures has made a special ally of the child or had secrets with him, giving him thereby a great gratification while at the same time arousing special anxiety about their betrayal. This situation may become almost inextricably bound up with guilt about the wish for oedipal betrayal. The old admonition of secrecy may then become a powerful reinforcement to keep the content away from the analyst. A complication may occur here through the use of the neurotic defense mechanism of denial which such patients have developed early in childhood and depended upon greatly throughout their lives.

It is also obvious that traumatic events in early childhood will tend to be repeated in acting-out episodes of which the traumatic neurosis is a paradigm. This occurs in the most clearly recognizable form, nonetheless often overlooked, in which the trauma has been an actual one with direct involvement of the child, though this naturally gains its significance largely from the degree to which the traumatic experience coincides with special fantasies of that period. It is my impression that the acting out is most forceful and persistent when the child has suffered humiliation in the traumatic episode, being forced from a desired active position to a seemingly devaluated passive one. When this situation is rearoused in the analysis, the acting out, representing an unconscious effort at regaining an active role, is usually carried out away from the analysis. The sense of humiliation which has originally promoted the repression now comes into play in the transference and therapy and is experienced temporarily but acutely as a degradation. Whenever this latter attitude crops out in the transference in a neurotic patient who does not generally suffer from a negative therapeutic attitude, the analyst may be alerted to the imminence of acting out outside of the analytic hour. It is in situations of this kind that patients may wish to discontinue the analysis.

A less well-focused type of acting out in connection with trauma occurs sometimes in a fuguelike re-enactment of some fairly well-organized fantasy of the past (Greenacre, 1950a). In such cases there has often been a minor sexual or aggressive incident in childhood which is based on and associated with elaborate fantasies derived from passive participation in (watching or hearing about) the behavior of adults. The original nucleus of this has generally occurred in the oedipal or immediately preoedipal period. But there may have been other, sometimes more extensive, re-enactments in prepuberty and early adolescence, and again in the course of analysis. These latter occur away from the analytic hour, are rationalized by the patient as things that have just unfortunately happened to him. Consequently they usually are reported in whole or in part in the analysis and can be worked with there.

There are other situations, too, in which a special premium has been put on the child's acting or acting up, rather than on his verbalization. This may amount to his being able to gain special indulgence by action in some way outwitting adult prohibition, when reasonable verbal communication would only have meant clearer frustration. The acting up may be the use of a stormy tantrum as blackmail, or it may be infantile delinquent behavior (e.g., taking surreptitiously that which is forbidden) or cute behavior which bypasses restrictions with charm. In any case, exhibitionism is greatly involved.

In an early paper on acting out (1950b) I described a small group of cases in which a tilted balance between action and speech had developed because speech itself had been deformed and devaluated for one reason or another. Infantilisms of speech were then paradoxically valued as part of the cute behavior but not as a means of communication. This was repeated subsequently during treatment and was usually associated with acting out in the analytic hour itself.

Acting Out in the Transference Relationship

General conditions which contribute in different degrees to the production of acting out have been reviewed because they appear in varying combinations and intensities in the type of *acting out in the transference* which is the special focus of this paper. But they have been referred to particularly in relation to acting out in the neuroses. The group of patients on whom I shall concentrate, however, does not belong to the anxiety hysterias or other anxiety and phobic states or the compulsive neuroses, which form the bulk of the conservative analyst's practice. Probably some clinicians would call them psychopathic or at least impulse-ridden characters. But in general they are not conspicuously impulse-ridden except under the pressure of analysis, and even there it is mainly within the transference relationship. Others would tend to put them in that general group of the "borderline" cases. But this seems too often not to define where the borderline approximately lies, or what is partially divided from what by it. I have thought that some were character neuroses with special deformations of the ego development. But I have also thought that some might be cases of major hysteria, a group which we have thought of as hardly existing any longer. It is possible that this is a clinical group that does exist but has been excluded from our vision by reclassification and the difficulty of their treatment. (This is referred to again later in this paper.)

Whether or not the acting out occurs mainly or exclusively outside of the immediate transference relationship and is excluded from the analytic hour, and whether or not it is reported to the analyst by the patient are considerations obviously of much importance in facilitating or hindering its understanding and its possible utilization through interpretation. This has been implicit in much of what has already been said regarding the place of acting out in the neurosis.

Massive acting out which is frequent, repetitive, and sometimes lasting over a considerable period of time is characteristic of the special group to be discussed. It mainly occurs in the analytic relationship and in the analytic hour. In some patients, it may on occasion extend into relationships outside of the immediate contact with the analyst. But it is then aimed directly at individuals known by the analysand to be associated with the analyst in either a positive or negative way. Such people are patently substitutes for the analyst. It is soon clear that whether the activity takes place inside or outside of the analytic hour, the analyst is the prime target and bears the force of the analysand's energetic efforts, whatever their content may be. During the period of acting out, the analysand generally loses all communication with the judging self-critical part of the ego and the therapeutic alliance is consequently diminished to the vanishing point. Interpretations therefore cannot be given at such times.

Once the period of acting out is over, the analysand has little inclination to examine it, and in some cases will neither spontaneously refer to it nor show any interest if the analyst tries to bring him to it. The analyst is then left almost emptyhanded until the next attack occurs. To be sure, by a gradual process of erosion through recurrent periods of this kind and the occasional possibility of linking up the content with material arrived at from associations to dreams in the intervals between the attacks, it is sometimes possible to get a gradually increasing wedge of therapeutic interest, but it is very slow going.

It might be thought that these patients were psychotic from the way in which emotions entirely incongruous to the setting in which they are expressed are allowed to color the total picture and to dominate the behavior usually without any apparent even superficial insight into their inappropriateness. Certainly the psychotic patient distorts reality in the interest of his displaced emotional reactions. But if the distortion invades the sensitive transference relationship, it generally has colored and continues to color aspects of reality relationships elsewhere as well. In these patients, reality outside of the transference relationship is hardly at all involved or impaired.

I have already referred to the acting out in *attack* form. This is generally but not invariably true. One of my patients described the attacks as being something like an addiction, a description also used by Fenichel (1945). But in what do the attacks of acting out consist; when do they occur? They are mainly provocative and seductive. The provocativeness takes many forms. But there is always the effort to seduce the analyst into some sort of reality involvement with him. The analysand may present himself as suffering and mistreated with a constant worrying over some current grievance which has a core or at least a kernel of realistic truth in it. But this is now brooded over in an obsessional way with a quiet drama aimed at getting the analyst to make an emotional response, form an alliance with the analysand, or intercede in his behalf. No other responses are acceptable. More frequently the other side of the coin is up and the analyst is represented as the misunderstander. There is then a persistent insidious nagging accusation with taunting ridicule. Anything the analyst says is taken out of context and distorted or shaded to fit the accusatory need. If the analyst says nothing, this is interpreted provocatively as indicating the justification of the complaints. There is a trying out of the analyst in a wearing-down effort to see where the limit of tolerance really is. This whole performance has a tantrum form, but of a special kind in which there is a relentless demand for reciprocation and discharge through or with the *other*, the analyst. One understands here a special significance of the term *projective identification*. Sometimes there is clearly a beating fantasy behind this provocativeness.

In the course of these episodes, certain details of behavior and verbal content may reveal quite clearly that a repetition of incidents of childhood is taking place. These may already be partly known to both the analyst and the analysand, but have not yet been adequately worked through. Attempts to point this out and to interpret the nature of the feelings toward the analyst are generally repudiated. The effort is to deny the past by making it come true in the present. It has been noticeable that quite often in patients with this kind of acting-out addiction, the tantrum occurred on the Monday following a "good" week or at least a good few days of analysis during which the analysand seemed to be gaining new ground of insight. This would be ruminated about over the weekend and followed by a violent effort at spewing out the gain and re-establishing the earlier state of affairs.

During the periods of acting out the analysand shows a heightening of alertness with a sensitivity to everything about the analyst (including his voice, expression, movement, etc.), all of which are pounced upon and felt as confirmatory of the analysand's emergent theme. There is also a mild kind of excitement which is sometimes detectable even before the attack has gotten well under way. In two patients, it was only possible to get some therapeutic leverage on the acting out when I was somehow able to get the patient interested in detecting this quiet excitement in himself preceding the attack which seemed to surprise him as well as me.

This is not a large group of patients. My material is drawn from five patients worked with during the last twelve to fifteen years. All five came into analysis with me in a state of anxious crisis, four coming from earlier analytic experience which had not worked out. All five were unusually bright and able people, distinctly above the average in intellectual ability; and four had a special flair for understanding and working with other human beings. Three of the five were women, and had no siblings. The fourth, a man, was the youngest, most gifted member of a large family and was distinctly the family darling.

The fifth also was the youngest child but in a smaller family. Bright and precocious, from infancy he had been abnormally adored by his father. His attacks of acting out differed from the others in that they consisted chiefly of glum angry silences. If there was any speech at such times, it was scanty and in so low a tone as to be scarcely audible. It was clear that this was a bid for me to come to him. Nonetheless, if I bent forward in my chair ever so little in order to hear better, he became more alarmed and bristled.

It will probably not be surprising to any analyst that these attacks, almost like states of being possessed, were especially precipitated by situations which stirred up the castration complex which was extraordinarily strong anyway. In the women, they were a good deal influenced by the menstrual rhythm. Separation, too, was a strong precipitant. Once accomplished, it was borne extraordinarily well. The first reaction to gaining of insight was exactly as though this had been a castrative attack, a phenomenon attributable to the fact that so much of the sense of ego strength and self-realization was narcissistically dependent on the feeling of ability to hold a negative attitude — to desert rather than be deserted.

Study of the genesis of these disturbances indicated that they had taproots in earliest infancy, i.e., in the oral phase and even into the preverbal part of it. In general, there was an overcloseness of the infant to both parents, not quite of the kind of focused tenacious interdependence described by Mahler (1952) as symbiosis, but with great physical contact and constant handling; being played with by the father as well as by the mother — understandable enough in immature parents with their first baby. This at least was the situation in infancy of the three women patients who were to grow up as only children.

But it is further conspicuous that in these three, the over-zealous devotion of the father to the infant daughter was rather abruptly withdrawn when the child reached the oedipal period. It was the sort of break which more frequently comes later and dramatically when the little girl begins to mature at puberty. In one instance this withdrawal of the father was clearly precipitated by the child who, being used to the closest physical intimacy including daily showering with the father, developed an overt and intolerably aggressive attitude toward his phallus. One may surmise, however, that the unconscious unresolved and peculiarly infantile oedipal problem in the father found outlet toward his young daughter and cooperated with her's in producing his climactic disturbance. The children in all five instances were exposed to extremely inconsistent and even erratic handling. Without exception the parents were inharmonious, held together by bonds of jealousy, with frequent quarrels, in some instances possibly worsened by the birth of the child. In all cases, at least one parent was subject to marked rages. Yet in only two instances did divorce occur, and in one of these the parents remarried before the child reached puberty.

The early infancy of these patients was not generally characterized by feeding problems, although in two cases they played some part. In one, this was early and soon righted itself; in the other, there was a prolonged siege of colic during much of the first year. In spite of there being no history of delay or of marked distortion in the development of speech in any case, all showed symptoms later which indicated a susceptibility for speech to become secondarily involved in the neurotic manifestations of young adulthood. This leads us at once to the obvious participation of speech in problems of exhibitionism and scoptophilia which in direct or inhibited form were conspicuous in all members of this acting-out group.

It should be emphasized that, in the oral phase, the mouth is not the only source of gratifying contact with the mother and then with other animate and inanimate objects. Although at birth it is the most active and organized in its function of taking in, this function is soon shared with vision and with general body contacts. At first, relatively passive since the infant is not then capable of great initiative, these become in-

creasingly more active and directed. Skin contact and kines-
thetic reactions to the mother's body and its movements are
partly superseded by more definite reaching and other outgoing movements to elicit and receive a response from the
other, i.e., mother or her substitute. In this balanced triangular interplay of functioning, the mouth and the hand soon become partners, with the eye generally acting as supervisor — the
whole setup fortified by the growing capacity for accessory
body movements and changes in posture. The latter part of the
oral phase is also characterized by the increasing strength and
rhythmical quality of the activity of the body sphincters and
merges into the early part of the period of gaining mastery of
these, synchronously with the development of speech. Hoffer's
paper (1950) on the early stages of development of the body
ego presents the reciprocity between hand and mouth, but
does not much emphasize the role of vision. As much as thirty-
five years ago, I. Hermann (1927) too pointed definitely to the
question of dominance of hand or mouth in the oral phase,
and was inclined to attribute the differences in balance
between them in different individuals to inherited constitutional factors. These doubtless may play a part comparable to
that played by the basic differences between the sexes, referred
to at the beginning of this paper. Still, it seems that the
emphasis on one or another part of this triangular interplay
may be determined by the degree to which that part has become specially libidinized by an erotization of its aggressive
activity.

Experience has led me to conclude that, in the group of
patients now being described, the disturbances in the oral
phase have been due largely to excessive and repeated visual
and motor stimulation. The mouth and speech problems as
such are, to a considerable degree, the result of secondary involvement, and may be accentuated by the confluence of the
exigencies of early speech with those of sphincter control. This
general state of affairs rests on two sets of conditions: *first*, the
abnormal closeness to one or both parents, an intensity of re-

lationship both enjoyed and suffered by the growing infant, and *second*, the infant's constant inclusion in both primal scenes and chronic marital quarreling. The combination of these two sets of factors interferes with the infant's sense of safety, reliability, and even reality of the parents. The image of one or both parents may then remain split into two components—the good and the bad. The tension of the child may become so extreme that it breaks through from time to time and precipitates some change in the patterns of family life. Already mentioned is the patient who had such aggressive interests in her father's phallus, both to possess and to degrade it, as to cause a family crisis. The two forms of outbreak most frequent, however, were tantrums and early frenzied or insistent masturbatory activity.

The abnormal closeness to the parents depends in these cases not so much on a symbiotic type of relationship, nor yet on what has elsewhere been referred to as an appersonation of the infant by the parent (Sperling, 1944), as on an almost total exposure of the young child to the gamut of the activities of the parents. Such children are loved by their parents—narcissistically to be sure—and often with more expressive warmth than discriminatory judgment. This means that the child's own maturational needs, his individuality, are not sufficiently appreciated and often can be expressed only through aggressive outbursts, the patterns for which may be furnished by the parents themselves. Separation, whether through endogenous maturational pressure or enforced by other circumstances, is felt as a hostile aggression or a counteraggression. Too much of the budding sense of independent self is bound up then in an ambivalence, in which the appreciation of power is through outburst.

Exactly these situations of primal scenes and of parental quarreling create a temporary milieu in which the infant, if present, is both in and out of the affair. He is, as it were, "included out." At the same time, he is greatly stimulated both visually and motorically with an implicit, fearful, and excited participation through primary identification.[1] The fact that he frequently cannot get the attention of the parents at such times may produce a situation approximating abandonment. It would probably be inaccurate to consider this as evoking a feeling of definite humiliation in so young a child. Yet this early state of helplessness and loss, combined with jealousy (something similar to what one sees in pets who are in disfavor), is a forerunner of and may predispose to the production of special reactions to humiliation later in life.

The infantile — even larval — masturbation which is set up may occur partly from the direct erotic stimulation of the primal scene and partly from the general excitement which may invade all zones overflowing into premature genital excitation. When this is early, it is nonorgastic and frenzied, with the child's inability to find relief by himself. He rather seeks a discharge of relief through further involvement with the parents. Above all, a response is desired which might be also a token restitution. Certainly this is sometimes achieved and may result in a spanking. Other autoerotic habits may develop alone or in combination with the genital rubbing. In any case, they generally do not resolve the tension. Although they may serve to focus and organize the diffuse stimulation into this activity until the child becomes tired out by himself, they have more often an oral rhythmic form than a true genital one.

What has already been described is the original nuclear form and background of the attacks of acting out in the transference relationship — the subject of our paper. It should be remembered, however, that attacks as they appear in and around the analyst's office carry with them a large burden of

[1] The nature of primary identification and its continued activity later in life in states of hysterical and religious fervor or frenzy is beautifully illustrated in some of the fifteenth- and sixteenth-century paintings of saints, receiving the stigmata through the appearance of an angel representing Christ on the Cross. I refer especially to paintings of St. Francis in which rays of influence from Christ's body parts to corresponding points on Francis's body are represented by dotted lines of light.

further accretions of later related experiences and develop-
ments. In configuration, they may vary from an almost endless, angry, brooding provocativeness (the oral form from the
first year or so of life) to a more clearly orgastic type of behavior. There is then a brooding prodrome gradually working
up to some generally self-destructive pitch of activity. It is
sometimes openly and directly self-destructive, but it is always
self-destructive if for no other reason than that it is clearly
driven by a wish to delay or demolish the analysis and so
achieve a negative therapeutic victory.

There is invariably a jealous identification with the analyst
who then naturally forms the eye of the hurricane. But this
jealousy is rarely consciously felt; and its component positive
and negative parts may be acted out consecutively, or divided
between the analyst and an accessory person in the general
transference area. In one patient, such orgastic activity seemed
to carry a total displacement of genital libido, for during these
attacks of acting out the patient had a genital "deadness," with
lack of interest in and inability to respond to genital stimulation.

One further element in the early genesis of the condition
should be mentioned. This has to do with the amalgamation of
the scoptophilia and the exhibitionism in a special fixation at
the state of imitativeness. This is *acting* in the sense of taking
on the behavior of another, in mimicry and simple forms of
impersonation. It is not so developed a form of identification
as to carry a really sustained wish to be like the person imitated. Yet it is distinctly more developed than the automatic mir-
roring reaction of the earliest months. It may be observed as
early as sixteen to twenty months when it appears as a trying
out of one's own capacities in comparison with others—
children, adults, or even pets—in the immediate environment.
But in these overexposed children who have grown up to become my patients and be discussed in this paper, it may have
become a highly developed skill. I have thought that it arose

not only from the enormous importance of the scoptophilic drives and the need to reverse these in exhibitionism, but that it was prolonged and perfected through the early years out of the child's necessity to observe quickly the mood and state of responsiveness of those around him.

In this paper no single clinical case report has been included. An attempt has been made rather to present in summary the common factors in the genesis of this type of acting out in all the patients I have worked with. I have omitted more personal clinical illustrations since, at this period in my practice, many of my patients come from fields of work adjacent to our own. Neither am I at a professional stage in which I can feel any assurance that I can afford to wait a number of years as a seasoning time to insure the stability of any therapeutic gain. I submit these findings, then, subject to these restrictions which are unavoidable.

Before closing, however, I wish to make a few comments and raise questions concerning the possible relationship of the conditions in these patients with similar but more intense conditions contributing to the production of certain forms of delinquency. Here I am largely speculating, since I have no well-worked-out cases and only limited experience. It has seemed to me, however, that the conditions of strong stimulation of the very early aggressive and sexual drives of the young child did not permit a separation of the two, and that sexuality developed in the service of aggression and narcissism; further, that inconsistency of handling was such as to interfere with adequate object constancy to an extent which might strike at the roots of object relationship, promoting ambivalence expressed through action with a minimum of self-awareness. Is it possible that in certain cases of delinquency or criminality in which there is clearly a repetitive patterned form of the offending behavior, there might have been, in addition, a particularly strong fixation at the imitative stage, acting somewhat like an early imprint or engram on the developing child?

Literature

In reviewing the literature on acting out as it bears on the findings presented in this paper, I have been impressed with how many of the factors just discussed have been described or mentioned in other clinical constellations. The relationship of neurotic acting out to delinquent activity especially in children is frequently stressed. These cases probably are rather different from those I have been studying. But even so, it is noteworthy that the cooperation through nonverbal communication between parent and child has been frequently observed as promoting impulsive acting out in which the child appears to gratify the poorly repressed aggressive drives of the parents, especially the mother. This was clearly emphasized in the work of Szurek et al. as early as 1942, and was further elaborated in later reports (Johnson, 1949; Johnson and Szurek, 1952; Giffin et al., 1954). Many of the papers dealing with acting out in adults in psychoanalytic treatment are expressed largely in dynamic and structural rather than predominantly in clinical genetic terms. It is not always easy then to extrapolate and interpret clearly the comparative findings.

Freud clearly indicated the reciprocal relation between memory and acting out when he stated that the patient reproduces instead of remembering (1914); and in his paper on the two types of mental functioning (1911) he gave a formulation of the different stages in the development of communication which furnishes the fundamental background for understanding the acting out by the individual. It is apparent, too, that there can be no absolute line between the development of tendencies toward action as a general way of communication and that of the more specifically organized forms of acting out which may replace conflict-burdened memories, as indicated by Freud. Fenichel (1945) pointed out that disturbances of the orality in the first months of life give an important etiological background for future acting out. This is emphasized again in a more recent paper by Altman (1957) in which there is the additional emphasis on the reciprocity of disturbance between mother and child in ways somewhat similar to those described by Szurek, Johnson, etc. In their cases, however, it would seem that the provocative stimulation of the child by the parent(s) was more severe and continuous, with greater impairment of superego development. Bird (1957) defined a somewhat comparable disturbance more specifically as resulting from a prolonged and accentuated symbiosis between mother and child causing a defective development with an incomplete differentiation between the child's ego and that of the mother. Ekstein and Friedman (1957), dealing especially with acting out of a delinquent type in adolescence, describe acting out not so much as merely a repetition of conflictful memory as an unconscious effort at solution of conflicts. They consider it to represent a more primitive stage of reality testing than is true in play action or play acting. The latter is seen as representing an effort to modify the past identification by new cue-taking. One suspects that such a condition might be more characteristic of acting out in adolescence than in other periods of life. Their conception seems related to that of Kanzer (1957b) on the relation of acting out to sublimation and reality testing.

The paper which gives a picture closest to the one I have presented is that of Spiegel (1954) who also stresses the massive nature of the acting out in his cases and the prominence of a sense of humiliation which is being warded off by the acting out. It is evident, however, that Spiegel's patients showed an extensive acting out both in and outside of the transference. He refers to their making acting out a way of life. The question has arisen in my mind how much some of my own cases, as well as the one reported by Spiegel, resemble the fate-neurosis type of hysteria described by Helene Deutsch in 1930. The precocious genital stimulation, with habitual masturbation generally without climactic discharge, would then form an important part of the "dispositional factor" mentioned by Deutsch, and would inevitably contribute to the peculiar malignancy of the Oedipus complex.

Jan Frank emphasized both the tendency to imitativeness and the influence of multiple (split) authoritative figures in the childhood of acting-out patients (see Kanzer, 1957a). Zeligs's paper on "Acting In" (1957) is also pertinent to my material. He describes special types of body activity on the couch with postural attitudes which proved to be compromise representations of conflicts. These protect the ego from unconscious unacceptable impulses. He recognized them as masturbation equivalents which were also associated with troublesome amnesias. His observations have special significance for the one of my cases in which there were periods of rigidity with provocative silence, followed by the later development of repetitive expressive movements, not as deeply automatized as tics but a bit suggestive of them.

The literature on transference naturally contains many references to acting out. I would especially mention the 1951 paper of A. Reich on "Countertransference." This points clearly to the fact that, in a countertransference overidentification with the patient, there may be a kind of acting out on the part of the analyst which cooperates with and intensifies that of the patient. It probably is a clear reproduction of some of the early childhood situations described by Szurek et al., Johnson, Giffin et al., Bird, Altman, and myself.

DISCUSSION

Dr. Helene Deutsch:

Dr. Greenacre defines "acting out" in analysis as "memory expressed in active behavior, without the usual sort of recall in verbal and visual imagery." Acting out, however, is not restricted to analysis. To some extent, we are all actors-out, because nobody is free of regressive trends, repressed strivings, burdens of more or less conscious fantasies, etc.

Artists are able to create in acting out their work of art, neurotics of every type and degree are using their symptoms to act out: hysterics in conversion symptoms, and often very dramatic twilight states; obsessionals in their ceremonies; psychotics in hallucinations and delusions; delinquents in their asocial behavior. In one word: everybody's "old memories seem to have found their resting place in action tendencies" (Greenacre).

Psychoanalytic practice gives us the best opportunity to observe the process of acting out *in statu nascendi*, to see its start, its functions, and very often the conditions under which it is arrested. One is able to understand what the patient expresses through his actions, and also to see what *specific* situations of analysis are provoking, reinforcing, or interrupting the acting out. Dr. Greenacre assumes a definite predisposition to acting out, generally and more specifically, in a group of patients she had under her analytic observation.

First of all, let us not forget that every patient brings into analysis his own personal predisposition which constitutes the roots and the form of his neurosis. As far as my experience goes every patient in analysis will, under certain psychological conditions, act out more or less intensively. The dispositional factors of *his neurosis* will give to his acting out a specific character.

Dr. Greenacre's paper is focused mainly on acting out inside the analytic situation. When we take the word *acting* in a motoric sense (as the word demands, and she is using it), there is very little room for *motoric* expressions in the analytic situation per se. Coming late or early, doing some chores such as fixing the window, moving the table, etc., certainly do not provide a sufficiently strong push toward activity. It happened once in my practice that a patient acted out his furious mood, and broke my wall with his fist; and another patient in a state of panic lost her bladder control on the couch. But these are rare and single events.

Inside the analytic locality there are only two ways of acting: (1) by actions of the body (see Felix Deutsch's "Thus Speaks the Body" [1950], "Analytic Posturology" [1952] and Zeligs's "Acting In" [1957, 1961]); and (2) by verbalization. We can define acting out inside the analytic situation as expression of revived emotions projected onto the analyst and communicated verbally to him.

Dr. Greenacre presented a group of patients who verbalize very strongly and actively, but their expressions of wild transference emotions still stay in the realm of verbal communication. In my opinion, we can speak of acting out proper only when a patient leaves the seclusion of the analytic room, and carries out the transference situation in the outside world, disregarding whether the place of action is nearby, for example, the patient's own family home, or the Far East, as it happened with one of my patients during his analysis. As long as the emotional center of the activities is connected with analysis, we can speak of "acting out."

We consider intensification of transference a resistance phenomenon against the recovery of memories. But transference, on the other hand, is the most important source of information, the most convincing part of the revival of the past. One can even ascribe to transference a certain degree of catharsis which may contribute more or less to the therapeutic efforts of analysis. Acting out during analysis is always a part of transference and one can say that every transference, even a mild one, is a form of acting out—let us say, "pre-acting." It takes the character of real acting out when the emotional cathexis of transference has reached a certain point of intensity.

The emotional forces of transference belong to various developmental periods of the past; they may represent primitive impulses of genital and pregenital character, or they may be repetitions of more consolidated emotional experiences.

We assume that, in a workable analytic situation, the ego of the patient does not participate fully in the regressive process, and has the power of "editing" the tendencies to repeat. Various situations may arise: in one, the impulsive elements of transference take over the field of analytic procedure, and the ego is not able to develop a rational control. Massive acting out, as in Dr. Greenacre's cases, will be the result. In another situation, the more effective ego will meet the impact of transference rationally and reinforce the therapeutic alliance with the analyst to analyze the transference.

Another possibility is that the controlling capacity of the ego will make attempts not only to rationalize the transference actions, but also to give it a pseudo-rational character. An example is the patient who energetically protested the "new edition" of his feelings for the analyst. He insisted on the realistic character of this love, courted the analyst with flowers, presents, theater tickets, etc. He became furious when the analyst rejected the courtship, and the analysis was on the brink of collapse. The analyst, in an act of professional despair, pretended to be at last convinced of the reality of his love, and asked the patient whether he thought that she should start divorce proceedings with her husband—whereupon the patient jumped from the couch and exclaimed: "That would be poison." Evidently somewhere in his preconscious, the patient was aware of the anachronism of his emotions.

But there also exists a danger on, so to say, the other side of the analytic situation. The transference may stay in the honeymoon stage of peaceful collaboration; the patient produces innumerable memories, finds connections, and works "through" the material. By and by, analysis passes on into the dangerous sphere of "intellectualization" and the situation collapses.

The progress of analysis fluctuates according to the interplay of these two factors: the recovery of memories, and the emotional experience of transference. The tension of these emotional experiences may rise very high and the patient is forced to look for outlets for these pent-up feelings—and he is doing that by "acting out."

As to Dr. Greenacre's patients, they represent a special group with a definite genesis. But I do not think that vicissitudes of the oral stage are always the reason for increased tendencies to act out. I also doubt that the primitive intolerance to frustration is always the culprit responsible for acting out. The atmosphere of the analytic situation is such that it may easily become a breeding place for various acting-out forces! Expectations and frustration, forced passivity, isolation from the outside world, onesidedness of the relation between the patient and the analyst, anonymity and secrecy of the latter, mobilization of latent emotions, etc. — all that plus the neurotic disposition are the provoking forces.

An excellent source of information comes from cases which acted out before analytic treatment and stopped the acting soon after the start of analysis; also from cases which acted out during an intermission or after an interruption. During analysis, the "acting-out" patients are either runners-away from a danger or stowaways in search of gratification missed in the analytic situation.

This symposium brought a wealth of observations on children and adolescents, as well as interesting theoretical contributions dealing with the problems of "acting out." To the clinical material presented by Dr. Greenacre, I would like to add some of my own experiences with "acting out" patients. I shall start with the one Dr. Greenacre mentioned in her paper.

"Fate Neurosis" is the case history of a young, beautiful, talented, attractive, and even intellectually outstanding girl (see H. Deutsch, 1930). Her life before analytic treatment consisted in a compulsive pattern in which it was not difficult to recognize the roots of the oedipal past. Love affairs with married men in the typical triangle situation, craving for gratification, provoking situations, and running away were her way of living. Every fresh experience had the quality of the previous one and the same unsuccessful end. The oedipal pattern of her acting out was evident, the secondary elaboration being simple and direct. Even the imaginary child of the little girl's fantasy was enacted by a nonsensical provocation of an illegitimate pregnancy.

A paradoxical situation arose in her acting out: when the man she loved was putting an end to the triangle by divorcing his wife and preparing for marriage with the patient, she made a serious attempt of suicide; after recovery, she came to analysis.

When you look into the case history you will see another pattern repeated in her verbalized, not acted-out desires. She had a sincere and burning wish to study; she was endowed with manifold talents; she had financial resources to engage in a professional and scientific training; but all her efforts in this direction came to grief, owing to an inhibition and feelings of inadequacy. She said in despair: "Why is it that I alone cannot do what every woman in my environment manages so easily and naturally?"

If we remind ourselves that this girl had a brother, born when she was four years old, that this brother not only was better equipped somatically than she was, but that he also took her place as father's favorite, we will be able to understand the compulsivity of her acting out. We see that this acting out is not a simple projection of an oedipal conflict. The jealousy and aggressiveness toward the little brother had evoked guilt reactions in her and the superego prevented her from entering into competition with him. She was using the unresolved oedipal conflict in a compulsive way to cover another one which she had solved by an unconscious act of sacrifice to fate by complete resignation. This act of resignation was triumphant; it interfered successfully with her capacity to sublimation.

In this case, we see that the acting out which impresses us as simple repetition of the conflicting inner situation represents an effort to cover another unresolved conflict, a defensive measure achieved under pressure of guilty feelings.

Discussing this case of fate neurosis, Dr. Greenacre saw the "dispositional factor in the preconscious genital stimulation, with habitual masturbation without discharge." I am very eager to accept this proposition. The traumatic situation which the patient was re-enacting was experienced in the period of strong genital masturbatory impulses, especially increased by the birth of a brother. But I doubt that this disposition would have been sufficient to produce the acting out without the intervention of the superego as described above.

This patient stopped acting out after a short period of analysis. Why? After the preliminary steps toward therapeutic alliance, I actively reinforced this alliance. My emphasis was not so much on her acting out, but on her inhibition of *acting*. I helped her to overcome this inhibition, supported her in finding teachers, passing examinations, and taking her full education in the field in which she had shown unusual talent. She is now a famous person in her chosen field. This was indeed a very unorthodox approach on the part of the analyst, but I knew that this was the only way to prevent the next wave of acting out, perhaps even suicide, and, above all, to make the analytic treatment work. Such a mechanism of utilizing one conflict-laden sector of the unconscious against another as defense and protection was observed by Spiegel (1954) in his acting-out patients.

In her paper on "General Problems of Acting Out" (1950b), Dr. Greenacre mentioned a certain type of patient with poor ego structure, shallow transference capacity, and great tendency to acting out. I am acquainted with quite a number of patients with very infantile personality, very narcissistic, and not able to establish a real object relationship. Their instinctual development is anchored in the pregenital and pre-oedipal period. These patients, outside and in the transference, dramatically act out emotions which they never experienced before, and, when in analysis with men, fake seducing oedipal situations.

I would like to give a very short report on Nora, who, like the case of fate neurosis, acted out before analysis, stopped during analysis, but started again in a more ominous way after the interruption of analysis necessitated by my departure. It is a case of a sixteen-year-old girl of an aristocratic and socially prominent Hungarian family.

She was educated in a convent, completed her schooling in an exclusive institution, and was to be introduced to society.

But instead of taking over the role of a fine lady, she started to act out in a nearly delinquent way, mixed with the wayward youth of the town, and continuously provoked public opinion. In analysis, all the acting out stopped like magic. She created an extremely positive transference, and analysis was progressing.

She was a typical oversized adolescent rebeller, with a furious anger against her demanding and devaluated mother. She was young and susceptible, and it was not difficult to rebuild a more respectable ego ideal by identification with the analyst. My leaving Vienna necessitated the interruption of her analysis after one year of treatment. I left her in the hands of a colleague, whom we all considered the best in working with adolescents.

When I returned, after some months, she was already back with her family in Hungary, after a period of wild acting out in Vienna and an abortion of pregnancy from an unknown man. I do not think it necessary to show you how the disappointment, the desertion by the once lost and newly found mother destroyed the still unconsolidated equilibrium, and provoked the revengeful acting out even more forcefully than before.

Whereas the two cases described above were actors-out outside the analytic situation, I want to mention now two cases whose acting out was purely the result of the analytic situation.

One is that of a highly cultivated, gifted woman in an important position with great responsibilities. She came to Vienna for "impressions," insights, etc. Her goal was very serious. We did not have at that time a properly organized Institute, and the patient, very respectable in her profession, was accepted for didactic orientation for a few months of analysis. The analysis was, so to say, going, but the anxiety connected with transference was overwhelming. Her behavior was very childish, she cried often, trembled, her whole attitude was in contrast to her real personality. On weekends, she used to travel, and I sensed that something was going on in those free days that was not reported to me. She left analysis very thankful, she learned a lot and planned to come back.

Some years later a friend of mine, an analyst in Switzerland, mentioned her name in a conversation. The fact was discovered that, on her week-end trips, she had been in analytic treatment with him. He had known that she had some professional contact with me, but he did not know that it was called analysis. This was an acting out *par excellence* of a situation in which the patient, endangered by the infantile and dependent form of transference, hurried under the guise of learning more into the protection of a man, and a better opportunity to reinforce her ego by masculine identification.

Another patient was a very mature, active, independent woman who never demonstrated any tendency to act out. She wanted to get acquainted with analysis for professional reasons — she was a social worker — and presented no real neurotic difficulties. During her treatment, I left for a vacation and we agreed to meet again in two months. She went on a little trip to Western Europe and came back refreshed and ready to work. There was no sign of anger or depression, but she confessed that she was depressed immediately after the interruption, and that she had the crazy idea to travel under the false name "French" (a variation on Deutsch-German) and that she introduced herself on many occasions as an analyst from Vienna, wife of a physician, and mother of a little boy. She herself was not married. Her rationalization was that I was better known in the countries she traveled in, and that it was a kind of expediency to travel under disguise. It was not difficult to convince her that she reacted to the separation depressively, and that the identification with her analyst was a helpful way to get rid of depression.

I could present many cases and many variations of acting out as expressions of transference. I have already mentioned that the atmosphere of the analytic situation and the forces inherent in the transference can be made responsible for various forms of acting out.

After this indirect discussion of Dr. Greenacre's paper, I now turn to the interesting group of cases with "massive acting out." I looked back for similar cases and found three patients whose attitudes correspond exactly with the description given by Dr. Greenacre. An abusive, hostile, demanding attitude toward the analyst is not unfamiliar to us, but Dr. Greenacre's cases are especially characterized by the intensity and periodicity in their behavior, and by the fact that they restrict their activity to the analytic hour and to verbalization—they do not carry their acting out to the external world.

One of these three patients was an alcoholic who drank periodically. In his alcohol-free periods, he was a man of very high ethical and intellectual standards, a distinguished personality, and an excellent father and husband. In his drinking bouts, he was a destructive, dangerous man. Oddly enough, he usually restricted his destructiveness to his immediate environment where he shattered to pieces everything breakable, beat his wife who adored him and whom he loved. In those days, he behaved like a wild animal.

In so-called analysis, he developed an excellent positive transference, gave up drinking, but soon demonstrated "massive transference attacks," exactly like Dr. Greenacre's patients. These attacks were periodic and continued throughout the treatment. He then gave up drinking and left after one and a half years in excellent condition. However, after some months of well-functioning, he started to drink again, deteriorated completely, and committed suicide (in "self-defense") when the police came to take him in custody.

His alcoholic bouts were *de facto* attacks of anxiety and the pleasure of intoxication was relief from anxiety and release of aggression. His transference behavior was a substitute for his dipsomaniacal attacks, and there is no doubt that the provocation which he could not tolerate was, like in Dr. Greenacre's patients, the lack of response on the part of the analyst.

Another patient was a morphine addict. He, too, stopped his addiction for the love of the analyst, but developed per-

iodically a behavior of anger and abuse similar to Dr. Greenacre's patients. During the period between the attacks, he was
a mild, rather submissive, depressive person. He was to some
degree accessible to analysis. After some months of complete abstinence, he declared that he could no longer tolerate
analytic treatment and left. He started again to take morphine and later committed suicide in the hospital where he
was admitted.

The third patient was a young nurse who came from
America to Vienna because of "hysterical fits." She was free
of her "fits" during the first months of analysis, but she did
not impress me as hysteric. In the analytic hours, especially at
the time of menstruation, she demonstrated a mounting tension. Usually a benign and inhibited person, during that time
she abused, cursed, degraded the analyst and the treatment.
Her companion reported to me that in those days she
behaved "peculiarly" after her analytic hour, and I had the
suspicion of *petit mal* attacks. Her fits reappeared and were
diagnosed as epileptic. I think that her transference behavior
was an equivalent of her epileptic attacks.

Describing her patients Dr. Greenacre used the term "this
kind of acting-out addiction." My two patients *were* addicts
and their acting out was a substitute for their addiction now
related to transference. Perhaps the accumulation of anxiety
and aggressiveness, mobilized by transference, creates in these
patients increasing tension which has to be discharged in
periodic attacks, in analogy to the dipsomaniac states of my
alcoholic patient or to the seizures of the epileptic girl.

When I review all the years of my analytic practice, I
come to the conclusion that there is hardly a case which,
during the long analytic treatment, did not seek in reality
outlets for aroused and frustrated emotions, inhibited activity, and, above all, compensations for narcissistic deprivation.

I am aware of a great omission in my discussion. The
most important part of Dr. Greenacre's paper is, as she
emphasized, the "genetic approach." I must confess that I am

a little bit lost: are the ideas expressed in this approach based on direct observations of infants, or on information from the child's environment, or on analytic recontructions?

In my discussion I was able to offer you only simple, clinical, empirical observations, a modest contribution to Dr. Greenacre's thought-provoking paper.

Dr. Phyllis Greenacre:

I want to thank Dr. Deutsch for her very full and interesting discussion. I was very much interested, of course, in her four cases. It seems to me that perhaps the nature of the addiction was more severe and multiform than in my cases. I think not one of mine has had an alcohol or drug addiction. In one case, smoking had very much this significance, however. The attacks of acting out were nonetheless experienced as addiction by the patient.

I would want to say just one or two things concerning the emphasis in my paper on the very early traumatic factors. It is perfectly clear from the fact of the nature of what I have written in the past that these early disturbances preoccupy me. I have written about them over and over again, in one form or another. But in this particular situation, I would like especially to point out that I do not wish to stress these as the only or even the main elements in the acting out. In one sense, however, they were of crucial importance since this set of factors produced a peculiar, bursting type of acting out which was so severe that, unless it was controlled, it might occlude access to other material. Without this, the latter could be worked with but not sufficiently in relation to the content of the acting out. Naturally anything that begins in as early a stage as this cannot be directly analyzed. I had no illusions about that. I have not been entirely successful by any means. But in a couple of cases I have met enough success to make me at least hopeful, and I learned as I went along. I would say that the more successful cases have been the later ones. I felt that, if I could understand the nature of the early pressure with the patient and sensitize his attention in regard to it, there was some degree of effort at mastery which the patient undertook, undoubtedly under the influence of the positive transference, which then allowed the analysis itself to progress. I think that is really about the only thing I want to say. I was very grateful to Dr. Deutsch for her unfolding her very wide experience for us.

Dr. Henry Wermer:

I would like to say a few words about the two admirable papers by Dr. Greenacre and Dr. Deutsch. Dr. Greenacre has made a real contribution in focusing on the etiology of acting out and in stressing the predisposing factors and the traumas that have occurred in early childhood. Dr. Greenacre has now again revived my own interest in the significance of severe traumatic experiences that occurred in actual reality rather than in fantasy. Dr. Helene Deutsch stresses in some cases that acting out may be provoked by the analytic situation. This is true. We should remember the experimental and rather misguided efforts of Ferenczi and his co-workers which led to very massive acting out on the part of their patients. Certain analytic situations promote acting out in patients in spite of all caution, tact, and skill of the analyst. This can occur in patients who are strictly neurotic. I have observed such situations on a number of occasions. If certain repressed memories of certain traumatic experiences link themselves up with reality difficulties of the analyst, such as illness or grief in the analyst, patients will often act out. Dr. Grete Bibring has described the situation where analysts and analysands encounter great difficulty because certain personal characteristics of the analyst clearly resemble the characteristics of important objects in the patient's past. This, too, when not recognized, may lead to acting out. One last comment about the family myth that has been mentioned: Dr. Joanne Fineman is currently treating a patient, a girl of ten whose mischievousness (stealing, lying, sexual provocativeness) has reached a peak of perversity. She is not a psychotic child but more likely a counterphobic personality. The family myth is an unusual one. She has been reared with a brother as a set of twins. Actually they are not of the same age and there is no biological relationship between them. They both were adopted from different mothers at about the same time. This myth is being maintained in the family and is coupled, as could be expected, with various other misinformation. Dr. Fineman and I feel that somewhere the children know that they are not really twins. I believe the little girl and her brother have a special need to act out because they are constantly told that two and two makes five. In this situation they have only two choices. They can accept that two and two makes five, deny reality, and be psychotic; they can act out against their misinforming adults, and this they do. They cannot, in this situation, like in the old joke, accept the fact that two and two does not make five and feel neurotically unhappy about it. They are children and the family myth introduced by the adult world is overwhelming.

Dr. Peter Blos:

We have enjoyed two extremely stimulating days. We were lavishly treated with a wide array of clinical and conceptual material focusing on acting out. It appears to me at the end of this conference that the concept of acting out is overburdened with references and meanings. The rather clear-cut definition of thirty years ago when acting out during analysis was considered a legitimate and analyzable form of resistance has by now been expanded to accommodate delinquent behavior and all kinds of ego pathology and impulsive actions. This expansion of the concept has reached a conceptual breaking point. I feel at the end of this symposium like groping my way through the underbrush of an overgrown concept eager to find a clearing which would permit a wider view.

This symposium has made us aware that the concept of

acting out needs further clarification. We have now reached the point of redefining, of subdividing, of organizing data along the lines of clear conceptual principles. What we all might do in the next years to come is to keep in mind certain aspects which this symposium has illuminated. For my own clarification I think of the concept of acting out as a system of coordinates. For instance, the coordinates of motoric discharge, of action, and of acting out; furthermore, of impulsive action in which acting is unorganized, and of acting out as an organized psychic process. Then, one might think of the coordinates relative to the predisposing, the developmental, the manifest, and the functional aspects of acting out.

Another pair of coordinates would differentiate acting out in male and female. It seems to me that we have not paid enough attention to this latter distinction despite the fact of its clinical obviousness. We all know, for instance, of the great difficulties in, or rather, of the relative ineffectiveness of, the treatment of the girl delinquent in contrast to the boy delinquent as has been observed by every residential treatment institution.

In conclusion, I suggest that we think of acting out in of these various coordinates in a multidimensional model and organize our clinical experiences within this framework. Then, in five or ten years, there will always be another anniversary of the Thom Clinic. On that occasion, we might bring together the mature fruits of our various investigations and thoughts which were conceived at this memorable symposium.

A SELECTIVE REVIEW
OF THE LITERATURE

Eveoleen N. Rexford, M.D.

The participants in this Symposium referred repeatedly to one or another aspect of several papers useful to them in understanding the clinical data they were presenting. This selective review summarizes the pertinent literature at somewhat greater length and, in keeping with the fact that we are presenting a revised edition, concludes with a summary of the more recent literature.

The term "acting out," long familiar to psychoanalysis as a description of a specific occurrence in the course of therapy, is now commonly used to denote a wide range of human behaviors. Frosch commented that the term today is applied to phenomena of action tending toward alloplastic rather than autoplastic modifications, or especially of actions with an antisocial bias (see Kanzer, 1957a).

The papers reviewed in this survey were written largely by psychoanalysts: the clinical material in certain instances was obtained in psychoanalytic therapy; in others, from clinical experiences of a different order. The conceptualizations presented vary according to the focus and type of material described. They differ for another important reason—the changes in psychoanalytic theory during the years from 1901 which are covered in these writings. Analytic theory has proved to be a constantly evolving body of propositions: clinical experiences have led to repeated amplifications and revisions from the time of Freud's first publications. I shall indicate the influences of important shifts in theory in relation to specific papers, so that the reader is reminded of the significance of the evolution of theoretical propositions in a sequence of writings presented largely in chronological order.

A further complication in presenting a survey of psychoanalytic literature on acting-out problems is that we have not yet achieved a general psychoanalytic theory of such behavior which encompasses all the various phenomena so characterized. The area most clearly defined thus far remains that of acting out in the course of psychoanalytic treatment. Following upon the elucidation of this phenomenon, various analysts have studied and written of neuroses and character disorders in which impulsivity and recourse to action are prominent features; there are both common and divergent points of view regarding the nature and interrelatedness of these emotional disorders. The work with antisocial children has not been well correlated with that described in the impulse disorders of adults. And finally, the influence of developmental crises upon the occurrence of acting-out behavior has yet to be integrated in a general psychoanalytic theory of acting out.

The reader of this survey of literature, therefore, needs to keep in mind that he is following an evolution of psychoanalytic concepts of acting-out behaviors, and that up to the present time the term acting out has had various meanings for different authors.

EARLY CONCEPTS OF ACTING-OUT BEHAVIOR IN ADULTS

Sigmund Freud (1901)

The earliest discussion of acting out in psychoanalytic literature is found in "The Psychopathology of Everyday Life" (1901) wherein Freud presented examples of faulty actions by healthy and neurotic persons, explaining them on the basis of the existence and operation of unconscious forces in psychic life. He illustrated in this publication the necessity to assume the presence of unconscious yet effective mental processes in order to understand forgetting, errors, lapses in speaking, writing, and reading, and in faulty actions.

For the purposes of his exposition, Freud divided his examples of faulty acts into two groups, and it is the second group which he termed the "symptomatic and chance actions" that we would today call acting-out behavior. His first group of erroneously carried-out actions or defaults were those in which the faulty *effect* seemed to be the essential element, that is, the deviation from the conscious intention (such as trying to open the door of a patient's home with one's own key rather than ringing the doorbell, or dropping and breaking objects valued by one's employer when going about housekeeping duties).

Chance and symptomatic actions appeared to Freud to differ from the first group in that there is no support of conscious intention: such acts appear independently and are accepted as having no aim or purpose. They escape inquiry because they are unobtrusive and they have slight effects. They may be habitual, as playing with a watch chain, or regular under certain circumstances, or isolated in occurrence. Freud pointed out that such playful occupations during psychoanalytic treatment regularly conceal sense and meaning to which other expression is denied.

However, meaningful symptomatic actions frequently occur in healthy people, and they can be understood as betraying an impulse, wish, or thought of which the person has no conscious awareness. Indeed, Freud related an incident reported to him by Dr. Hanns Sachs which concerned an elderly couple at the supper table. "The lady suffered from a gastric complaint and had to observe a very strict diet. A piece of roast meat had just been set before the husband, and he asked his wife, who was not allowed to join in this course, to pass him the mustard. His wife opened the cupboard, reached inside, and put her little bottle of stomach drops on the table in front of her husband. There was of course no resemblance between the barrel-shaped mustard pot and the little bottle of drops which might have accounted for her picking up the wrong one; yet the wife did not notice her confusion of the two until her husband laughingly called her attention to it. The meaning of the symptomatic act needs no explanation" (p. 201).

Freud concluded that we could assume a general principle, namely, that certain inadequacies of our psychic function and certain performances which are apparently unintentional prove to be well motivated when subjected to psychoanalytic investigation, and that their meaning can be elucidated through bringing into consciousness the underlying motives. While an inner conflict clearly governs the phenomena of erroneously carried-out actions, Freud stated, the inner conflict in the chance or symptomatic act, in contrast, withdraws into the background. "These motor manifestations, to which consciousness attaches little value, or which it overlooks entirely, thus serve to express a wide variety of unconscious or withheld impulses; for the most part they are symbolic representations of phantasies or wishes. . . . we can say that in a number of cases it is easy to show that the disturbing thoughts are derived from suppressed impulses in mental life. In healthy people, egoistic, jealous and hostile feelings and impulsions, on which the pressure of moral education weighs heavily, make frequent use of the pathway provided by parapraxes in order to find some expression for their strength, which undeniably exists but is not recognized by higher mental agencies" (p. 276).

Freud found that the mechanism of the faulty and chance actions was that already discovered in dream formation. "In both cases we find condensations and compromise-formations (contaminations). We have the same situation: by unfamiliar paths, and by the way of external associations, unconscious thoughts find expression as modifications of other thoughts" (p. 278).

Throughout Freud's presentation in "The Psychopathology of Everyday Life," he was clearly viewing psychic phenomena according to his topographical model of mental functioning, that is, in terms of conscious and unconscious processes. In his investigations of the meaning of the specific incidents he described, Freud was particularly intent upon discovering what other elements in the current situation were displaced upon or concealed by the actions.

The later development of the structural theory of mental processes brought with it conceptions of such actions far more complex. Nevertheless, Freud's early conceptualizations involved a number of important elements: such actions have psychological meaning; they express in modified form an inner conflict; the motivations are unconscious and related to unacceptable instinctual impulses, wishes, and thoughts; and, finally, the motor system provides a particularly apt vehicle for the expression of unconscious motives.

Freud (1914)

By 1914, when Freud published his technical paper, "Remembering, Repeating and Working-Through," the phenomenon we call acting out in the transference or acting in the transference was so commonly observed by psychoanalysts that he devoted a paper to this frequent source of difficulty in therapeutic management. He began by reminding his readers of the nature of the hypnotic treatment of the neuroses. "In these hypnotic treatments the process of remembering took a very simple form. The patient put himself back into an earlier situation, which he seemed never to confuse with the present one, and gave an account of the mental processes belonging to it, in so far as they had remained normal; he then added to this whatever was able to emerge as a result of transforming the processes that had at the time been unconscious into conscious ones" (p. 148).

Freud noted, however, that when psychoanalysts reviewed their experiences with the free-association technique, they observed that some patients behave differently from the beginning while others conduct themselves as patients did with the old hypnotic treatment only up to a point. Freud characterized the difference as follows: "we may say that the patient does not *remember* anything of what he has forgotten and repressed, but *acts* it out. He reproduces it not as a memory but as an action; he *repeats* it, without, of course, knowing that he is repeating it. For instance, the patient does not say that he remembers that he used to be defiant and critical towards his parents' authority; instead, he behaves in that way to the doctor" (p. 150).

Freud noted that the beginning of the treatment sets in with a repetition of this kind, and as long as he is under treatment a patient never escapes from this compulsion to repeat. Freud concluded, "in the end we understand that this is his way of remembering. . . . We soon perceive that the transference is itself only a piece of repetition, and that the repetition is a transference of the forgotten past not only on to the doctor but also on to all the other aspects of the current situation. We must be prepared to find, therefore, that the patient yields to the compulsion to repeat, which now replaces the impulsion to remember, not only in his personal attitude to his doctor but also in every other activity and relationship which may occupy his life at the time — if, for instance, he falls in love or undertakes a task or starts an enterprise during the treatment. The part played by resistance, too, is easily recognized. The greater the resistance, the more extensively will acting out (repetition) replace remembering. For the ideal remembering of what has been forgotten which occurs in hypnosis corresponds to a state in which resistance has been put completely on one side" (pp. 150-151).

In this 1914 technical paper, Freud was viewing the psychoanalytic situation as one characterized by the patient's compulsion to repeat in action; he saw therapists and analysands carrying on a continual struggle to bring within the context of verbal communication in the therapeutic hours the memories, the impulses connected with them, and the defenses against them which press for expression in action rather than in recollection in thought and word. These formulations reflect Freud's assumption that memories and thoughts were being repressed and returned by way of action—for instance, the repetition "is the patient's way of remembering." Freud was still working with the topographical model of mental functioning and with the concept of repression as a forgetting. Freud's later recognition that it was the unconscious wishes, not the memories, which were the motivating unconscious forces and that repression was an active keeping out of consciousness of these wishes led to a more complicated picture of acting out in the transference in later psychoanalytic papers.

LATER CONCEPTS OF ACTING-OUT BEHAVIOR IN ADULTS

Anna Freud (1936)

By 1936, when Anna Freud published *The Ego and the Mechanisms of Defense*, the structural theory of the psychic apparatus (that is, of three psychic institutions, the id, the ego, and the superego) brought significant changes in the understanding of acting-out behavior in psychoanalytic treatment. Anna Freud defined transference as "all those impulses experienced by the patient in his relation with the analyst which are not newly created by the objective analytic situation but have their source in early—indeed, the very earliest—object relations and are now merely revived under the influence of the repetition-compulsion" (p. 18).

She then distinguished different types of transference phenomena according to the degree of their complexity; transference of libidinal impulses, transference of defense, and acting in the transference.

Anna Freud wrote, "Now an intensification of the transference may occur, during which for the time being the patient ceases to observe the strict rules of analytic treatment and begins to act out in the behavior of his daily life both the instinctual impulses and the defensive reactions which are embodied in his transferred affects. This is what is known as acting in the transference, a process in which, strictly speaking, the bounds of analysis have already been overstepped. It is instructive from the analyst's standpoint, in that the patient's psychic structure is thus automatically revealed in its natural proportions. Whenever we succeed in interpreting this 'acting,' we can divide the transference activities into their component parts and so discover the actual quantity of energy supplied at that particular moment by the different institutions. . . . Although in this respect the interpretation of 'acting' in the transference affords us some valuable insight, the therapeutic gain is generally small. The bringing of the unconscious into consciousness and the exercise of therapeutic influence upon the relations between id, ego and superego clearly depend upon the analytic situation, which is artificially produced and still resembles hypnosis in that the activity of the ego institutions is curtailed. As long as the ego continues to function freely or if it makes common cause with the id, and simply carries out its behests, there is but little opportunity for endopsychic displacements and the bringing to bear of influence from without" (pp. 23-24).

In her formulations, Anna Freud placed "acting" or acting out in the transference within the context of the relationship of the functioning of the ego to the id impulses and to the superego. Her conceptualizations resemble more closely those of later writers in reserving the concept of acting or acting out in the transference for more circumscribed phenomena occurring at specific points in the analytic treatment and related to the intersystemic balance within the patient's psychic structure at that particular time. She spoke of instinctual impulses or wishes and the defenses against them as being expressed in action, in contrast to Freud's earlier assumption that memories were being recalled in the acting out.

Otto Fenichel (1945)

Otto Fenichel's paper, "Neurotic Acting Out," read in San Francisco in April, 1941, is a wide-ranging discussion to which all subsequent writers on this subject refer. Fenichel offered a definition of the phenomenon and formulated the preconditions for its appearance. He compared and contrasted acting out with transference, displacement, and symptom formation. He noted the universal influence of the individual's past upon any human action and commented upon impulse control in children and their mastery of traumatic events by repetition of these experiences in play. Fenichel differentiated the psychic state of predisposition to acting out from the occurrence in acute or chronic fashion of this behavior, describing acting out within psychoanalytic treatment and presenting suggestions for its management. His formulations regarding acting outside of psychoanalysis led him to remarks upon the impulse neuroses, the traumatic neuroses, the addictions and depressions that suggested their interrelatedness, and the role of the "acting-out" pattern in each.

In what he termed "an inexact definition, . . . an approximative description," Fenichel wrote, "Obviously, all neurotic acting out has the following in common: It is an acting which unconsciously relieves inner tension and brings a partial discharge to warded-off impulses (no matter whether these impulses express directly instinctual demands, or are reactions to original instinctual demands, e.g., guilt feelings); the present situation, somehow associatively connected with the repressed content, is used as an occasion for the discharge of repressed energies; the cathexis is displaced from the repressed memories to the present 'derivative,' and this displacement makes the discharge possible" (p. 296).

Fenichel found his definition inadequate because displacement, symptom formation, and transference accord with it,

yet they are not acting out as he conceived of it. He noted, at
the same time, that all these phenomena do have in common
the fact that the pressure of repressed forces toward discharge
disturbs the ego's reality-testing and other adaptive functions.
Fenichel distinguished acting out from the other phenomena
by its characteristic of complex motility; it is "an acting, not a
mere feeling, not a mere thinking, not a mere mimic expression, not a mere single movement" (p. 296).

Transference and acting out have "in common an insufficient differentiation between the present and the past, an
unwillingness to learn, a readiness to substitute certain rigid
reactive patterns for adequate responses to actual stimuli. But
these reactive patterns . . . are not necessarily real actions—
sometimes they consist in mere emotional attitudes; and we
rather call it 'transference' if the attitude concerns certain
definite persons, and 'acting out' if something has to be done
regardless toward whom" (p. 297).

Fenichel pointed out that any human action is influenced
by the individual's past and may, to a certain extent, give discharge to other impulses of the associative neighborhood. "But
the normal individual recognizes the differences between the
present situation and the patterns he has acquired in his past,
and is able to modify these patterns according to the present
situation. The higher the pressure of repressed impulses
toward motility, the more actuality is taken as a mere precipitating factor which brings occasion to let out something quite
different. . . . 'Acting out' is more dangerous than mere transference feelings, because it may have more real consequences"
(p. 297).

Fenichel found that "the analytic situation furthers transference as well as acting out in a twofold way: (a) the unemo-
tional and steady attitude of the analyst diminishes the component of 'actual adequate response' in the patient's utterance
and increases relatively the 'irrational' component; (b) the
analytic process, by educating the patient to produce less and
less distorted derivatives of his repressed impulses, mobilizes

and provokes all repressed impulses" (pp. 297-298). He found it useful, therefore, to distinguish between acting out outside of psychoanalysis and acting out inside analysis.

Fenichel discussed the reciprocal relationship between the symptom and the character neuroses and referred to a group of the latter, formed by people who not only develop rigid defense attitudes, but who also repeatedly provoke certain experiences corresponding to unconscious needs. He noted that these have been called the "neuroses of fate." He disagreed with Alexander's suggestion (1930) that these are easier to analyze because such persons are ready to act; Fenichel observed that they use other people in attempts to solve their intrapsychic conflicts, to which they must be brought back in treatment. "The higher the pressure from the repressed, the more compulsive and the more irresistible their impulses to neurotic action become" (pp. 298-299).

The irresistible impulses of the "impulse neuroses" appeared to Fenichel to "serve the purpose either to escape from a (real or imaginative) danger, or to deny a danger, or to reassure against a danger . . . this formula is valid only if we include the possibility of depression into the conception of 'danger.' This defensive purpose of the pathological impulses does not exclude that they may bring simultaneously a distorted instinct satisfaction of a sexual or aggressive nature. But only the fact that this satisfaction is condensed with a defensive purpose . . . explains the irresistible nature of the impulse" (p. 299).

These impulse neuroses, Fenichel believed, "are certainly rooted in an early phase of development in which striving for security and striving for sexual satisfaction were not yet differentiated from each other. The infant is dependent on the mother's care in physical, sexual, and self-esteem respects simultaneously" (p. 299).

Persons with fixations on oral types of self-esteem regulation depend upon external supplies, on being loved, on getting. Since they are fixated at the oral level of development, "they tend to react to frustrations with violence, and their main conflict is a conflict between a tendency to take by violence what was not given to them, and a tendency to repress all aggressiveness, out of fear of loss of love, that is, fear of getting still less in the future. It does not make much difference which person gives the necessary supply; the objects are not yet persons — only the deliverers of supply, and therefore interchangeable. And actually such a relative unimportance of the partner's personality is characteristic of all 'acting out,' too" (p. 299).

Fenichel had found that the same oral type of regulation of self-esteem formed the dispositional basis for depression. It may be said that if the necessary supplies are missing, depression is the state into which such persons fall. "The identity of the basic disposition for pathological impulses and for depression corresponds to the fact that most impulsive acts serve the purpose of avoiding depressions. Naturally it makes a great difference whether the supply is demanded from a real object, or whether the subject is regressed to narcissism and directs his demands to the own superego only" (p. 300).

He viewed the structure and clinical pictures in addicts as similar to those of the acting-out neurotic characters, with the added complications introduced by the chemical effects of drugs.

Fenichel noted the similarities of spontaneous acting out and the characteristic repetitions of the traumatic neuroses. The symptoms of the latter, he wrote, serve the purpose of achieving a belated mastery of overwhelming experiences which brought too great an amount of excitation to be dealt with in a normal way. Children in their play often repeat traumatic experiences, with the difference that they try to master actively what they once experienced passively. Certain types of acting out, he had observed, served the same purpose, namely, the attempt to get rid of or master a disturbing, overwhelming experience by an active repetition, while the ego maintains the dosage of excitement at a bearable level. In the combinations of traumatic neuroses and psychoneuroses, people overwhelmed by an infantile trauma — a primal scene, for instance — have the compulsion to repeat the traumatic experience again and again for the sake of belated mastery, and at the same time they are burdened by the fear of the repetition of the trauma.

In regard to acting out within psychoanalytic treatment, Fenichel observed that when persons of the acting-out type undergo analysis, they will act out in their therapy. Analysands with the same psychic structure who have not previously produced spontaneous acting out because these tendencies were not strong enough or were counterbalanced by opposite forces may be induced by the mobilization of unconscious impulses to begin to act out during treatment. He noted, however, that even patients with other psychic structures may demonstrate, as a form of transference, acting out in analysis.

Fenichel concluded that we "formulate the preconditions for 'acting out' (as contrasted to mere 'transference' of feelings): (a) a (perhaps constitutional) 'alloplastic readiness'; (b) fixations on orality, high narcissistic need, and intolerance toward tensions; (c) early traumata" (pp. 300-301).

Phyllis Greenacre (1950b)

Greenacre in "General Problems of Acting Out" (1950b) was concerned with the genesis of habitual acting out in severe neuroses and with the therapeutic management of the difficulties this tendency creates in analytic treatment. Beyond her agreement with Fenichel's formulations of the predisposing factors to acting out, Greenacre presented the suggestion that "the common genetic situation which combines with or sometimes partly produces these characteristics, and the accompanying general tendency to act out, consists in a distortion in the relation of action to speech and verbalized thought, arising most often from severe disturbances in the second year and showing its effects in the following months as well" (p. 227). From this point of departure, she discussed the disturbances of severe acting-out patients in the use of speech for communication, the reliance upon magic, the heightened exhibitionism, the faulty development in reality sense, disturbances which are related to this imbalance between verbalization and motor activity. It was the relationship between the specific acting-out pattern in the adult and the early history of the patient which engaged Greenacre's attention.

Greenacre observed that not much had been written about problems of acting out in analysis despite the difficulties they create. She regarded Fenichel's description as the most systematic and summarized his definitions as follows: "Acting out, in other words, is a special form of remembering, in which the old memory is re-enacted in a more or less organized and often only slightly disguised form. It is not a clearly conscious visual or verbal recollection, nor is there any awareness that the special activity is motivated by memory. His behavior seems to the subject to be plausible and appropriate, although to the analyst and to the patient's friends it [his action] appears singularly disproportionate and inappropriate" (p. 225).

Greenacre had noted that "there may be special problems in accepting and understanding current reality either because of (a) specific problems in the immediate and real situation; (b) special persistence of memories of earlier disturbing experiences; or (c) an inadequate sense of reality" (p. 225). She underlined the compulsion in acting out to reproduce repetitively a total experience or episode rather than to select some small part of it as a token representation. Despite a translation into new terms or forms, the original organization of the remembered experience is retained to a considerable degree.

Greenacre contrasted habitual neurotic acting out with psychotic acting out, in which the unconscious memories and attitudes take over the current situation so completely that the stimuli of the latter may be barely discerned. Isolated, occasional, or truly symptomatic acting out during the course of analysis, she similarly differentiated from the frequent, habitual, or characteristic acting out evident in the entire life of the neurotic patients whom she had studied.

To Fenichel's list of genetic factors, Greenacre added two others: "a special emphasis on visual sensitization producing a bent for dramatization . . . and a largely unconscious belief in the magic of action. The need for dramatization may be one of the factors which is most influential in turning tendencies to neurotic action into acting out, in that it predisposes to retention of the episode in memory as a scene or an organized memory rather than to the selection of parts of it for repetition. Such people often believe that to do a thing in a dramatic or imitative way — to make it look as though it were true — is really the equivalent of making it true. It is obvious that this works also to ward off with magic activity as well as to produce by imitative approximation" (p. 227).

Greenacre suggested that "a distortion in the relation of action to speech and verbalized thought, arising most often from severe disturbances in the second year," may partly produce or combine with such characteristics to produce the habitual acting-out tendencies. She had observed in her patients that, "Even when the action involved in acting out includes speech, the latter was usually secondary to the action which is the more important function. Sometimes the speech itself seems . . . to participate in the motor discharge of tension rather than through establishment of communication or any distillation of the situation into thought" (p. 227-228). Further, such periods of acting out were often characterized by an extraordinarily large number of distortions of language.

Greenacre described the second year of life as a period in which speech and other motor functions, especially those of locomotion and of imitative action, may be subject to a special complex involvement. It was Greenacre's impression that the motility of acting out came from these rather than from inherently constitutional sources, at least in the sense of the congenital constitution.

The orality which Fenichel emphasized Greenacre, too,

viewed as important: the orally frustrated child expressed his distress through heightened diffuse motility and oral frustration, or special forms of indulgence may produce a general inability to tolerate other frustrations. Oral demands may persist as the most conspicuous focus of a general state of emotional tension and remain as a source from which heightened disturbances at a later date occur. "The special character of an early oral trauma may further play into delay, distortion, or diversion of speech functioning" (p. 229).

However, during the second year of life, when mastery of speech and walking is being accomplished, sphincter control is in process of being established. The character of speech and mouth movements may be marked by imprints from the bodily ejecta. "General motor behavior, too, is influenced, but not so often involved in an inhibitory way, by the struggle for mastery of the body excretory processes. Activity seems rather to be increased by the effort to control the excreta, and the first communications in regard to these are often in terms of gestures or infantile . . . terms which may persist . . . into adult life" (pp. 229-230).

Greenacre found in her habitually acting-out patients "often . . . more or less emotional disturbance in early months of infancy with increased orality, a diminished tolerance for frustration, and a heightened narcissism" (p. 230) along with disturbance in speech development relatively more than in motor discharge. The latter took over the burden of the need for increased communication because of the greater tensions of the period of toilet training. It is, however, the disturbance of the functions of speech, rather than merely of the form, which is important. Speech may be exploited for exhibitionistic or imitative purposes or it may be inhibited, leaving the burden of communication almost entirely on action. In either case, an increase in rapport by looking sets in. Greenacre commented that Anny Katan had remarked to her upon the importance of repeated primal-scene exposure in influencing acting out. Greenacre concluded that the transition the child ordinarily makes to "The capacity to verbalize and to think in verbal terms seems to represent an enormous advance not only in the economy of communication, but also in a focusing of the emotions . . . associated with the content of thought. This, I believe, is a very important consideration in understanding the problems of acting out" (p. 231).

This disproportion between verbalization and motor activity characteristic of most habitual acting out varies in importance, Greenacre had found, according to "the pressure of the specific content of the individual piece of acting out, which will then be reproduced repeatedly as it is elicited by current stimuli, as though to ward off danger 'by doing it first,' or to repeat the past event as though 'to see it again' and prove it to be less noxious, very much after the fashion of the stages in the development of a sense of reality. Indeed, an incompletely developed sense of reality has appeared characteristic of many of these patients" (p. 231).

Greenacre wrote, "But chronic or habitual acting out is a repetition of past events and an establishing of transference relationships with too great a burden, from the second year of life. Both are lived out and presented without the sufficient emotional equipment or the methods of communication that belong to later development. This symptom complex is intensified when, in addition, a weak and narcissistic ego persists due to other causes. In most instances this very narcissistic weakness of the ego, with its accompanying overdependence on dramatic activity rather than on work-directed activity as a means of expression, is associated further with tendencies to exaggerated and somewhat detached fantasies which, in turn, impair the sense of reality or at the very least jade the perception of reality" (pp. 231-232).

Panel Discussion of the American Psychoanalytic Association (1956)

In a panel discussion on "Acting Out and Its Relation to Impulse Disorders" reported by Kanzer (1957a), the participants sought to clarify the variety of meanings given to the concepts of acting out and impulse disorders. The chairman, John Frosch, and the succeeding speakers repeatedly emphasized the influence of these differing concepts upon evaluation of patients and technical procedures used in treatment as well as upon theory building. Frosch himself divided the impulse disorders into symptomatic and character disorders. These have in common ego syntonicity, a pleasurable component, a minimal distortion of the original impulse, and an irresistible quality. The symptomatic disorders he included were the impulse neuroses, perversions, and catathymic crises; the character impulse disorders resemble, in his opinion, the impulsive psychopathic character described by Michaels. In exploring the genetic and dynamic factors operative both in acting out and in impulse disorders, he postulated a series of models for patterns of delay in response to a given impulse. These delay mechanisms go through "successive levels of evolution such as hallucination, motor play, fantasy formation, thought and successful action. Interference with the development of this delay structure could lead to the establishment of action patterns which are more direct, primitive and autonomous at early levels, more elaborate and distorted at higher levels, depending upon the stage of ego development at which the interference took place" (Kanzer, 1957a, p. 137).

Joseph J. Michaels in his paper "Character Disorder and Acting Upon Impulse" described the impulsive psychopathic character with primary acting out "as endowed with the following characteristics: a disproportion between motor activity and verbalization, an emphasis on the sensory and concrete rather than the abstract, and a minimum capacity for sublimation and fantasy. Often there is retardation in language development and the presence of reading disabilities which may result either from overcathexis of the preverbal state or impairment in the differentiation of ego and superego. In support of this idea, Michaels outlined the evolution on various levels of psychophysiological functioning of the impulsive character with persistent enuresis, aggressiveness and delinquency, whose impatience and inability to control his tension must be evaluated physically, psychologically and socially. The impulsive psychopathic character, he believes, may be closely related to the traumatic neuroses and epilepsy" (Kanzer, 1957a, pp. 136-137).

Ralph Greenson described impulse disorders "as on the borderline between the transference and the narcissistic neuroses. They include perversions, nonsexual symptomatic behavior such as kleptomania, and finally the impulsive character, with a generalized disposition to seek outlets in external activities. The accident-prone and the fate neuroses belong to the latter type. In all the impulse disorders, the main symptoms consist of irresistible, pleasurable actions" (Kanzer, p. 138). The etiology seems based on traumata in the early years of life.

Greenson stressed the difference between acting out and other forms of neurotic action such as reliving and symptomatic acts: "unlike simple reliving, acting out is a distorted memory and is ego-syntonic. It is well organized, in contrast to symptomatic actions. It occurs in all neurotics as a temporary and benign manifestation, usually under the impact of the transference situation. There is, however, a chronic and malignant form in the acting-out character disorder. The latter shows traits commonly ascribed to the impulse disorders: action instead of thought; orality; defective ego functions in regard to memory; a corruptible and isolatable superego" (Kanzer, p. 138). Greenson indicated that the "chronic acting-out patients are prone to confuse identification with object relationships. Their eyes become important devouring organs. To look and to be looked at means to share, to participate, and to be close to the object, They have fragmented identities, multiple identities, or screen identities . . . they need an audience to reassure them and to satisfy their exhibitinoism" (Kanzer, 1957a, p. 138). He also discussed their disturbances in speech and described their use of verbal communication to get close to others and to induce them to participate in some form of intimacy.

L. L. Robbins preferred to speak of "disorders in the control over impulses" rather than impulse disorders and to define acting out as more the defensive reaction of a mature ego. In referring to Frosch's hierarchy of model delay mechanisms, Robbins observed that the "newborn child needs to be able to anticipate consistently the experiences to come," making it possible for him "to explore the world about him instead of being overcome by accumulating tensions. Failure to mature in this way leads to therapeutic problems distinct from acting out as a flight from memory by a more mature ego" (Kanzer, p. 139).

Hanna Fenichel, limiting herself to a discussion of acting out, described this as "a fairly organized activity, a pantomime, a nonverbal and preverbal communication of some part of a past life experience" (Kanzer, 1957a, p. 139).

She called attention to a third form of memory, namely, the hallucination, "which is intermediate between acting out and memory proper in its ability to bind energy." She, too, stressed "the primitive nature of the identifications in acting out, with impulse controls often being dependent upon the fantasy of being part of the body of another person." Controls are externalized, as in the person of the analyst, so that impending separation even for a brief vacation is especially threatening. "The acting out directs itself to the future and presumes that the infantile wish has not been frustrated and need not be abandoned; in this, it resembles the hallucination." The person who acts out "avoids insight for fear that frustration will occur at the height of conscious awareness of the wish. Ultimately, the problem is the trauma of separation from the mother" (Kanzer, pp. 139-140).

The paper by Rudolf Ekstein and S. W. Friedman brought into the discussion (within the context of the psychotherapy of a neurotic delinquent boy) the occurrence of acting-out behavior in children. The authors suggested that

acting out may be regarded as a form of experimental recollection to be understood in relation to developmental stages
of impulse expression, mastery, and utilization in problem
solving.

They placed play action, fantasy, and play-acting as
different components of acting out developing between the
infant's action to attain the immediate gratification of his
wishes and the delay and adaptive direction of impulse expression which distinguishes the mature ego. The first, most
primitive, problem solving consists primarily of instant impulse discharges, and even the attempts at hallucinatory gratifications are but substitute means of immediate need satisfaction: these take place within the symbiotic relationship to
the mother.

Ekstein and Friedman noted that, as the psychic apparatus develops, modes of problem solving grow richer and impulsive action is supplemented by play action, which is delayed action as far as reality is concerned and combines the
quasi gratification of play with an attempt at resolution of a
conflict. It is still near the primary-process mode of thinking.
It is, however, already a very complex mental phenomenon, which includes the act, the fantasy, advanced elements of language, and, frequently, strong aspects of reality
testing.

As the mental development of the child continues, he will
slowly replace more elements of play action by expressed fantasy and higher forms of thought. Play-acting, a preconscious
trial solution, contains rudimentary secondary-process domi-
nation and is the first attempt to master the future by role-
taking. It marks the beginning of autonomy and reflects
identification by imitation. The mature stage of delay and
adaptive direction of impulse expression achieves resolution
in thought and adaptive action, the secondary process is
established, as are object relationships and reality testing.

Ekstein and Friedman comment that while this schema is
a convenient classificatory device to follow a child's behavior,

such stages of mental development should be seen not as separated from each other but as arrangements in which any of these modes of thought might be dominant while the other coexisting forms are more or less submerged.

In the therapy of the child, his play takes the place of free association in adult analysis. The play may be invaded by less mature modes of communication and impulse control as evidences of increased resistance, increased defense against anxiety, and inner instinctual demands. The child whom the authors described could not sustain his play in treatment; rather than becoming silent or changing the topic, he tended to erupt into acting out. The assumption was made that the acting out, play action, and play acting which the boy demonstrated were in the service of adaptation: rather than being merely a substitute for recollection, this behavior represented experimental recollection, a primitive mode of the ego to bring about reconstruction.

Mark Kanzer agreed with Ekstein's description of acting out as "experimental recollection"; he added that it was also experimental action. The discharge patterns beginning with impulses and proceeding through play, "finally become anchored in reality-tested action. In acting out, this process is not completed; the final action is suffused with primary-process energy" (1957, p. 142).

Adelaide Johnson, in her contribution to the panel discussion, introduced the factor of the role of the parents in acting-out behavior of children. She referred to her clinical findings that certain delinquent children and others demonstrating perversions give the expression to ostensibly forbidden impulses under the pressure of the unconscious wishes of the parents, who are gratified by the supposedly unacceptable behavior of the child. The superego defect in the child represents an identification with the lacunae of the parental superego, and the apparent defect in reality testing of the child is actually an orientation to the unconscious wishes of the parent.

During the years that have elapsed since the 1962 Symposium, child psychiatric and child mental health facilities have been preoccupied with extending the range and variety of services for children, giving very little emphasis to acting out and delinquency. The criminological and sociological literature has been equally unfruitful. Whether other clinicians and students have developed a larger measure of sophistication in the conceptualization of acting out and a clinical usage reflecting newer concepts is hard to say. The community mental health field tends to emphasize the role of adverse social conditions in so-called acting out — e.g., aggressive destructive behavior of children and adolescents — and the number of carefully studied cases in psychiatric centers has apparently declined. Among psychoanalysts, however, an increasing awareness of the complexity of current concepts of acting out and of the ambiguous uses to which the term has been put persists, and the topic remains one to which they address themselves at professional meetings and in their literature.

The 25th International Psychoanalytic Congress Symposium

The main Symposium of the 1967 Copenhagen International Psychoanalytic Congress which concentrated upon concepts of acting out offered no major conceptual breakthroughs or marked advance in the measure of agreement among psychoanalysts regarding the term and when and how it should be applied. The familiar differences between the group working to retain the term of acting out for the behaviors stimulated by the psychoanalytic process and those seeking to extend it to the wider groupings of behaviors outside as well as within the analytic setting remained. Certain participants, such as León Grinberg (1968) who conceived of the phenomena in a broader sense, still thought it preferable to restrict the term to the analytic situation where it could be scrutinized in the setting of the bipersonal relationship.

It was notable that sharp differences of opinion arose in

the discussion groups about the nature and significance of acting out within the analytic situation. While those opting for a restricted use of the term appeared, in their general remarks, to agree on the dynamics of the behavior, they not infrequently differed in more specific clinical applications of the concepts which earlier had seemed obvious to everyone. According to David Beres (1968), members of a Kris Study Group for the New York Psychoanalytic Institute reported that after two years of working together on the problems of acting out, they were still not agreed about the meaning of the concept.

Anna Freud set the tenor of the Congress meeting in her introduction to the Symposium. In an admirably lucid paper in which she confined herself to the psychoanalytic situation, psychoanalytic theory and technique, she moved from a succinct description of the original meaning and significance of the term acting out in psychoanalysis to the changes in psychoanalytic preoccupation, patient population, theory, and teaching that have been responsible for shifts in the use of the term. She illustrated how the widening scope of theoretical interest and of analytic practice had stimulated an expansion of the use of the term acting out without the differentiations and distinctions which the changes warranted.

After describing the concept of acting out as defined in the original setting, Miss Freud focused on the technical changes resulting from theoretical changes. ". . . acting out is at a mimimum, i.e., nipped in the bud, so far as the technical devices of free association and dream interpretations are concerned. It is allowed latitude, within the limits of the analytic rules, in the transference and for the sake of transference interpretation. And it endangers the progress of analytic treatment where it cannot be confined either within the physical sphere (short of motor action) or within the analytic setting (i.e., within the transference)" (1968, p. 167).

Within the analytic situation, the balance between recovery of the past by way of free association and dream interpretation (i.e., remembering) and by way of transference behavior (i.e., reliving, repeating, acting out) was fairly even until changes in theoretical outlook altered that technical balance decisively. The first such change, Miss Freud pointed out, was the shift of interest from oedipal to preoedipal events, especially the early mother-infant interactions, a phase that is under primary repression and is not recoverable in memory; it is therefore only apt to be relived (repeated, acted out, in behavior).

Secondly, the shift to a concentration on the ego required the analyst to focus upon the transference of infantile attitudes to provide material for interpretation. Furthermore, "the widening of the instinct theory to include aggression had similar technical consequences . . . [since] the aggressive drive is more closely linked with action and the motor apparatus, i.e., more liable to be acted out than to be remembered" (p. 167).

Miss Freud remarked upon the growing disbelief in the therapeutic effectiveness of remembering and the preference for insisting on reliving emotional experience and repeating it in the transference. She called attention to the widening scope of psychoanalysis which brought other diagnostic categories and ages into the therapeutic experience. The original concept, which described neurotic adult individuals who acted out under the pressure of the analytic situation, has been used to earmark these other types of patients as well.

Prominent examples are "the impulsive and delinquent character disorders, the pre-psychotic, psychotic, and especially paranoid states, the alcoholics and other addicts who are now considered amenable to psychoanalytic therapy" (p. 168). They tend to be referred to as "acting-out patients," and discussions of difficulties in their therapy often is carried out under the heading of the expected transference behavior of neurotic patients. This confusion not only disregards the changes in meaning of the concept, "it obscures thereby the differences between the neurotic and the delinquent or psychotic type of analysand instead of helping to highlight them. Unlike the neurotic, the delinquent, the addict, and the psychotic act out habitually, i.e., also without the releasing benefits of the analytic technique. . . . We have to disregard the misleading factor that under the influence of analysis neurotic patients behave as if they were impulsive characters. It remains a mistake to reverse the statement and regard the analytic behaviour of the impulsive types as on a par with the neurotic ones" (p. 168). Miss Freud stressed the quantitative differences between the two types and the area in which the behavior originates. In the neurotic, it takes place within the analytic situation, in the other types, it starts outside and must be drawn into the transference.

While acknowledging that young children in analysis by definition could be called "acting-out patients," Miss Freud observed that since this fact is developmentally determined, it does not carry the same significance as it does later in life "neither for highlighting alternating states of treatment alliance and resistance to treatment nor for the quality and historical level of the material which is produced." The child analyst "has to be content with reducing reality actions to play activity and to find his way from there via fantasy elaboration to verbalization and secondary process thinking. His final aim remains the same as in adult therapy: to submit all psychic content to the synthetic function of the patient's ego, regardless of the manner in which it has appeared (acted out with the original objects, acted out in the transference, in reality behavior, in role play, in play with toys, in fantasy, etc." (p. 169).

The analysis of adolescents is rendered problematic by the adolescent's often violent acting out within the transference, a function of his heightened tendency toward re-enactment. Whether his "dramatized form of acting out can be turned into analytically useful material depends above all on two conditions: on the analyst's side on his skill in differentiating between past and present, i.e., between transferred and new material and between pathological and developmentally adequate elements; on the patient's side above all on the economic aspect, i.e., on the degree of cathexis of the reawakened and of the newly-arrived strivings and the relative strength of the anxieties and defences mobilized against them" (p. 169).

In her conclusion, Miss Freud noted that reliving in the transference has been increasingly taken for granted in analytic circles, "and the longer this happened, the more often was the term 'acting out' not applied to the repetition in the transference at all, but reserved for the re-enactment of the past outside the analysis." She personally regretted this change of usage since "it obscures the initially sharp differentiation between remembering and repeating and on the other hand it glosses over the differences between the various forms of 'acting out'. To my mind, there is merit in preserving the distinctions between the consecutive steps which in this respect form a sequence in the analysand's behaviour" (pp. 169-170).

Miss Freud's clear definitions, her descriptions of the sequences in psychoanalytic activity and theory and of the nature of the different conditions involving "acting out" provide at once the guide and the framework within which the analytic clinician can sort out his preconceptions and confusions regarding the concepts of acting out in the area of psychoanalysis.

Leon Grinberg (1968, p. 171) discussed acting out in a clinical context, with emphasis upon the etiology and the functions of acting-out behaviors. He saw one of its essential roots as associated with experiences of object loss and separation with inadequate mourning. Acting out is a process which always involves an object relationship, generally of a narcissistic nature and patterned upon an early conflictual mother child relation. The patient persists in a search for someone to take away his pain, for someone Grinberg refers to as "a container object." At times this object is found in his own body as a psychosomatic or hypochondriatic disturbance or in a peculiar dream.

Grinberg would prefer to restrict the application of the term acting out "to psychoanalytic experience in order to limit one of the fields in which it appears more clearly. . . . the psychoanalytic framework offers the best possibility of understanding what happens in a bipersonal relationship. Acting out is basically a process that develops in an object relationship" (p. 177).

Hedwig Schwarz reported on the Hampstead Clinic project on Problems of Delinquency. In her view the delinquent act is a symptom formation, a compromise arising from conflicts acted out repeatedly and compulsively and evolving from different agencies in the psychic structure. Schwarz considered the dynamics of acting out in the neurotic patient undergoing analysis and in the patient habitually acting out sufficiently similar to render the use of the term helpful despite the ambiguities admittedly involved.

Schwarz indicated the work of the Hampstead project suggests that we may relate the origin of the acting-out pathology to "a break in the mother-child relationship at the very height of the ambivalent phase of development when only the presence of the mother and her tolerance make it possible for the child to express his libidinal and aggressive feelings, his love *and* hate of her whilst gradually accepting the unavoidable frustrations and restrictions set by her and others. If at that period of development (tentatively put at 18 months-2½ years) a break in the mother-child relationship occurs which interrupts this phase of development, the child's capacity for a relationship to an object above and beyond the need-satisfying, giving role is interfered with" (p. 181). Since a child of this age can cope with extreme pain and anxiety only by massive repression, later situations which threaten to evoke the pain may lead to acting out which represents either eruptions of the repressed or the struggle against painful affect. Schwarz suggested that all acting out could be seen as a seeking for a new object, one who will restore the original union with the mother in early childhood, protected by her presence and by her lending him certain standards of behavior from which he could have progressed gradually by using these for his own internalized superego.

Schwarz's suggestions regarding the genesis and time of onset of the acting-out pattern remind us of Greenacre's hypotheses. These latter were derived from clinical work with adults, and emphasized the rapid maturational growth, the impact of the onset of speech and walking, the presence of heightened sensibility, and the child's vulnerability to trauma during this period. In general, limited attention was paid to genetic factors in the Congress discussions.

Rangell proposed that we separate action from acting out and regard it as one of the possible end-products of the multidimensioned and complex intrapsychic process. Such final action depends on the particular configuration of id, ego, and superego interaction in the living experience and the internal-external continuum of that particular individual at that dynamic and economic moment of his life.

Serge Lebovici argued from clinical experiences in child analysis that acting out is "an elaboration of behaviour which, technically, should lead to interpretative elaboration and which has special metapsychological characteristics, i.e., that of primitive forms of the ego when the secondary processes start to appear" (p. 205).

Thorkil Vanggaard spoke for defining acting out in the classical and narrow sense. He contrasted with it what he called the therapeutic trial and error, which plays a quite different role in analysis, and he described various clinical syndromes in which varieties of action play different roles due to the ability of the patients' egos to handle anxiety and the drives, and particularly differences in ego strength. Vanggaard had little confidence in the success of interpretation or analysis proper in the chronically acting-out patient: he himself resorts rather to a pedagogical approach.

Greenacre likened the process of psychoanalysis to the creative process — as one of recreative growth. She was concerned with whatever facilitated this process and whatever interfered with it, conspicuously the phenomena of acting out. She reviewed certain of her prior theses regarding this phenomenon and explored particularly the role of the patient's misuse of speech in the transference and in acting out. She found it hard to distinguish sharply between action and acting out, and she was reluctant to confine attention exclusively to the analytic situation because she thought "certain repetitive actions — no matter what we call them — may occur even where there is no analysis" and resemble closely those occurring under the stimulus of the analytic process. She found Anna Freud's differentiation in the origin and in the texture of acting out in the neuroses, impulsive characters, and psychoses important in view of the recent tendency to over simplify the application of our theories in a way to exaggerate common factors and sometimes overlook fundamental differences. Greenacre doubted the specific ascriptions of etiology given by several speakers and implied her preference for a multidimensional concept in which early ego development involving the relationship of speech to motor activity plays a prominent role.

Mark Kanzer explored the concept of "ego alterations" in relation to acting out and its improved management when a better understanding of the ego and modifications takes place in the course of treatment. Samuel Ritvo pointed out that various analysts have sought to link each developmental stage with its own accompanying form and content of acting out. He pointed to the complexities of dealing with the inherited aspects of the ego, the autonomous areas and the impact of experience and environment on ego development. He noted that Greenacre had specified one form of ego development as particularly prone to acting out, and others may be teased out as longitudinal studies and child analyses provide detailed data from which to conceptualize.

Beyond the clear difference of opinion regarding both clinical and metapsychological formulations of acting out, the Congress speakers and discussants displayed a more organized consideration of the phenomena called acting out, neurotic actions, and symptomatic acts than noted in previous psychoanalytic meetings. There seemed to be a greater tendency to seek technical measures for dealing with acting out in analysis and more tolerance or acceptance of the likelihood that analysands of whatever make-up would at some point tend to act out. The extreme views, namely, that acting out could be avoided by permissiveness on the part of the analyst or that, conversely, those who act out almost by definition cannot be analyzed, were held by very few.

Those who wished to restrict the term and concept to the analytic situation gave as broadly based an explanation of acting out as did those who preferred a much wider application of the concepts. The tendency to seek for a specific trauma, a specific ego weakness or a specific developmental phase or constellation as the source of acting out persists, but the variety of theses put forward suggests the sensed inadequacy of each one. The discussion in one English Language Section lent itself to a division into four categories: the clinical descriptive aspects of acting out, the genetic considerations, the dynamic formulations, and its technical management. Despite this more comprehensive approach to the clinical data, the reporter concluded that "we still have the need for a more specific dynamic understanding of the term acting out."

Panel on Acting Out
American Psychoanalytic Association

A second panel on acting out took place at the 1969 Fall Meetings of the American Psychoanalytic Association. Its purpose, as reported by Norman Atkins (1970), was to follow Leo Rangell's suggestion made (at the Copenhagen Congress) "to establish the role of acting out within the major realm of human action and to distinguish it particularly from neurotic action." The discussion itself centered largely upon the phenomena of acting out and the symptomatic act in relation to illustrative case material.

There was rather general agreement that the symptomatic act during an analysis, whether directly involving the analytic situation or not is apt to represent a communication to the analyst. Elizabeth Zetzel put forth the proposition that these acts more often indicated the re-emergence of long-defended-against infantile wishes than a resistance to the analytic work. She in particular sought to emphasize the distinction between an action that represents some active participation on the part of the ego and acting out, which is essentially passively experienced by the ego and which may have a different kind of underlying meaning.

The panel largely agreed that many analysts have regarded all acting out unfavorably. "Pejorative" was the word most frequently used to indicate the pessimistic attitude taken in the past and even currently about the analyzability and technical management of patients resorting a great deal to one or another form of action. Most of the members of the panel were more tolerant of these occurrences, regarding action or acting out in analysis inevitable in a patient whose life pattern is characterized by neurotic action, an action that cannot be analyzed if it does not take place within the purview of the treatment. They reminded others that the analytic process itself predisposes to action, acting out, or symptomatic acts, depending upon the make-up of the patient and the nature of the transference at a certain point in the analysis.

Martin Stein described a patient who, in analysis, developed complex and self-destructive patterns of neurotic action during which his habitual judgment, caution, and reality sense were suspended. Although the patient acquired some understanding of and partial control of the episodes, the tendency toward action never disappeared. Stein hypothesized altered states of consciousness as the predisposing factor in his patient and wondered if such subtle neurophysiological changes might not be more common than is realized in acting-out patients. Other panelists, who noted that the episodes began in analysis and were related to the transference, were skeptical, although Zetzel recalled EEG tracings during sleepwalking or bed wetting that were different from those during the subjects' dreaming. She added that perhaps the acting-out patients resemble the sleepwalkers in their neurophysiological patterning.

In their closing comments, the panelists pointed to the broader range of clinical material open for study in the current pattern of psychoanalytic practice. The influence of the current social and political scene, its orientation toward action and confrontation, must be added to the natural proclivities of certain action-oriented patients. However, action must be analyzed, and both analysts and patients encouraged toward introspection.

The participants of this panel dealt more extensively with clinical than with theoretical issues. The repercussions of the action pattern upon the analytic process took up much of the discussion. The distinction between patterns of neurotic action occurring before and during analysis, patterns making their appearance as massive transference resistances, patterns of symptomatic acts serving largely as a communication and less as a resistance and complex episodes of acting out was pursued, with fair agreement about their definition and less about their significance. Clearer was the general inclination to regard these manifestations of action rather than verbalization, as material of the analysis and for analysis, neither more perilous nor less desirable than other obstacles to the analytic process. The discrimination between acts in which the ego clearly participates and those which by-pass the ego or in which the ego appears largely passive seemed a promising tool for setting up a hypothetical hierarchy of acts and relating them to other human phenomena.

Charles Brenner

Charles Brenner (1969) in discussing the effects of theory on psychoanalytic technique referred to acting out in the limited sense: "Actions which are motivated by transference conflicts and wishes may be momentary or extended in time; they may be of great or little practical importance in the patient's life; they may be variously motivated by those forces within the mind which we designate as ego, superego, and id; all these characteristics may vary from case to case. What applies equally to every case is the general principle that it is the patient's resistances which determine how accessible to analysis are the underlying motives of the actions in question" (p. 340).

Brenner pointed out that the relationship between action in general and intrapsychic conflict is understood today much better than was the case fifty years ago. "One does not at present attempt to separate the normal from the neurotic in the field of human action in a qualitative way . . . the separation between the two is one of degree rather than of kind. We are accustomed to observing the part played by unconscious, infantile conflict in actions of every sort; we are familiar with the fact that it is not only in so-called neurotic behavior that such motivation plays a part" (p. 340).

Sandler, Holder, and Dare

Sandler, Holder, and Dare (1973) in a critique of basic psychoanalytic concepts observed that of all the clinical concepts considered in their series, "acting out has probably suffered the greatest extension and change of meaning since it was first introduced by Freud. . . . The term now tends to be used (by psychoanalysts and others) to include a whole range of impulsive antisocial or dangerous actions, often without regard to the contexts in which such actions arise." They note that relevant recent literature "shows the great variety of current usages, the only common denominator appearing to be the assumption that the particular action referred to as 'acting out' has unconscious determinants" (p. 94).

The authors in their review of the evolution of the concept within psychoanalysis, emphasize semantic factors. For instance, they believe that Fenichel's use of the term acting out to characterize a group of people tending to express their unconscious impulses in action more readily than others reduced the link that previously existed between acting out and transference resistance. They suggest that some such term as "enactment" should be used to distinguish the general tendency to impulsive or irrational action from acting out linked with the treatment process.

Sandler et al. noted the frequent characterization of the extra-analytic form of acting out as "habitual modes of action and behavior which are a consequence of existing personality and pathology and which are related to the type of individual rather than to the treatment process (p. 102)." They regard as "the most lucid statement concerning such individuals" Hartmann's (1944) comments: "There is . . . a large number of people in whom active social conduct represents not a rational action but an 'acting out,' which is more or less neurotic, in relation to social reality. In this 'acting out,' they repeat infantile situations and seek to utilize their social conduct to resolve intrapsychic conflicts. A strong reliance on reality can also be used to overcome fear. It can, but it does not need to have, the character of a symptom. It also depends on the peculiarities of the social milieu, what conflicts and anxiety tensions are overcome by the social behavior. On the other hand, sometimes a modification of the social structure which limits this activity . . . leads to a reappearance of those conflicts which were temporarily overcome and serves to precipitate a neurosis" (pp. 27-28).

Sandler and his colleagues believe that the difficulties in applying the concept of acting out to behavior arising in contexts other than that of psychoanalytic treatment "do not arise if we use the concept in its widest sense, i.e., as relating to individual tendencies, for these exist apart from the treatment situation. In the narrower and technical sense, however, a problem arises if we adhere to the view that acting out is a substitute for remembering. Other forms of treatment . . . may not involve or stimulate the recall of the patient's childhood past. Nevertheless the concept would, it seems, be capable of extension if it were linked with those situations (therapeutic and otherwise) in which an intense relationship fosters a tendency to a revival of earlier, especially infantile states and impulses. Enactments of these earlier states can occur, and these could, in our view, be legitimately referred to as acting out" (pp. 102-103). These may occur in staff relationships, institutional arrangements, and other human groupings. "There is no doubt, however, that such an extension of the concept does imply a certain change in meaning from the original psychoanalytic usage. This will render it somewhat less precise in its application" (p. 103).

American Journal of Psychotherapy

A group of papers on acting out appeared in a 1974 issue of the *American Journal of Psychotherapy*. Silvano Arieti in his discussion of such behavior in schizophrenics made a pertinent distinction between action and behavior. He noted that actions of all types are the result of a last stage of a process unfolding at the cognitive level, passing through many steps, of which only the last ones are conscious. "Contrary to action, simple external behavior can be reflex, conditioned, automatic, instinctive and not necessarily accompanied by a cognitive component. . . . When thought, conscious or unconscious, precedes behavior one should speak of action, rather than of behavior, in spite of the common use of the latter term" (1974, p. 335).

James Masterson (1974) descibed his point of view regarding acting out in the adolescent whom he called an actor, a playwright, or a novelist whose greatest artistic creation is his behavior pattern. His behavior is like a drama which constantly reproduces his past in the present in symbolic form in order to avoid the painful feelings associated with the conflicts of the past. Externalization is the mechanism for ridding the self of the intrapsychic conflict. Reality is denied so that conflict can be projected, replayed, or reworked when an infantile conflict is causing great internal stress.

Martin Symonds addressed the problems of acting out in children and young adolescents. He identified individual behavior which is seemingly unrelated to other people as different from that in which the individual is fully aware of others through whom he acts out. "All acting-out behavior is essentially an unrelated act." This point of view is in contrast to that of many others who believe it always involves two people.

Symonds found the concept of "action-oriented" useful in the study of delinquent and antisocial children who show defects from the early process of socialization. When the early parent-child relationship was hopeless, the child, in despair, becomes depressed or resorts to action. They "live in egocentric time, the immediate present," exhibit little fantasy life, and their feelings of guilt and anxiety appear minimal. They show fright and anger instead, which interfere greatly with interpersonal relationships. Symonds found that they often show "reflexive behavior": opportunity, not impulsiveness directs their behavior.

ACTING-OUT BEHAVIOR IN CHILDREN

The literature regarding acting-out behavior in children has emerged largely from clinical experiences with antisocial boys and girls in clinics, courts, and residential settings. Rarely has it been possible to subject these children to classical analytic therapy, and the clinical material usually consists of observations of and psychotherapy sessions with the child, psychological testing, and interviews with parents and other

interested adults. A few of the neurotic children described
display compulsive antisocial acts, but the studies most often
concern the child with the habitual impulsive behavior
pattern of the antisocial character disorder.

While acting-out behavior in adults obviously may involve
antisocial acts, the papers summarized above did not deal
with delinquency or crime as a central focus. The literature
regarding children, however, is immediately concerned with
the issues of predelinquent and delinquent behavior. The few
psychoanalysts who carry out such studies or include in their
conceptualizations the clincal work of others have usually had
to relate their ideas to the subject of delinquency.

The introduction of a subject as complex as delinquency
into considerations of acting-out behavior may appear to
complicate still further an already difficult task of conceptualization. The term delinquency is itself a legal one, the
area the center of attention of several disciplines, not all of
which regard it as germane to the central concerns of the
psychoanalyst or psychiatrist. Psychoanalysts, in view of the
paucity of direct analytic data from which to draw conclusions, have tended to leave the area of antisocial behavior outside their theoretical formulations of psychopathology.

Nevertheless, for over fifty years, a small but important
number of psychoanalysts and psychiatrists have used analytic
concepts to further their understanding and guide their
therapeutic efforts with delinquent children. They have
written of the evolution of impulse control in the
development of the child's personality and have described the
different clinical pictures related to difficulties in control
shown by boys and girls of varying ages. Because their subjects have been young, these psychoanalysts and psychiatrists
have used available data regarding the family life, parental
personalities, and early developmental histories to help them
explain the failures of such children to move from the
expectable stages of infantile impulsivity to the establishment

of ego and superego controls which marks the usual course of a child's development.

Perhaps the fact that social and environmental factors loom so large in the life situations of antisocial children has slowed the process of correlating the understanding gained of acting-out children with that obtained in the treatment of acting-out adults. The majority of psychoanalysts have studied acting out in their consulting rooms, and the phenomena have been considered within the realm of neurotic disorders. They have not become familiar with the milieu of youth authorities, probation officers, and courts, and the work of their colleagues who have interested themselves in antisocial children has not received the attention it deserves.

William Healy (1915)

The extensive clinical research studies of William Healy, first reported in *The Individual Delinquent* (1915), have strongly influenced students of antisocial behavior and remain the most substantial systematic investigation carried out by clinicians. Healy revolutionized the thinking about delinquent children by his emphasis upon the uniqueness of each boy or girl who commits delinquent acts. He demonstrated that one must understand the child himself to understand and to deal with his acts: the child's inner life, his physical and intellectual status, his family relationships, his neighborhood and school — all must be studied before one can properly offer a diagnosis and a plan for treatment. In the many case records and analyses of clinical data collected over nearly forty years, Healy demonstrated the high incidence of a history of serious physical injury or illness, of repeated separations from the mother, of broken homes, of highly pathological emotional and social factors in the homes and neighborhoods in which the child grew up. He was the first of many students of antisocial behavior to emphasize the impact of the emotional and social milieu in which the child lives upon the development of such ego functions as impulse

controls and reality testing, of object relations, and of superego functions.

Alexander and Healy (1935)

It was Healy who arranged for Franz Alexander to spend
a year in Boston in 1931-32 to psychoanalyze adult offenders.
In *The Roots of Crime,* Alexander and Healy (1935) presented the summaries of the analytic treatment carried out
with eleven prisoners who had been studied at the Judge
Baker Guidance Center when they were children. They investigated the origin of those character traits which make an
individual receptive to the criminal influences of his environment. They agreed that a cure of crime cannot be achieved
without considering its social bases, but they sought other
factors which might be responsible for the dissatisfactions
likely to disturb the equilibrium between gratifications and
social restrictions. They found a dependent receptive attitude
highly prominent in these patients and traced the cause of the
fixation or regression to this infantile position to: (1) early
intimidations of the instinctive life through fear and sense of
guilt; (2) indulgence; and (3) early deprivations.

Alexander and Healy declared the chief difference between neurosis and criminal behavior to be that in neurosis
the emotional conflict results in symbolic gratifications of unsatisfied urges, whereas in criminal behavior it leads to overt
misdeeds. The emotional conflicts and deprivations in childhood, the resentments against parents and siblings, find a
powerful ally in resentments against the social situation, and
this combined emotional tension seeks a realistic expression in
criminal acts and cannot be relieved merely by fantasy
products which are exhibited in neurotic symptoms.

The authors noted that in some individuals certain fundamental constitutional characteristics cannot be entirely dis-
regarded: "Certain unacquired bases of the instinctive life
(constitution), apart from environmental influences, must be
partly responsible for the fact that similar emotional conflicts

may, depending upon the make-up of the individual, result either in criminality or in neurosis" (p. 289).

August Aichhorn

August Aichhorn's *Wayward Youth* (1925) presented a review of his pioneering application of psychoanalysis to the pedagogical task of re-educating delinquent children. "Psychoanalysis," he wrote, "enables the worker to recognize dissocial manifestations as the result of an interplay of psychic forces, to discover the unconscious motives of such behavior, and to find means of leading the dissocial back to social conformity" (p. 3). He included problem and neurotic children as well as delinquents in his grouping of wayward youth.

Aichhorn differentiated the phases of dissocial behavior. "Every child is at first an asocial being in that he demands direct primitive instinctual satisfaction without regard for the world around him" (p. 4). The task of rearing him is to bring him from this asocial state to a social one, since behavior normal for the young child is considered asocial or dissocial in the adult. This training or education proceeds concomitantly with normal libidinal development, but if certain disturbances in the latter arise, the child either remains asocial or else behaves as though he had become social without having made an actual adjustment to society. In the latter instance, the child has not renounced his instinctual wishes, but suppressed them so that they remain in the background awaiting an opportunity to break through to satisfaction. "This state we call 'latent delinquency'; it can become 'manifest' on provocation" (p. 4). It may change over to "manifest delinquency" very gradually during a period in which no definite symptoms are present, but a susceptibility can already be perceived. This concept of a latent and a manifest stage of delinquency is reminiscent of the important distinction Otto Fenichel made between the psychic structure underlying the propensity to chronic acting out in adults and the state of acting out on the basis of that psychological make-up.

Aichhorn taught that re-educational and treatment methods should be applied to children in the latent delinquent stage, which often coincides with the time at which observant parents bring a child to a guidance clinic. He warned that a symptom troubling the parents may suddenly disappear, suggesting a return to the latent condition. "The instinctual wishes may have been suppressed because of the child's attachment to the worker or because of some anxiety or fear which is not recognized. Our work is finally successful when a recurrence is made impossible, that is, when the suppression of instinctual wishes is transformed into an actual renunciation of these wishes through the laying bare of unconscious relationships" (p. 5).

Aichhorn's view of psychic development constituted the theoretical basis for his premise that "the treatment of the delinquent is a matter of re-education" (p. 5). He pointed out that in the history of human development, the first task of early man was to develop a certain primitive capacity to cope with reality in order to escape annihilation. "The human being has had to learn to endure pain, to postpone and renounce satisfaction, and to divert primitive instinctual urges into socially acceptable channels. Thus through the centuries a civilization has developed within which man, with his technical achievements, strides steadily forward conquering nature and continuously creating artistic, scientific, and social works. From this it follows that the lower or primitive cultural level is characterized by less restriction of immediate satisfaction of instinctual drives, and that the original primitive capacity to cope with reality increases with cultural development. This heightened capacity to cope with reality we regard as the capacity of the individual to share in the general culture of his age, and this we term culture-capacity. This may be assumed to vary quantitatively, according to the cultural level achieved. The original primitive reality-capacity remains as a constant" (pp. 5-6).

Each child in the course of his development must traverse the path "from the unreal pleasure-world of his nursing period to the real world of the adult, parallel[ing] that of mankind from primitive times to the present. It may be longer or shorter according to the particular cultural level, but must be traversed by the child in those few years during which he ripens to maturity. . . . Although the newborn child brings with him traces of the accummulated experience of his ancestors, this endowment is not sufficient equipment for adjustment to the society in which he finds himself. His inherent capacity must be expanded through education and experience. Thus man becomes civilized through experience and training. Life forces [man] to conform to reality; education enables him to achieve culture" (pp. 6-7). The need for self-preservation continually leads the child toward further social conformity. "To the child who lacks the constitutional endowment necessary for primary adaptation to reality, education has little to offer. Education is no more than a means for unfolding existing potentialities and cannot add anything new to the individual" (p. 7).

Aichhorn stated categorically that the predisposition to delinquency cannot be explained by heredity alone. It "is not a finished product at birth but is determined by the emotional relationships, that is, by the first experiences which the environment forces upon the child" (p. 40). He therefore believed that, "To find the causes of delinquency we must not only seek the provocation which made the latent delinquency manifest but we must also determine what created the latent delinquency. It is the task of re-education to weaken the latent tendency to delinquency. Later we shall learn that this is tantamount to altering the ego structure of the child" (p. 41).

Aichhorn discussed the different types of parental relationships and various traumatic life experiences which may result in the failure of the young child to adapt to reality and to renounce immediate gratification of his instinctual impulses. His emphasis on the crucial role of the positive transference to the educator or therapist of delinquent children is based upon his understanding that only through meaningful libidinal relationship can the child progress beyond the level of the pleasure ego. He pointed out that, frequently, parts of the delinquent child's ego have matured and that in many cases a delinquent can react in a reasonable and sensible way. This cleavage of the ego seen in many delinquents offers the opportunity of enlisting this more critical and reasonable ego sector in the therapeutic process.

Aichhorn devoted a chapter to the ego ideal, using this term as we would now use superego. He remarked that the ego ideal (superego) sits in judgment over the rest of the ego, and thus ideally takes on features which exclude the possibility of later censorial conduct. After outlining briefly the psychoanalytic theory of the development of the ego ideal (superego), he described various types of distortions arising out of individual reactions to specific family situations. He emphasized the role of identification with the educator in the correction of such distortion, stating, "The teacher, as a libidinally charged object for the pupil, offers traits for identification that bring about a lasting change in the structure of the ego-ideal [superego]. This in turn effects a change in the behavior of the formerly dissocial child" (p. 235).

Aichhorn concluded, "The difference between the delinquent and other people is a question of the ego-ideal [superego], the ego, and the relation of these to each other" (p. 223). Throughout his skillful weaving of psychoanalytic theory with case illustrations, Aichhorn adhered to the central issue of the child's endopsychic structure; and through his vignettes of the child's reaction to his experiences at the hands of his parents, this pioneering educator showed us how the parents' child-rearing methods and individual personalities contributed to the child's faulty ego and superego development. Although in each instance the child's responses to his upbringing and his solution of emotional conflicts with family members were uniquely his own, the outlines of the whole picture illustrated what the child was reacting to and what he was trying to solve in the course of his early life.

Kate Friedlander (1947, 1949)

Kate Friedlander's long experience with antisocial children in child guidance and psychoanalytic work led her to a psychodynamic formulation of the antisocial character (1945, 1947). She described the various crucial steps in the development of the child's social adaptation, highlighting the key roles of his early relationship to his mother, the nature of his oedipal conflicts, the formation of the superego, and group formation in his family. She defined the antisocial character formation as follows: it "shows the structure of a mind where instinctive urges remain unmodified and therefore appear in great strength, where the Ego, still under the dominance of the pleasure-principle and not supported by an independent Super-Ego, is too weak to gain control over the onrush of demands arising in the Id. This character formation is at the basis of the condition which Aichhorn calls the state of 'latent delinquency' and it will depend on the various factors exerting their influence in the latency period and puberty whether delinquent behavior becomes manifest or not" (1947, p. 94).

In a paper titled "Latent Delinquency and Ego Development," Friedlander (1949) emphasized the great importance of Aichhorn's conception of latent delinquency to the understanding of the personality deviations of child and adult offenders. She reviewed her formulations that environmental factors lead to a disturbance in early instinct modification and object relationship resulting in the antisocial character formation. From the analysis and psychotherapy of a number of children, she had found that this character deviation could be seen to be the result of a disturbed ego development.

Normally, the child's ego at the age of three is strong enough to enable him to endure a certain amount of tension and to cope with primitive instinctual urges, the expression of which is not favored by the environment. If the child enters the oedipal phase with his ego thus underdeveloped and still more or less under the dominance of the pleasure principle, it is very unlikely that this phase can pass without further disturbance.

Friedlander remarked, "The most important outcome of the decline of the oedipal phase is the consolidation of the superego by a process of internalization and desexualization, which together lead to the oedipal identifications. This process of identification is based on the *slow* renunciation of oedipal desires. . . . If the ego is weak, castration anxiety is unbearable and the oedipal desires are quickly repressed. But such an ego is not strong enough to maintain an effective defense. The tension of ungratified desires becomes unbearable, and the instinctual drives then seek gratification by regressing to a pregenital level . . . this defective ego permits the gratification of these desires without building up new defenses against them. The relationship to the parents or other adult remains sexualized, usually on the anal-sadistic level and as a result of this the superego is defective. Contact with adults outside the family circle does not lead to the usual identifications of the latency period, which enrich the personality, but remains on the same level as the sexualized relationship to the original love objects. . . . Since there is no functioning superego, there is no internal demand and consequently no tension between ego and superego to produce guilt feelings" (p. 207).

Friedlander concluded with a statement that the most important result of the studies of the underlying basic disturbance in the delinquent personality is the elucidation of the effect of gross environmental disturbances on the child's ego development and the subsequent disturbance in superego function.

John Bowlby (1944, 1951)

John Bowlby has stressed the role of physical and emotional separation from the mother during the first three years of life as a crucial factor in the formation of the antisocial disorders (1951). In his study of forty-four juvenile thieves (1944) he attempted to classify the characters of the children. Almost without exception he found that the "affectionless characters" had suffered the complete emotional loss of their mothers or foster mothers during infancy and early childhood. Bowlby's work has contributed to the concept of delinquency as a disorder due to early object loss and the chronic acting-out pattern in children as rooted in problems of the oral phase of development.

Adelaide Johnson

Adelaide Johnson's paper "Sanctions for Superego Lacunae" (1949), first read in Chicago in 1947, is perhaps the best known of a series of publications by Johnson, Szurek, and their co-workers concerning the hidden links between the superego of the parent and child even in cases in which the parent himself does not act out. Through concomitant psychiatric and psychoanalytic therapeutic study of both parent and child, they had found the chief dynamics of the situation to be the unconscious encouragement of the amoral or antisocial behavior in the child. Johnson reviewed the various discussions of the etiology of superego disorders in the acting out of forbidden, antisocial impulses and emphasized that her aim had been to study the subtle parent-child interrelationships for clues to an understanding of the superego structure of the acting-out child and adolescent.

Johnson wrote, "The astonishing observation emerging repeatedly in our studies was the subtle manner in which one child in a family of several children might unconsciously be singled out as the scapegoat to act out the parent's poorly integrated and forbidden impulses. Analytic study of the significant parent showed unmistakably the peculiar meaning this child had for the parent and the tragic mode in which both the parent and the child were consciously but much more often *unconsciously*, involved in the fatal march of events" (p. 227).

Another finding was that the child's "very acting out, in a way so foreign to the conscious wishes of the parent, served often as a channel for hostile, destructive impulses that the parent felt toward the child. . . . Similarly the child consciously but more often unwittingly exposes the parents to all degrees of suffering through acting out" (pp. 227-228).

Johnson commented, "We must first understand the behavior of a well-integrated parent, and the subtle conscious and unconscious ways in which this behavior directs the child's superego development in order to be able to recognize the evidence of such destructive sanctions in less integrated parents. To be sure, the dissolution of the oedipus conflict puts the real seal on the superego, but it is well to be aware of all the preoedipal and oedipal subtleties in the family which are part and parcel of this development. To the child in the early and middle latency period there may be alternative modes of reacting on an ego level, but when the superego is involved the child normally is reared as if there could be *no* alternative reaction in regard to the suppression of the impulses to theft, murder, truancy, etc. The well-integrated, mature mother issuing an order to a child does not immediately check to see if it has been done, or suggest beforehand that if it is not done, there will be serious consequences. Such constant checking or such a warning means to the child that there is an alternative to the mother's order and an alternate image of *him* in the mother's mind. Identification with the parent does not consist merely of identification with the manifest behavior of the parent. It necessarily includes a sharing by the child of the parent's conscious and unconscious concept of the child as one who is loved and honest or sometimes unloved or dishonest" (p. 228).

Johnson elaborated her understanding of the etiology of superego lacunae by giving samples of clinical material describing her therapeutic management of both children and parents. Her discussion of therapeutic errors with such acting-out children led her to consider carefully Freud's (1914) meaning and intention when he made his suggestion for offsetting acting out in analysis by interpreting and warning ahead of time. She decided that he was speaking of the "'acting out' of the neurotic patient on the couch who was repeating in the transference the salient episodes of his earlier life. This is an entirely different matter from warning a patient about some antisocial impulsive behavior. In fact, if I understand Freud correctly, he warned analysts against mobilizing and interpreting too rapidly any impulse that might be dangerously expressed outside the analytic hour — particularly sadism. A loose and unclear concept of what is meant by 'acting out' had led a number of analysts to carry over Freud's suggestions about transference 'acting out' in a serious antisocial way" (p. 233).

Anna Freud

Anna Freud (1949) wrote of disturbances of social functioning based "not on the early stunting of object-love but on conflicts which belong to the normal realm of the child's emotional attachments, especially to the attitudes of the oedipus complex of which they are derivatives and distortions. They do not originate from a weakening of the ego functions and identifications though secondarily their existence may harm the integrity of the ego. These social maladjustments are, therefore, in their content nearer to the neurotic than to the common dissocial abnormalities. But they cannot, on the other hand, be classed with the neuroses since their manifestations are not, like the neurotic symptoms, compromise-formations designed to hold the inner balance between id and ego forces, but rather irruptions of more or less undistorted libidinal and aggressive material into

the sphere of the individual's dealings with the real environment" (p. 195). She noted that such disturbances arise at
approximately the same time, that is, the first half of the
latency period, and show a symptomatology similar to those
types of social maladjustment based on early disturbances of
object love.

Anna Freud commented that many workers and authors
in all countries have confirmed and extended Aichhorn's
theories and observations regarding the social maladjustments
which are based on early disturbance, namely, the inadequate binding of the destructive urges in the child resulting
from the blunting of libidinal development which stems from
the familiar early deprivations to which such children have
been subjected. She wrote, "Where the child's love-life is deficient, the destructive urges remain more isolated and manifest
themselves more independently in various ways, from merely
overemphasized aggressiveness to wanton destructiveness, i.e.,
in attitudes which are in themselves the most frequent sources
of delinquency and criminality" (p. 194). Discussing the
period of normal social maladjustment, Anna Freud
commented that we do not apply the term dissocial to the
emotional upsets which occur between the young child and
his environment. He passes through various stages in developing his sense of reality and in accepting restrictions, renun-
ciations, or postponements of his instinctual wishes. However, when infantile modes of mental functioning — remnants
of the primary process — persist beyond their normal time, the
behavior based on them is then classified as dissocial.

"One of these instances, namely, the distortion of reality
owing to the projection of the individual's own inner urges into
the external world, and the consequent hostile, aggressive or
anxious behavior toward the external world has been studied
and described in detail by Melanie Klein and her followers"
(p. 196).

Anna Freud described a second source of social maladjustment (not due to the early stunting of object love) as the

transference of the family situation upon the wider community. In normal cases, the child learns by experience to distinguish between adults in a positive or an indifferent relationship to him, and this realization gradually reduces his tendency to transfer emotion indiscriminately. However, this step in development from the family circle to the wider community is not taken when the preoedipal and oedipal attitudes are too violent and remain unresolved. "In such cases the environment is merely—throughout the latency period and sometimes forever—an extended battleground for the fighting out of family conflicts" (p. 196). In the difficult task of growing beyond the family relationships, the child receives varying, often insufficient, help from the adults who are responsible for his upbringing. The old-fashioned kindergartens and nurseries were based upon the principle of merely widening the family circle. Anna Freud noted with approval that modern nursery schools are built upon completely different lines. "The nursery school teacher takes the place in their life, not of a mother substitute for the gratification of unsatisfied emotions, but of an ideal figure farther removed from instinctual life, with whose sublimated interests and demands the child can identify himself" (p. 197).

Another important source of maladjustment is the transference of preoedipal and oedipal fantasies upon the wider community. The aggressive and destructive images of the oral phase, the sadomasochistic fantasies of the anal level, exhibitionistic fantasies with the defenses against them, fantasies of castration, the family romance with the feeling of being isolated and unloved, all these can distort the child's picture of the teacher as they originally distorted the picture of the parents. Transference of these fantasies to the school cannot but act as a hindrance to social adjustment.

A still further step in social maladjustment occurs when the fantasies displaced to the environment do not remain in the realm of thought and feeling but lead to direct action. "The environment is, then, not merely understood in terms of

fantasy but treated on the same basis. Life, in these circumstances, is a form of psychodrama with the child concerned
acting as stage manager and as a central figure. . . . Children
who, in this manner, act out *passive-feminine*, or *masochistic
fantasies* in school actually succeed in being punished more
often or more severely than others. . . . In the absence of personal persecutors the maltreatment may be ascribed to im-
personal factors. . . . The corresponding *sadistic fantasies* are
usually acted out with either animals or younger children as
object" (pp. 199-200). They may also be lived out in the role
of spectator, when other children are criticized or punished.
Life in a classroom offers special opportunities for the acting
out of exhibitionistic fantasies. While the acting out of positive exhibitionistic fantasies may fall into social channels and
thus serve the aim of adjustment to the community, there is a
socially disruptive element in the fact that it is compulsive.
"Whatever the circumstances, under the pressure of this
fantasy, the child has to excel at all costs, his interest is primarily concentrated on being conspicuous; the activities
which help him to achieve his aim are of secondary importance" (p. 201).

"In a similar way," Anna Freud continued, "children
become involved in continual battles with their environment
when an *observation of intercourse* or fantasies concerning
intercourse between the parents have had a traumatic effect
on their sexual development" (p. 201). The fantasies expressing their ideas of intercourse as a violently aggressive and
sadistic act which is continued until one of the partners or
both are severely damaged are then displaced on the environment and acted out. "Their hate-relations are as important
to them as love-relations are to normal children, i.e., the
hated enemy is for their unconscious the representative of the
sexual partner" (p. 201).

Anna Freud concluded with a discussion of grave disturbances of social adjustment which can be traced back to
the complete suppression of phallic masturbation and the

consequent flooding of the ego activities with sexual content. She believed that this sexualization of the ego activities produces certain familiar forms of psychopathic behavior. The acting out of fantasies, whether passive or active, sadistic or masochistic, exhibitionistic or scoptophilic, is a derivative of phallic masturbation and in these cases its substitute and representative. "The driving force behind it [social maladjustment in these children], which makes adults and childdren in the environment join in the acting-out, is the full force of infantile sexuality; the monotony and repetitiveness of the child's behavior corresponds to the endless monotony of the crude fantasies which accompany masturbatory acts; the compulsive and periodic character of the acting-out corresponds to the periodic need for masturbation which arises from the id and appears in the child's ego as an unrelated foreign body" (p. 203).

Edward Glover

Edward Glover (1954), in a critique of the contributions of psychoanalysis to criminology, discussed the problems of classification derived from etiological variables considered important by psychoanalysts. He criticized the current tendency to convert a traumatic circumstance (such as early separation from the mother or a broken home) into a direct determining environmental factor in delinquency, to the neglect of the central proposition of psychoanalysis that these predisposing elements acquire their pathological force and form in accordance with the effect of their passage through the varying phases of the unconscious oedipus situation. Glover declared further that if delinquency is to be regarded in the main as an object-relation disorder, we must distinguish between transient crisis disorder due mainly to functional stress and symptomatic reactions due principally to oedipal conflict. Equally unsatisfactory to him was the use of such generic terms as "superego" to arrive at etiological generalizations.

Glover questioned the validity of Friedlander's classification of delinquents as insufficiently related to the clinical
manifestations or syndromes. He pointed out that she sub-
divided her antisocial character group in accordance with the
degree to which (a) environmental stress, (b) neurotic conflict, and (c) acting out of neurotic fantasy combine with
varying degrees of antisocial character formation to form distinct delinquent groups. He emphasized his opinion that each
of these secondary factors also owes its importance to the
relative strength of the three domains of the mind, for, even
in the case of environmental stress, the effect of psychic
trauma depends on the specific sensitivity of the endopsychic
receptors. Schwarz's study, as reported at the 1967
Symposium (see p. 276, above) is the principal contribution
to our literature from the child psychoanalytic field to the
problem of acting out and delinquency since 1962.

DISCUSSION

This summary of a series of papers written by psychoanalysts and psychiatrists over a period of half a century
presents a number of differing concepts of acting-out behavior, differences that reflect the gradual shift of emphasis
from the analytic treatment of neurotic symptoms to the
analysis of character defenses and of patients with disturbances in their early character formation. Significant changes
in theory accompanied the widening of clinical experience.

The group of articles dealing with adults put forth three
principal approaches to acting-out problems. Freud's papers,
based on the topographical theory, described chance and
symptomatic acts as symbolic representations of fantasies and
wishes which seek for expression; in his later writing on acting
out in the transference, Freud placed in the central role a
specific repressed memory leading to an act.

Anna Freud and Otto Fenichel, writing after the structural theory had been developed, conceived of acting out as

the expression in action of unacceptable instinctual impulses, effected by a shift in the balance of the three psychic institutions. The impulse that cannot be contained within the system does not emerge in thought content or fantasy when a shift in balance occurs, but in a short-circuiting of the delaying and controlling mechanisms. It is discharged in a single act or series of acts.

Greenacre's concept of acting out as a special form of remembering differs from that of Freud, in which a specific memory once repressed now returns and leads to action. From her study of analytic patients, she believes that acting out replaces remembering: a situation from the past is revived, but because it belonged to the preverbal period of development the situation returns, not in the form of thoughts, fantasy, or verbal content, but in the form of action.

The problems of acting out in children and adolescents which have been explored in the literature reviewed above are manifested in the antisocial patterns of behavior and hence become involved in the general area of juvenile delinquency. These papers on children center upon developmental issues, such as the expectable course of the acquisition of impulse control and socialization, the nature of the various deviations from that course, and the factors in the child's environment which predispose to encourage or provoke dissocial acts in boys and girls. Healy, who pioneered in the study of the individual delinquent child, pointed to how the impact of unfavorable psychological and social factors on the development of his ego and superego functions and his object relations contribute directly to his acting-out patterns. Friedlander, in her psychoanalytic formulations of antisocial character formations, utilized her extensive clinical data as evidence of the crucial influence of early gross emotional deprivation upon the processes of socialization. She postulated that, given certain degrees of antisocial or acting-out character formation, the vicissitudes of future stages of development and of life experiences would determine the presence and extent of actual acting out. Aichhorn explained dissocial behavior of children in terms of the development of psychic structures and their interrelationships in latent and in manifest delinquency. He described the phylogenesis and ontogenesis of the socialization process in the child, emphasizing the crucial role of object relations in the attainment of controls. Johnson's focus in her work with antisocial children and their parents was the exploration of the hidden links between the parents' unconscious wishes and the superego functioning of the children. Although she did not belittle the importance of the oedipal period of the child in the development of such superego lacunae, she called attention to the role of pregenital conflicts in both parents and child in the formation of a secret system in which the acting out of the child's ostensibly forbidden impulses was unconsciously condoned and encouraged by the parents.

Anna Freud's 1949 paper dealt with children of latency age who may show the same evidences of social maladjustment as those boys and girls whose antisocial disorder is based upon early emotional deprivation. The disturbances in social functioning of the children in her study, however, she considered to be based upon conflicts which belong to the normal realm of the child's emotional attachments and particularly to the attitudes of the oedipal phase, of which the disturbances were derivatives and distortions.

All of these writings contribute to our understanding of factors which predispose to acting out. In each instance, they are describing causes for certain defects in ego and superego development which interfere with impulse control. By implication, these defects are related to the capacity to postpone instinct gratification and to tolerate instinctual pressures without having to resort to action as a way of tension relief.

Let me summarize here certain points emerging from or given emphasis in the papers contained in the present volume and the ensuing discussions that have particular relevance to our search for a more precise understanding of acting-out be-

havior. Two clinical papers describing different groups of
preschool children raised identical issues. The first concerns
our understanding of normal personality development in the
young child and the significance of deviations from it. Anna
Freud (1965) designated the areas to be studied in assessing
an individual child's development as follows: (1) the maturational history of the drives and the ego; (2) the adaptation of
the child to his environment and his relationship to his
objects; and (3) the development of the organization within
his psychic structure and the conflicts noted at various points
within this structure. We have available from accumulated
data the progress expected along such developmental lines of
children of different chronological ages. While the expectations at each period are phrased in terms of ranges, we do
have clear-cut pictures of normal development in a four- or
four-and-a-half-year-old nursery school child, a seven-year-
old second grader, and so on.

The level of adaptation of a four-year-old in a nursery
school class is normally subject to temporary regressions, and
the usual behavior at this period varies at different times
because of regressions followed by progressions. Developmentally, the attainments of the normal four-year-old indicate that maturation of the drives and of the ego occurs simultaneously, that the impulses have lost their original urgency and are under control of an ego which is stronger.
However, it is important to note that the ego controls are not
identically effective with all impulses at the same time: when
we can find the weakest point of ego control, we probably
have found the points from which later pathology will
develop.

The second important issue is that of relating the personality structure and behavior of an individual at one period
of his life to probabilities regarding his character and behavior at a later time. Freud (1920b) observed, in relation to
predictions in analysis, that synthesis is not so satisfactory as
analysis. "Even supposing that we have a complete knowledge

of the aetiological factors that decide a given result, nevertheless what we know about them is only their quality, and
not their relative strength. Some of them are suppressed by
others because they are too weak, and they therefore do not
affect the final result. But we never know beforehand which
of the determining factors will prove the weaker or the
stronger" (p. 168).

Manifold observations of small children in normal settings
and in clinical facilities testify to the frequent occurrence of
deviations from our scheme of normal development. Preschool children may show temporary or more permanent regressions from a level of adaptation once attained, they may
show moderate or severe developmental delays in libidinal or
ego growth, and they may present evidence of fixation at
earlier points with a concomitant tendency toward regression
to that point or limited capacity to move on from it. Our
ability to predict the outcome of later personality development in children displaying such deviations is certainly
limited by our lack of knowledge, although current analytic
research studies in child development promise to place our
prognoses on a sounder basis. However, when we are dealing
with such young children, our capacity to prognosticate more
than "vulnerable to" or "a tendency toward" is repeatedly
hindered because we cannot know what interplay of life
experiences and maturational forces will ensue for a child;
and, hence, we do not know what his patterns of adaptation
will be later in life.

Malone's group of nursery school children had been referred by social workers who knew their disorganized families
and unfavorable sociocultural milieu. The children presented
impulsive, action-oriented, and generally immature behavior:
most conspicuous was their deficiency in object relations,
manifested in a lack of emotional separation from their
mothers and a reaching out to adults in the nursery school as
need-fulfilling objects. Malone's studies demonstrated the deficits in ego functions which have to do with the development

of secondary processes of thought as experimental action, of judgment and memory. These deficits may predispose to acting, in Greenacre's sense of acting out, and take the place of remembering or thinking. Malone suggested that, in view of their personality development when studied in the nursery school and their continued exposure to homes and neighborhoods providing little support for impulse control and delayed gratifications, these children might be predisposed to impulse disorders or acting out. He considered "acting on impulse" the most suitable term to designate their rather nonspecific and unorganized behavior. The discussants hesitated to offer a diagnosis beyond that of developmental delays and were concomitantly cautious about predicting the outcome in view of their age and our limited knowledge of the development of such children.

Reiser's groups of preschool children were brought by their parents to a psychiatric clinic because of unmanageable, aggressive, and destructive behavior. These boys and girls were far more explosive and overactive than the children studied by Malone and were given to impulsive acts of a more organized nature. The description of their dissocial acts closely resembled that with which we are familiar in older antisocial children and adolescents. These boys and girls came from intact homes of a higher sociocultural background than did those in Malone's studies, their parents were apparently less disturbed, and the children had not been exposed to similar gross early deprivations and inconsistencies; Rieser emphasized the pervasive influence which the parental infantile neuroses nonetheless had on their children's development. He described a combination of parental difficulty in helping the child resolve his conflicts at various maturational levels and of persistent encouragement and condoning of impulsive behavior as characteristic of the histories of these parent-child relationships, a finding paralleled in the Thom Clinic studies of older antisocial children and their parents.

Reiser labeled these children antisocial or acting-out, and

his clinical material provided support for the position that if such a diagnosis appeared premature, the children's behavior patterns could then be considered precursors to acting-out or antisocial syndromes. He and his co-workers put their conjectures about prognosis to the test of a follow-up study to see whether those preschool children for whom they had predicted later delinquency were indeed known to the community for antisocial behavior in their preadolescent and adolescent years. Nine of the twenty-six considered predelinquent were reported to be antisocial upon follow-up, while none of a comparison group of preschool children studied for neurotic symptoms was found to be antisocial in his teens.

The Thom Clinic studies reported by van Amerongen, Schleifer, and Rexford consisted of clinical investigations of children from six to twelve years of age and of their parents. Despite common histories of persistent aggressive and destructive behavior, these boys and girls did not present a specific form of psychopathology. Some of the children had pervasive character disorders manifested by primitive ego defenses, paucity of object relations with adults and peers, inability to concentrate, tenuous reality testing, and marked disorganization and lack of impulse control. Others with much the same behavior showed a predominantly neurotic picture. However, all of the children had manifested at an earlier age several of a variety of other symptoms, such as marked hyperactivity, accident proneness, learning difficulties, immaturity, and a propensity for regression.

Each of the children, moreover, had been subjected in the past and was currently being subjected to the united parental attitudes of permitting, promoting, or provoking acting-out behavior. Again, there was no clear-cut relationship between the parents' specific individual psychopathology and the child's behavior, but the parents' conflicts and ambivalence interfered with their inability to help the child attain age-appropriate and effective ways of managing the aggressive and sexual impulses. For some of these families, acting out was a familiar mode of instinct gratification, tension relief, and rebellious self-assertion. For other parents, action and activity were signs of independence and health and represented their own defense against passivity, dependency, and depression. In still other parents, the boy's manifestations of dependent needs and of ego and sexual drives strongly reactivated their own conflicts over instinct gratification, frustration, and control. These and the similar findings of Reiser coincide with those of Johnson and her co-workers, who studied the relationship between the child's acting out and the parents' unconscious attitudes.

The findings regarding the personalities and attitudes of the fathers toward their sons raise a specific developmental issue. The father's relation to his son takes on a particular importance in latency, when he represents the external world of reality for the boy and provides a model for identification whose modes of dealing with authority, learning, and achievements in the world beyond the home are highly significant to the son. Those fathers whose own acting out in childhood and adolesence had apparently been curbed obtained a lively vicarious gratification from their sons' antisocial behavior: far from helping the boys find acceptable and growth-promoting ways of adapting to outer reality, they encouraged and, indeed, provoked the acting-out pattern. As a group, the fathers of the Thom Clinic study resembled one another more closely in personality structures than did the mothers. They were a conspicuously passive, resentful, dependent group of men with strong homosexual orientations. They allied themselves with their sons in warfare against the mother and reinforced the existing developmental delays in object relationships and in ego and superego growth.

The Gluecks (1950) found that the presence in the home of a father who was to some degree effectively responsible for the boy's discipline was one of the most important factors that differentiated a group of nondelinquent adolescent boys from those who were delinquent. Since the role of the father in providing a crucial developmental influence during the latency years may determine whether an acting-out pattern persists or is given up, this area is worthy of further study.

The histories and characters of these men remind us of another difficult and fascinating problem of acting out, namely, the disappearance of the pattern and the ways in which this comes about. Aichhorn and others have described their therapy of antisocial children as converting the acting-out disorder into a neurosis and then treating the neurosis by classical measures. This formula implies the strengthening of ego and superego functions, which are weak for a variety of reasons. Aichhorn was explicit in describing the development of an object relation with the child as the principal vehicle whereby the education of the ego can take place. It is by way of cathexis of an important object that ego functions can develop, or be re-established if they have been lost as a result of regression.

We know very little about the spontaneous curbing of an acting-out pattern in individuals who have not been studied during a treatment process. When such a pattern disappears in the circumstances of a progressive personality development, we assume that the following factors are involved: the presence of a cathected object, the strengthening and developing of certain ego and superego functions, and the modification of modes of dealing with inner tension states resulting from id pressures, ego weaknesses, or superego lacunae.

The Thom Clinic group did not have the opportunity to learn enough about the fathers they studied to explore the issue of how their earlier delinquent patterns had been modified. The men as they presented themselves were, in the main, not neurotics: they appeared to suffer from chronic pervasive restricting character disorders of a passive, dependent, and hostile type. They gave the impression of needing to invest so much energy in maintaining their defenses that they had few resources for achievement, rewarding relationships, or growth. A group of adolescent boys who had been treated at the Thom Clinic during their grade-school years for antisocial behavior did not in most instances act out; they were, however, remarkably passive, uninterested, unachieving youths. It appeared that the therapeutic relationship had helped them attain more effective impulse controls, but relatively limited psychic energy was available to them for expectable development. In other individuals who have acted out conspicuously at one period of their lives, the disappearance of the pattern does not appear to have coincided with the institution of counterforces so strong that the likelihood of further maturation is precluded.

Several speakers at the Boston University-Thom Clinic Symposium had referred to the lack of material about the fathers of antisocial children and about delinquency in girls. This revised edition contains papers contributing to both of these important areas.

Dr. Lewis and her group are among the very few clinical teams in the nineteen-seventies providing not only consultation to a court but an ongoing clinical and epidemiological study of different aspects of the problems of the children and their families referred to them by court officials.

Lewis and her colleagues had earlier (1973) reported on the heavy proportion of severe chronic psychopathology they had found in the children and youth in the court clinic. Later investigations (1976) revealed a high percentage of parents with histories of prior psychiatric treatment, of criminal records and of current psychopathology. The present report summarizes an epidemiological investigation of the clinical observations made in the course of psychiatric and pscyhological evaluations of a large number of the delinquent children and their families conducted in a psychiatric clinic within a juvenile justice setting.

Readily verifiable global measures of parental psychiatric disorder, antisocial behavior, and delinquency were utilized, namely, actual contact with the psychiatric system, the adult criminal justice system, and the juvenile court. The writers found in all cases significantly greater use of two major psychiatric institutions in the community was found by parents of children identified as delinquent than by a random sample of a lower socioeconomic New Haven population. When the authors turned to criminal histories of the parents, they found a highly significant association of paternal criminality and paternal psychiatric treatment.

The findings regarding patterns of intermarriages among the various men and women Lewis et al. studied open up other avenues for the investigation of families of antisocial children and of the family interactions among them. While fathers with psychiatric histories tended to marry mothers with psychiatric histories, fathers with criminal histories also tended to marry mothers with psychiatric histories. Two marital constellations therefore emerged, but criminal mothers and criminal fathers did not tend to marry one another nor did criminal mothers on the whole marry psychiatrically treated fathers. The emphasis upon the adaptive failures of both individuals and of the family which clinical observation suggested was borne out by the epidemiological studies.

The studies of Lewis and her co-workers illustrate a current trend toward bringing together clinical modes of working with delinquent children and clinical ways of thinking about them and their families with epidemiological approaches to serious social and psychiatric problems. These studies constitute a bridge between the older investigations which centered upon the individual case study and the more recent emphasis upon larger scale research investigation. Just as newer understanding of biological factors in development have enriched our capacity to follow more of the intricacies of the growth of a specific child, the epidemiological techniques can bring to the more microscopic investigation of individual behavior a perspective that both illuminates that study and puts new questions before us.

At our Symposium, Blos presented an admirably supported thesis that acting out is a phase-specific manifestation of adolescence. He carefully differentiated direct outbursts of relatively unmodified libidinal and aggressive impulses from the more organized motor acts directed toward the outer world to achieve solutions for troubling and typical adolescent conflicts. He discussed the adaptive purposes to which action and acting out may be put during this period and reminded us that trial action is one of the principal modes whereby an adolescent tries to find his own identity.

Blos also indicated that the adolescent period, because of its natural upheaval, can predispose to acting out as a way of relieving tension, as a way of repeating an earlier object relationship, and as a special way of remembering (reminiscent of Greenacre's concept).

Blos added another important dimension to Greenacre's formulation that acting out can also constitute a way of actively mastering what one had experienced passively at an earlier age. The concept of attempting to master a traumatically overwhelming experience through repetitive compulsive acting reminds us of the links to certain types of children's play and to the traumatic neuroses of which Otto Fenichel wrote.

It is worth noting that the basic studies of the quarter-century before our Symposium had concentrated on antisocial behavior and delinquency in boys. The general assumption was that the majority of delinquent girls were adolescents caught up in sexual acting out. Certainly the girls seen in clinics and casework agencies were referred for aggressive behavior, stealing, or truancy far less often than the boys.

Child psychiatrists and psychoanalyst staff members of child guidance clinics had accumulated years of experience during wartime in the pragmatic management and psychotherapy of prepuberty and adolescent girls whose principal symptomatology was that of "sexual acting out." But thera-

peutic management rarely included psychoanalytic treatment, and the dynamic formulations of the individual case
usually rested upon scanty general data. Peter Blos's paper on
delinquency in girls was all the more welcome in that it rests
upon the psychoanalytic understanding of the phases of
female adolescence built up by Helene Deutsch, Ruth Mack
Brunswick, and others in the nineteen-forties and fifties. He
detailed a typical personality configuration leading to delinquency at puberty, specifying that this configuration is but
one of several that might eventuate.

The usefulness of Blos's formulations regarding delinquency in girls began to be questioned as the nineteen-sixties
brought a loudly heralded sexual revolution in which adolescents played a prominent role. If sexual activity among
even young adolescent girls were as frequent as reported,
could we or should we consider sexual relations during the
teens as the essence of female delinquency?

In his Postscript to his 1957 paper, Blos set the tone for
his reconsideration of the terms and concepts of female
"sexual delinquency" and "sexual acting out." He proposed
three categories or types which offer a framework for the purpose of assessment, each to be understood according to psychoanalytic concepts, each to be assessed according to the
etiological and dynamic factors in the girl's sexual behavior.
Blos acknowledges that the designation of "sexual acting out"
loses much of its meaning when it largely ceases to be in open
conflict with society. He corroborates the conclusions Helene
Deutsch reached more tentatively a decade ago, namely, that
rapid and significant cultural changes appear to alter patterns of behavior previously considered largely determined by
biological forces. Her studies of "Special Problems of Adolescence" concerned older young people, but the underlying
thesis of the vulnerability of psychosexual development of the
young to social and cultural mores appears similar.

Greenacre brought the B.U.-Thom Clinic Symposium
back to the circumstances under which acting out has been

most carefully studied, namely, in the transference relationship during psychoanalytic therapy of adults. She described a small group of analysands with massive acting out within the analytic situation, which continued despite the patients' gain of some degree of insight into the underlying conflicts and the peculiar excitement which often initiated a burst of acting out. "Such stubbornly held-to patterns seem then to be expressing hostility of a deeply ambivalent nature." She pointed out that these patients belonged neither to the classical neuroses nor to the psychopathic or impulse-ridden except under the pressure of analysis, and even there, it is mainly within the transference relationship. She thought some were character neuroses with special deformations of ego development and others perhaps cases of major hysteria.

Greenacre (see p. 231) speculated upon the possible relationships between the conditions under which her patients' acting-out pattern had arisen and those leading to certain forms of delinquency suggesting two possibilities: (1) that the early conditions are similar but more intense in the latter type of disorder; and (2) that a particularly strong fixation at the imitative stage might have been added to the above conditions in certain cases of delinquency or criminality. A third possibility might be inferred from Greenacre's note of the studies indicating cooperation through nonverbal communication between parent and child in promoting impulsive acting out in which the child appears to gratify the poorly repressed aggressive drives of the parent, especially the mother.

It is interesting to note the questions regarding acting out which Deutsch brought out in her discussion of Greenacre's paper. She reminded us that to some extent, we are all actors-out, because none of us is free of regressive trends, repressed strivings, burdens of more or less conscious fantasies, and the like. She agreed that psychoanalytic practice provides the best opportunity to observe the process of acting out in *statu nascendi*, its functions, and very often the conditions under which it becomes contained. One is able to understand what the patient expresses through his actions, and also to see what specific situations of analysis provoke, reinforce, or interrupt the acting out.

Deutsch offered her own definitions of acting out in the analytic situation, the first, as the expression of revived emotions projected onto the analyst and communicated verbally to him, the second, which she called acting out proper, occurring "only when a patient leaves the seclusion of the analytic room and carries out the transference situation in the outside world."

In conclusion, several general comments may be in order regarding the scope of the Symposium papers and the literature most frequently discussed by the participants. Problems of acting out involve such a wide range of clinical and theoretical issues that not all the relevant material available could be included in one program. The focus upon the developmental approach was planned to explore the usefulness of this theme in clarifying confusions and indicating areas for further study. The deliberate emphasis upon clinical material from studies of children coincided with this choice of focus.

Acting-out disorders in adults did not, therefore, receive the same degree of attention as those in children; however, it was our hope that the developmental theme would help clarify certain questions about the adult acting-out manifestations. The topic of acting out in the transference in certain adult patients appeared to us a happy choice for the paper on adults.

Discussion of Papers Published Subsequent to the Symposium

The review of papers on acting out, again a selective one, published and discussed since 1962, illustrates the trend within psychoanalysis toward focusing on specific well-defined and agreed-upon symptoms, personality structures, ways of viewing acting out, and its analytic management.

Acting out has been variously described as a resistance, as an ingrained mode of behavior, and/or as a communication to the analyst, depending upon the particular patient and the point in his psychoanalytic treatment and upon the analyst's understanding of him. The varieties of analytic management proposed were related to these concepts, namely, the "permissiveness" of the good tolerant analyst proprosed by the French analysts such as Nacht (1968), or the acceptance of the phenomenon which can lead to ego growth through the supportive object relation between analyst and patient, and, lastly, interpretation leading to an exchange of motor patterns for thoughts and action for fantasy.

Despite the manifest increment of agreement among psychoanalysts about the nature and management of acting out in their patients, the papers reviewed and particularly those of the 25th International Congress offered a confusing array of opinions which were, at times, difficult to relate one to the other and difficult to place within the framework of basic psychoanalytic theory. The repeated shifts from considering the patient whose specific acting out was viewed as almost inevitable somewhere in the course of psychoanalytic treatment, to the patient prone to chronic neurotic action, and then to the patient whose severe action-prone behavior usually excludes him from psychoanalytic treatment, illustrated the necessity to build up a more general theory through which to understand the different manifestations of action behavior. If one decides to reserve the term "acting out" for the classical events during psychoanalytic treatment, one has still to place, at least in theory, the far-from classical neurotic, action-prone patient who does come into analysis and psychotherapy and the patients whose habitual impulsive, action-oriented behavior is often a professional problem and certainly a social one.

These discussions of the phenomena of acting out leave

many of us dissatisfied, as did the material of the 1962 Symposium. Despite the greater clarity in concept and use of the term demonstrated by these later papers, they seem to fall short, particularly in the scant attention given to the origins and developmental aspects of action behavior, of which the acting-out pattern is one manifestation.

Those analysts who wish to restrict the term to the behavior stimulated by an intensified transference during psychoanalytic treatment have a far simpler conceptual task; the patient's defenses are gradually loosened up in the course of systematic interpretation, and infantile wishes can surge to the surface, appearing in the transference or translated into action within or outside the analytic setting. Several speakers reminded their colleagues that the very nature of the analytic process predisposes to acting out, even in neurotic patients who have not exhibited such tendencies in their adult daily lives. Shifts in the intrasystemic relationships of the psychic apparatus can readily be hypothesized to explain the appearance of acting out under such circumstances.

Understanding the patient who comes into psychoanalysis with a chronic action pattern or one whose past history contains many episodes of serious neurotic action requires more comprehensive conceptualizations. Such analytic patients may resemble in many ways delinquent or impulsive characters who rarely enter psychoanalysis but may be seen in psychotherapy or ego supportive casework. It has been amply demonstrated that patients with a propensity for action in dealing with painful affects and conflicts will act out under the pressure of intense transference during analytic treatment. Clinical experience with these patients was the basis for many of the conclusions and suggestions offered by the authors reviewed in this postscript.

Nonetheless, the differences of opinion regarding both definition and significance of the acting-out patterns in this action-disposed group of patients were striking. A combination of a cross-sectional view and a less than rigorous application of basic psychoanalytic theory seemed responsible for some of the confusion.

Two fundamental developmental questions appear in order at this point: how old and how vulnerable was the child when the universally hypothesized early traumata were experienced, and how reversible are the effects of the early insults in a particular individual. We are handicapped when we turn to the neurophysiologists working with young infants for answers to such questions because no one yet knows enough of the factors involved to do more than speculate or perhaps extrapolate from neurological findings. Norman Geschwind (personal communication), among other neurologists, has observed that the younger the child, the larger the sphere of functions influenced by what might seem to be relatively limited insults; the older the child, the more severe or extensive the insults must be to provide a global effect. The focus of such investigations has tended to be the cognitive and motor functions, but the conclusion rests upon solid embryological principles. An embryo damaged by rubella in the first trimester of pregnancy tends to show far more extensive, diffuse, and irreversible damage than an infant who contracts a comparable infection during his first year. We cannot as yet lay out a parallel schema to say with confidence what the equation of psychic trauma to character defect at different ages is apt to be, but the correlation of serious infant neglect or the remoteness of the depressed mothering person during the first year with a child's later states of developmental retardation or ego defect is a common clinical finding.

Schwarz (1968) hypothesized that it was during the second and into the third year of life that a serious rupture in the mother-child relationship occurred in the children studied in the Hampstead delinquency project. She implied that relatively good relations between baby and mother had obtained earlier, but that the child faced with the mother's inaccessibility at a critical time (eighteen months to three years) regressed to a need-satisfying type of relationship with a limited capacity for moving on to a trusting object relation thereafter.

In our Thom Clinic studies we found more commonly a highly ambivalent maternal attitude toward the baby from relatively early days; the ambivalence seemed to be related to the mother's identifying the child with a person or with qualities that aroused considerable anxiety in her. The mothers were not remote or cold with their babies so far as we could tell, but their inconsistent attitudes with regard to impulse gratification and control strongly influenced their methods of child rearing. The phenomenon of a serious rupture in the relationship during the second or third year would indeed interfere with the progress of the child's object relations and ego controls, but we found that whether that break took place in a heretofore benign atmosphere or in a climate already fraught with conflict and confusion was a significant factor.

Perhaps this question involves the quantitative issue to which Brenner referred, namely, that we no longer view modes of action as qualitatively different in the normal and in the action-prone persons, but that intensity and amounts and frequency of acting or acting out are the characteristics to be weighed in evaluating an individual. From this point of view, we might expect a more pervasive and less often controlled action-orientation in persons with a history of a serious conflictual up-bringing from his early months on in a parent-child relationship fraught with anxiety and struggles about problems of ego controls leading to poorly internalized standards and object representations.

The related subject of the reversibility of early insults calls for considerable study. What type and severity of insult can be reversed in what child, and how? Some young children react very strongly to serious early blows, but under optimal conditions of care and affection can recoup and develop progressively. Other children seem to react mildly to early separation experiences, for instance, but appear to display a vulnerability to separation thereafter. Some children are quick to regress or readily become physically ill. The rapidity with which other young children under stress resort to serious withdrawal can be observed in any infant intervention program. One gains the impression that some are not prepared to tolerate very much strain while others can be subjected to chronic stress or to a multitude of severe insults and yet, with devoted care or skillful intervention, display an astonishing resiliency.

These are significant developmental questions which can be answered satisfactorily only in the detailed longitudinal studies such as those now being carried out by various psychoanalysts and child development specialists. Moreover, if therapists consider such issues in their clinical studies of acting-out children and adults, they may be able to provide correlative information regarding the origins of the pattern, the matrix out of which it emerged, the nature of traumatic experiences involved, and the climate in which some degree of amelioration of the action pattern was obtained. The two types of studies brought together might dispel many of the uncertainties and some of the confusions revealed by the latest discussions on acting out.

At any rate, the tendency to ascribe a single event or a specific constellation of events and reactions to them as the primary etiological agent of a chronic acting-out pattern does not appear consonant with contemporary concepts of personality development. Such reasoning by-passes the potential effects of progressive ego functioning as the child's mental apparatus develops and defensive and adaptive patterns become available which may achieve a partial or more complete assimilation and mastery of the original traumata. The serendipitous appearance of a well-placed, patient caretaker or a fortunate placement in a supportive nursery or elementary school may provide a richness of object relations and stimulation to growth in ego functioning, making it possible for the child to acquire controls and internalize standards not expected in the ordinary course of events. We are perhaps more apt to notice the unexpected which is traumatic, but serendipity does enter into the lives of some children.

The influence of the oedipal struggles upon distorted and infantile object relations as well as upon ego functions in general tends to receive little attention, although the effect of early traumatic experiences upon the form and nature of the oedipal complex is more commonly mentioned.

In a paradoxical fashion, our increased understanding of the earlier phases of ego development and object relatedness seems to accompany a tendency to oversimplify our concepts of the psychic apparatus and to leave to one side subtle and complicated interactions within the world of object representations and among the various psychic agencies we hypothesize. Anna Freud reminded the 25th Congress membership that it is the synthetic function of the ego that determines how curative the regained material from the acting-out pattern tends to be. There was a similar aptness in Hanna Segal's remark that the transference is related to an attitude toward inner objects; in acting out, the patient attempts to carry over such transference attitudes to outside objects. Those who protested the facile assignment of equivalency of somatic symptoms, dreams, or other psychic phenomena with acting out seemed to be on sound logical grounds in wishing to describe relationships among the different manifestations with all due respect for the nature of the psychic structure, rather than to hypothesize an identity that obscures the different processes probably involved.

SUMMARY AND CONCLUSIONS

The term acting out refers to a variety of phenomena characterized by an inability to refrain from action under different sets of circumstances. The lack of an agreed-upon definition of a concept of acting out is an important hindrance to clarification of existing confusions and differences. It is clear that today the term is no longer restricted to the special phenomenon observed as a form of resistance in psychoanalytic treatment. The current use in many professional circles of the label acting out for a wide variety of behaviors involving motor activity and impulse discharge greatly complicates the task of sorting out a clinical entity, describing its characteristics, and relating it to other behavioral phenomena. A concept of acting out so broad as to include every human impulsive act of whatever nature and without regard for the person's age, history, or life circumstances is unlikely to contribute to a better understanding of intrapsychic processes.

It appears to me that *there is merit in reserving the term acting out for a highly organized purposeful ego activity, a complex action pattern which can be described in predispositional, developmental, defensive, and adaptive terms.* Acting out in this sense can then be differentiated from direct motor discharge of instinctual tension and from outbursts of relatively unmodified primitive aggressive or libidinal drive derivatives. We may infer that it occurs in the setting of a shift in the balance of psychic forces, due to the revival of partially repressed impulses or memories and affects connected with them. Relief of tension is sought through discharge in a complex act or series of acts. Some event or relationship in the person's current life situation provides the stimulus for the acting out through its associative links with the repressed impulses or their derivatives. While acting out brings relief of tension and so may provide direct gratification, an examination of the functional aspects of the particular episode may be the most profitable avenue for understanding its occurrence.

A predisposition to acting out has been described by a number of authors who have distinguished between the presence of a predisposing character structure and the specific behavior. What role a constitutional proclivity for action in conflict solution plays in certain predisposed individuals we do not know.

Investigations of developmental aspects of problems of acting out thus far contribute the following possibilities: (1) acting out in the sense defined above may occur when the psychic apparatus are sufficiently developed to produce a highly organized motor activity under the conditions hypothesized; (2) acting out may appear as a phase-specific phenomenon with well-defined defensive and adaptive functions, as Blos postulates for adolescence; such behavior may serve similar functions in other periods of stress, as in the involutional phase; (3) the context in which acting out occurs may clarify which situations predispose to acting out and which counterforces militate against it; (4) the role of parent-child relationships in encouraging or curbing a tendency toward acting out is a significant factor; (5) acting out in one period of life or at one point in time cannot be taken as an indicator of the likelihood of the presence or absence of the pattern in future periods of life, since life experiences and maturational forces can bring about alterations in the relative strengths of acting-out tendencies and counterforces mobilized against them.

The *defensive aspects* of patterns of acting out have been noted or inferred in many papers on this subject. Otto Fenichel's dictum that all acting out ultimately serves to defend against depression was complemented by Hanna Fenichel's statement that the basic fear defended against is that of loss of the mother. Here we find a link to Kaufman (1955) work with antisocial children and adolescents, which led to the conclusion that the acting out served to defend against a depressive core and object loss. Careful examination of episodes of acting out in individuals not prone to a chronic pattern of this behavior usually reveals a specific conflict, and affects connected with it, which the acting out defends against.

The *adaptive aspects* of acting out have received less attention. Blos's paper on adolescent acting out could stimulate a reconsideration on the part of various clinicians regarding their interpretations of the functions of such behavior in their patients. It is well known that a period of acting out may precede the outbreak of a psychosis or may occur when the individual begins to emerge from his psychosis. The defensive functions of the acting out under such circumstances have been clearly seen; to what extent the behavior can be understood in specific instances as the most satisfactory mode of adaptation of a sick person to what is for him an intolerable life situation is a question not often put in such terms.

And finally, emphasis can profitably be placed upon *the economy* of the acting out, upon the relative strength of the psychic forces at the time the behavior takes place. Acting out frequently emerges when an imbalance of impulses over ego controls occurs in certain critical developmental phases, as in the oedipal, adolescent, and involutional periods. During such stages of relative ego weakness, the shifting balance of psychic forces permits more ready recourse to the more highly organized episodes of motor activity as well as to impulsive action in general.

Acting out may occur in the context of relative ego weakness vis-à-vis the anxiety aroused by certain specific instinctual wishes or affects connected with them, as in the transference relationship. In such an instance, highly specific episodes of acting out take place, stimulated by events or persons linked associatively to the repressed material. A more general ego weakness may lead to the chronic pattern of acting out.

Disturbances in superego development in which an archaic superego with little tolerance for any impulse gratification overrides the ego and allies itself with the id may lead to massive destructive acting out as a defense against intolerable feelings of guilt.

Such a concept of acting out appears to bring together in as coherent a form as possible the findings and inferences of the work done thus far. As a working hypothesis, this conceptual scheme may be useful in examining clinical data from various sources. One important deficiency in the literature both from analysts and other professional persons is the paucity of actual details of the acting out behavior, the individual's developmental history, and his current life situation. As Greenacre observed at the Thom Symposium, discussions of dynamic and structural implications tend to take precedence over actual clinical material so that it becomes difficult to compare and contrast cases and to ascertain whether one is dealing with similar or different phenomena. In a very real sense, we are in the stage of data collection regarding acting-out behavior. We need detailed clinical data from individuals of varying ages, of differing personality structures, of widely differing current life situations to help us arrive at a more satisfactory understanding of acting out and its relationship to ubiquitous human phenomena, on the one hand, and to specific pathological syndromes, on the other.

REFERENCES

Abt, L. E. & Weissman, S. L. eds. (1965), *Acting Out, Theoretical and Clinical Aspects.* New York: Grune and Stratton.

Aichhorn, A. (1925), *Wayward Youth.* New York: Viking Press, 1935.

———— (1949), Some remarks on the psychic structure and social care of a certain type of female juvenile delinquent. *The Psychoanalytic Study of the Child,* 3/4:439-448. New York: International Universities Press.

Alexander, F. (1930), The neurotic character. In: *The Scope of Psychoanalysis, 1921-1961.* New York: Basic Books, 1961, pp. 56-73.

———— & Healy, W. (1935), *The Roots of Crime.* New York: Knopf.

Alpert, A. (1957), A special therapeutic technique for certain developmental disorders in prelatency children. *Amer. J. Orthopsychiat.,* 27: 256-269.

Altman, L. L. (1957), On the oral nature of acting out. *J. Amer. Psychoanal. Assn.,* 5:648-662.

Andry, R. G. (1960), *Delinquency and Parental Pathology: A Study in Forensic and Clinical Psychology.* Springfield, Ill.: Charles C. Thomas.

Atkins, N. (1968), Contribution to Symposium on acting out. *Internat. J. Psycho-Anal.,* 49:221-223.

————, reporter (1970), Panel on "Action, Acting Out and the Symptomatic Act." *J. Amer. Psychoanal. Assn.,* 16:631-643.

Arieti, S. (1974), Acting out and unusual behavior in schizophrenia. *Amer. J. Psychother.,* 28:333-343.

Baldwin, J. (1956), *Giovanni's Room.* New York: Dial Press.

Barker, R. G. & Wright, H. F. (1954), *Midwest and Its Children.* Evanston, Ill.: Row Peterson.

Beres, D. (1952), Clinical notes on aggression in children. *The Psychoanalytic Study of the Child,* 7:241-263. New York: International Universities Press.

———— (1968), Panel discussion on acting out. *Internat. J. Psycho-Anal.,* 49:506-512.

Bibring, E. (1954), Psychoanalysis and the dynamic psychotherapies. *J. Amer. Psychoanal. Assn.,* 2:745-770.

Bird, B. (1957), A specific peculiarity of acting out. *J. Amer. Psychoanal. Assn.,* 5:630-647.

Blos, P. (1957), Preoedipal factors in the etiology of female delinquency. *The Psychoanalytic Study of the Child.* 12:229-249. New York: International Universities Press.

327

328

_____ (1962), *On Adolescence: A Psychoanalytic Interpretation.* Glencoe, Ill.: Free Press.

Bonnard, A. (1961), Truancy and pilfering associated with bereavement. In: *Adolescents: Psychoanalytic Approach to Problems and Therapy,* ed. S. Lorand & H. I. Schneer. New York: Hoeber, pp. 152-179.

Bowlby, J. (1944), Forty-four juvenile thieves. *Internat. J. Psycho-Anal.,* 25:19-53.

_____ (1951), *Maternal Care and Mental Health.* New York: Schocken Books, 1966.

_____ (1969), *Attachment and Loss, Vol. 1, Attachment.* New York: Basic Books.

Brenman, M. (1952), On teasing and being teased: and the problem of moral masochism. *The Psychoanalytic Study of the Child,* 7:264-285. New York: International Universities Press.

Brenner, C. (1969), Effects of theory on psychoanalytic technique. *J. Amer. Psychoanal. Assn.,* 17:333-352.

Briffault, R. (1927), *The Mothers.* New York: Macmillan.

Brunswick, R. M. (1940), The preoedipal phase of libido development. In: *The Psychoanalytic Reader,* ed. R. Fliess. New York: International Universities Press, 1948, pp. 261-284.

Cantwell, D. P. (1975), *The Hyperactive Child: Diagnosis, Management and Current Research.* New York: Spectrum Publications.

Carroll, E. J. (1954), Acting out and ego development. *Psychoanal. Quart.,* 23:521-528.

Chance, E. (1959), *Families in Treatment.* New York: Basic Books.

Chien, I. (1956), The family of the addict. Paper read at Bellevue Hospital, New York.

Cloward, R. A. & Ohlin, L. E. (1960), *Delinquency and Opportunity: A Theory of Delinquent Gangs.* New York: Free Press.

Cohen, A. K. (1955), *Delinquent Boys: The Culture of the Gang.* New York: Free Press.

Demaria, L. (1968), Contribution to Symposium on acting out. *Internat. J. Psycho-Anal.,* 49:219-220.

Demos, J. (1974), The American family in past time. *American Scholar,* 43:422-446.

Deutsch, F. (1947), Analysis of postural behavior. *Psychoanal. Quart.,* 16:195-213.

_____ (1950), Thus speaks the body. II. A psychosomatic study of vasomotor behavior (capillaroscopy and plethysmography). *Acta Med. Orient.,* 9:199-215.

_____ (1952), Analytic posturology. *Psychoanal. Quart.,* 21:196-214.

_____ (1957), A footnote to Freud's "Fragment of an analysis of a case of hysteria." *Psychoanal. Quart.,* 26:159-167.

Deutsch, H. (1930), Hysterical fate neurosis. In: *Neuroses and Character Types.* New York: International Universities Press, 1965, pp. 14-28.

_____ (1942), Some forms of emotional disturbance and their relationship to schizophrenia. In: *Neuroses and Character Types*. New York: International Universities Press, 1965, pp. 262-281.

_____ (1944), *The Psychology of Women*, Vol. I. New York: Grune & Stratton.

_____ (1955), The imposter. *Psychoanal. Quart.*, 24:483-505.

Dittman, A. T. & Goodrich, D. W. (1961), A comparison of social behavior in normal and hyperaggressive preadolescent boys. *Child Develop.*, 32:315-327.

Douglas, J. W. B. & Ross, J. M. (1968), Characteristics of delinquent boys and their homes. In: *Genetic and Environmental Influences on Behavior*, ed. J. M. Thoday & A. S. Parkes. New York: Plenum Press, pp. 114-127.

Duncan, P. (1971), Parental attitudes and interactions in delinquency. *Child Development*, 42:1751-1765.

Eissler, K. R. (1953), The effect of the structure of the ego on psychoanalytic technique. *J. Amer. Psychoanal. Assn.*, 1:104-143.

Eissler, R. S. (1949), Riots: Observations in a home for delinquent girls. *The Psychoanalytic Study of the Child*, 3/4:449-460. New York: International Universities Press.

Ekstein, R. & Friedman, S. W. (1957), The function of acting out, play action and acting in the psychotherapeutic process. *J. Amer. Psychoanal. Assn.*, 5:581-629.

El-Guebaly, N. & Offord, D. R. (1977), The offspring of alcoholics: A critical review. *Amer. J. Psychiat.*, 134:357-365.

Fenichel, O. (1939), Trophy and Triumph. In: *Collected Papers*, 2. New York: Norton, 1954, pp. 141-162.

_____ (1945), Neurotic acting out. In: *Collected Papers*, 2. New York: Norton, 1954, pp. 296-304.

Fraiberg, S. (1959), *The Magic Years*. New York: Scribner.

Freud, A. (1936), *The Ego and the Mechanisms of Defense. The Writings of Anna Freud*, 2. New York: International Universities Press, 1966.

_____ (1949), Certain types and stages of social maladjustment. In: *Searchlights on Delinquency*, ed. K. R. Eissler. New York: International Universities Press, pp. 193-204. Also in: *The Writings of Anna Freud*, 4:75-94. New York: International Universities Press.

_____ (1965), *Normality and Pathology in Childhood. The Writings of Anna Freud*, 6. New York: International Universities Press.

_____ (1968), Contribution to Symposium on Acting Out. *Int. J. Psychoanal.*, 49:165-170. Also in: *The Writings of Anna Freud*, 7:94-109. New York: International Universities Press, 1971.

Freud, S. (1901), The psychopathology of everyday life. *Standard Edition*, 6. London: Hogarth Press, 1960.

_____ (1905), Fragment of an analysis of a case of hysteria. *Standard Edition*, 7:3-122. London: Hogarth Press, 1953.

_____ (1911), Formulations on the two principles of mental functioning. *Standard Edition*, 12:215-226. London: Hogarth Press, 1958.

———— (1914), Remembering, repeating and working-through. *Standard Edition*, 12:145-156. London: Hogarth Press, 1958.

———— (1920a), Beyond the pleasure principle. *Standard Edition*, 18:3-64. London: Hogarth Press, 1955.

———— (1920b), The psychogenesis of a case of homosexuality in a woman. *Standard Edition*, 18:146-172. London: Hogarth Press, 1955.

———— (1925), Some psychical consequences of the anatomical distinction between the sexes. *Standard Edition*, 19:243-258. London: Hogarth Press, 1961.

———— (1933), New introductory lectures on psycho-analysis. *Standard Edition*, 22:3-182. London: Hogarth Press, 1964.

Friedlander, K. (1945), Formation of the antisocial character. *The Psychoanalytic Study of the Child*, 1:189-204. New York: International Universities Press.

———— (1947), *The Psychoanalytical Approach to Juvenile Delinquency*. New York: International Universities Press.

———— (1949), Latent delinquency and ego development. In: *Searchlights on Delinquency*, ed. K. R. Eissler. New York: International Universities Press, pp. 205-215.

Garbarino, H. (1968), Contribution to symposium on acting out. *Internat. J. Psycho-Anal.*, 49:193-194.

Gardner, G. E. (1959), Separation of the parents and the emotional life of the child. In: *The Problem of Delinquency*, ed. S. Glueck. Boston: Houghton Mifflin, pp. 138-143.

Giffin, M. E., Johnson, A. M., & Litin, E. M. (1954), Specific factors determining antisocial acting out. *Amer. J. Orthopsychiat.*, 24:668-684.

Glover, E. (1954), Recent advances in the psycho-analytic study of delinquency. In: *Roots of Crime*. New York: International Universities Press, 1960, pp. 292-310.

———— (1956), Psycho-analysis and criminology. In: *Roots of Crime*. New York: International Universities Press, 1960, pp. 311-324.

Glueck, S. & Glueck, E. T. (1950), *Unraveling Juvenile Delinquency*. New York: Commonwealth Fund.

———— ———— (1956), *Physique and Delinquency*. Millwood, New York: Kraus Reprint Company.

———— ———— (1970), *Toward a Typology of Juvenile Offenders*. New York: Grune & Stratton.

Goodrich, D. W. & Boomer, D. S. (1958), Some concepts about therapeutic interventions with hyperaggressive children. *Social Casework*, 39:207-213, 286-291.

Gorer, G. (1948), *The American People: A Study of National Character*. New York: Norton.

Greenacre, P. (1944), Infant reactions to restraint: problems in the fate of infantile aggression. In: *Trauma, Growth, and Personality*. New York: International Universities Press, 1969, pp. 83-105.

———— (1950a), The prepuberty trauma in girls. In: *Trauma, Growth, and*

Personality. New York: International Universities Press, 1969, pp. 204-223.

_____ (1950b), General problems of acting out. In: *Trauma, Growth, and Personality*. New York: International Universities Press, 1969, pp. 224-236.

_____ (1968), The psychoanalytic process, transference, and acting out. In: *Emotional Growth*. New York: International Universities Press, 1971, pp. 762-775.

Grief, E. B. (1976), Fathers, children and moral development. In: *The Role of the Father in Child Development*, ed. M. E. Lamb. New York: Wiley Interscience, pp. 219-236.

Grinberg, L. (1968), Contribution to Symposium of acting out. *Internat. J. Psycho-Anal.*, 49:171-178.

Guze, S. B., Wolfgram, E. D., McKinney, J. K., & Cantwell, D. P. (1967), Psychiatric illness in the families of convicted criminals: A study of 519 first-degree relatives. *Dis. Nerv. Syst.*, 28:651-659.

Hartmann, H. (1939), *Ego Psychology and the Problem of Adaptation*. New York: International Universities Press, 1958.

_____ (1944), Psychoanalysis and sociology. In: *Essays on Ego Psychology*. New York: International Universities Press, 1964, pp. 19-36.

_____ Kris, E. & Loewenstein, R. M. (1946), Comments on the formation of psychic structure. *The Psychoanalytic Study of the Child*, 2:11-38. New York: International Universities Press.

Healy, W. (1915), *The Individual Delinquent*. Boston: Little Brown.

Hendrick, I. (1951), Early development of the ego: Identification in infancy. *Psychoanal. Quart.*, 20:44-61.

Hermann, I. (1927), Charles Darwin. *Imago*, 13:57-82.

Heston, L. (1970), The genetics of schizophrenia and schizoid disease. *Science*, 167:249-256.

Hoffer, W. (1950), Development of the body ego. *The Psychoanalytic Study of the Child*, 5:18-23. New York: International Universities Press.

Hollingshead, A. B. & Redlich, F. C. (1958), *Social Class and Mental Illness*. New York: Wiley.

Hutchings, B. & Mednick, S. A. (1974), Registered criminality in the adoptive and biological parents of registered male adoptees. In: *Genetics, Environment, and Psychopathology*, ed. S. A. Mednick, F. Schulsinger, J. Higgins, and B. Bell. Netherlands: North Holland Publications, pp. 215-227.

Jacobson, E. (1957), Denial and repression. *J. Amer. Psychoanal. Assn.*, 5:61-92.

_____ (1961), Adolescent moods and the remodeling of psychic structure in adolescence. *The Psychoanalytic Study of the Child*, 16:164-183. New York: International Universities Press.

Jenkins, R. L. (1966), Psychiatric syndromes in children and their relation to family background. *Amer. J. Orthopsychiat.*, 36:450-457.

———— (1968), The varieties of children's behavioral problems and family dynamics. *Amer. J. Psychiat.*, 124:1440-1445.

Jessner, L. & Pavenstedt, E. eds. (1959), *Dynamic Psychopathology in Childhood.* New York: Grune & Stratton.

Johnson, A. M. (1949), Sanctions for superego lacunae of adolescents. In: *Searchlights on Delinquency*, ed. K. R. Eissler. New York: International Universities Press, pp. 225-234.

———— & Szurek, S. A. (1952), The genesis of antisocial acting out in children and adults. *Psychoanal. Quart.*, 21:323-343.

Jonsson, G. (1967), Delinquent boys, their parents and grandparents. *Acta Psychiatr. Scand.*, 43 (Suppl.), 195.

Kanzer, M., reporter (1957a), Panel on "Acting Out and its Relation to Impulse Disorders." *J. Amer. Psychoanal. Assn.*, 5:136-145.

———— (1957b), Acting out, sublimation and reality testing. *J. Amer. Psychoanal. Assn.*, 5:663-684.

———— (1968), Ego alteration and acting out. *Internat. J. Psycho-Anal.*, 49:431-435.

Kaufman, I. (1955), Three basic sources for predelinquent character. *Nerv. Child*, 11:12-15.

———— & Makkay, E. F. (1956), Treatment of the adolescent delinquent. In: *Case Studies in Childhood Emotional Disabilities*, 2. New York: American Orthopsychiatric Association, pp. 316-352.

Kestenberg, J. (1968), Acting out in the analysis of children and adults. *Internat. J. Psycho-Anal.*, 49:341-344.

Kirkegaard-Sorenson, L. & Mednick, S. A. (1975), Registered criminality in families with children at high risk for schizophrenia. *J. Abnorm. Psychol.*, 84:197-204.

Lamb, M. E. (1976), The role of the father: An overview. In: *The Role of the Father in Child Development*, ed. M. E. Lamb. New York: Wiley Interscience, pp. 1-63.

Layman, E. M. (1961), Discussion: Symposium: Father influence in the family. *Merrill-Palmer Quart.*, 7:107-111.

Leary, T. (1956), *Multilevel Measurement of Interpersonal Behavior.* Berkeley, Calif.: Psychological Consultation Service.

———— (1957), *Interpersonal Diagnosis of Personality: A Functional Theory and Methodology for Personality Evaluation.* New York: Ronald Press.

Lebovici, S. (1968), Contribution to the Symposium on acting out. *Internat. J. Psycho-Anal.*, 49:202-205.

Lewis, D. O. & Balla, D. A. (1976), Delinquency and Psychopathology. New York: Grune & Stratton.

———— ———— Sacks, H. L., & Jekel, J. F. (1973), Psychotic symptomatology in a juvenile court clinic population. *J. Amer. Acad. Child Psychiat.*, 12:660-674.

———— ———— Shanok, S., & Snell, L. (1976), Delinquency, parental psychopathology and parental criminality; Clinical and Epidemiological findings. *Amer. J. Child Psychiat.*, 15:665-678.

_____ & Shanok, S. S. (1977), Medical histories of delinquents and non-delinquents: An epidemiological study. *Amer. J. Psychiat.*, 134:1020-1025.

Litin, E. M., Giffin, M. E., & Johnson, A. M. (1956), Parental influence in unusual sexing behavior in children. *Psychoanal. Quart.*, 25:37-55.

Mahler, M. S. (1952), On child psychosis and schizophrenia: Autistic and symbiotic infantile psychoses. *The Psychoanalytic Study of the Child*, 7:286-306. New York: International Universities Press.

Masterson, J. (1974), The acting out adolescent: a point of view. *Amer. J. Psychother.*, 28:343-351.

McCord, W. & McCord, J. (1959), *Origins of Crime: A New Evaluation of the Cambridge-Somerville Youth Study*. New York: Columbia University Press.

Michaels, J. J. (1955), *Disorders of Character: Persistent Enuresis, Juvenile Delinquency and Psychopathic Personality*. Springfield, Ill.: Charles C. Thomas.

_____ (1959), Character disorder and acting upon impulse. In: *Readings in Psychoanalytic Psychology*, ed. M. Levitt. New York: Appleton-Century-Crofts, pp. 181-196.

Milebamane, B. M. M. (1975), Perception des attitudes et pratiques educatives du pere par les delinquants et les normaux. *Can. Psychiat. Assn.*, 20:299-303.

Mitscherlich-Nielsen, M. (1968), Contribution to Symposium on acting out. *Internat. J. Psycho-Anal.*, 49:188-192.

Moore, B. E. (1968), Contribution to Symposium on acting out. *Internat. J. Psycho-Anal.*, 49:182-184.

Mussen, P. H. & Distler, L. (1960), Child-rearing antecedents of masculine identification in kindergarten boys. *Child Development*, 31: 89-100.

Nacht, S. (1968), Discussion to Symposium on acting out. *Internat. J. Psycho-Anal.*, 49:229.

Neavles, J. C. & Winokur, G. (1957), The hot-rod driver. *Bull. Menninger Clinic*, 21:28-35.

Neubauer, P. B. & Beller, E. K. (1958), Differential contributions of the educator and clinician in diagnosis. In: *Orthopsychiatry and the School*, ed. M. Krugman. New York: American Orthopsychiatric Association, pp. 36-45.

Nye, F. I. (1958), *Family Relationships and Delinquent Behavior*. New York: Wiley.

Parsons, T. (1947), Certain sources and patterns of aggression in the social structure of the Western world. *Psychiat.*, 10:167-181.

Provence, S. & Ritvo, S. (1961), Effects of deprivation on institutionalized infants: disturbances in development of the relationship to inanimate objects. *The Psychoanalytic Study of the Child*, 16:189-205. New York: International Universities Press.

Rangell, L. (1968), A contribution to Symposium on acting out. *Internat. J. Psycho-Anal.*, 49:195-201.

Rank, B. (1949a), Aggression. *The Psychoanalytic Study of the Child*, 3/4: 43-48. New York: International Universities Press.

——— (1949b), Adaptation of the psychoanalytic technique for the treatment of young children with atypical development. *Amer. J. Orthopsychiat.*, 19:130-139.

Rapaport, D. (1960), *The Structure of Psychoanalytic Theory. Psychological Issues,* Monogr. 6. New York: International Universities Press.

Rausch, H. L., Dittman, A. T. & Taylor, T. J. (1959), Person setting and change in social interaction. *Human Relations*, 12:361-378.

Reich, A. (1951), On countertransference. In: *Psychoanalytic Contributions.* New York: International Universities Press, 1973, pp. 136-154.

Rexford, E. N. (1959), Antisocial young children and their families. In: *Dynamic Psychopathology of Childhood*, ed. L. Jessner & E. Pavenstedt. New York: Grune & Stratton, pp. 186-220.

——— Schleifer, M. & van Amerongen, S. (1956), A follow-up of a psychiatric study of 57 antisocial young children. *Mental Hygiene*, 10: 196-214.

——— & van Amerongen, S. (1957), The influence of unsolved maternal oral conflicts upon impulsive acting out in young children. *Amer. J. Orthopsychiat.*, 27:75-87.

Reider, R. O. (1973), The offspring of schizophrenic parents: A review. *J. Nerv. Ment. Dis.*, 157:179-190.

Robins, L. N. (1966), *Deviant Children Grown-up.* Baltimore: Williams & Wilkins Press.

——— West, P. A., & Herjanic, B. L. (1975), Arrests and delinquency in two generations: A study of black urban families and their children. *J. Child Psycho. & Psychiat.*, 16:125-140.

Rosenthal, D., Wender, P. H., Kety, S. S., Schulsinger, F., Welner, J., & Ostergaard, L. (1968), Schizophrenic offspring reared in adoptive homes. In: *The Transmission of Schizophrenia*, ed. D. Rosenthal, & S. S. Kety. Oxford: Pergamon Press, pp. 377-391.

Rosenthal, M. J., Ni, E., Finklestein, M. & Berkowits, G. K. (1962), Father-child relationships and children's problems. *Arch. Gen. Psychiat.*, 7:360-373.

Ritvo, S. (1968), Comment on Dr. Kanzer's paper. *Internat. J. Psycho-Anal.*, 49:435-437.

Rochlin, G. (1959), The loss complex. *J. Amer. Psychoanal. Assn.*, 7: 299-316.

Rouart, J. (1968), Contribution to Symposium on acting out. *Internat. J. Psycho-Anal.*, 49:185-187.

Sandler, J. (1960), On the concept of superego. *The Psychoanalytic Study of the Child*, 15:128-162. New York: International Universities Press.

——— Holder, A., & Dare, C. (1973), *The Patient and the Analyst.* New York: International Universities Press.

Schafer, R. (1960), The loving and beloved superego in Freud's structural theory. *The Psychoanalytic Study of the Child*, 15:163-188. New York: International Universities Press.

Schmideberg, M. (1956), Delinquent acts as perversions and fetishes. *Internat. J. Psycho-Anal.*, 37:422-424.

Schwarz, H. (1968), Contribution to Symposium on acting out. *Internat. J. Psycho-Anal.*, 49:179-181.

Short, J. F., Jr., & Nye, F. I. (1958), Extent of unrecorded delinquency. In: *Society, Delinquency and Delinquent Behavior*, ed. H. L. Vose. Boston: Little, Brown, pp. 52-59.

Siegman, A. W. (1966), Father absence during childhood and antisocial behavior. *J. Abnorm. Psychol.*, 71:71-74.

Sperling, O. (1944), On appersonation. *Internat. J. Psycho-Anal.*, 25:128-132.

Sperling, S. J. (1953), On the psychodynamics of teasing. *J. Amer. Psychoanal. Assn.*, 1:458-483.

Sperry, B. (1962), The internal opponent in thought in relation to children's learning errors. Read at the Meeting of the American Orthopsychiatric Association.

_____, Staver, N., Reiner, B., & Ulrich, D. (1958), Renunciation and denial in learning difficulties. *Amer. J. Orthopsychiat.*, 28:98-111.

Spiegel, L. A. (1954), Acting out and defensive instinctual gratification. *J. Amer. Psychoanal. Assn.*, 2:107-119.

Stephens, W. N. (1961), Judgment by social workers on boys and mothers in fatherless families. *J. Gen. Psychol.*, 99:59-64.

Sunley, R. (1955), Early nineteenth-century American literature on child rearing. In: *Childhood in Contemporary Cultures,* ed. M. Mead and M. Wolfenstein. Chicago: University of Chicago Press, pp. 150-167.

Symonds, M. (1974), Therapeutic approaches to acting out. *Amer. J. Psychother.*, 28:362.

Szurek, S. A. (1954), Concerning the sexual disorders of parents and their children. *J. Nerv. & Ment. Dis.*, 120:369-378.

_____ Johnson, A. M. & Falstein, E. (1942), Collaborative psychiatric therapy of parent-child problems. *Amer. J. Orthopsychiat.*, 12:511-517.

Tallman, I. (1965), Spoused role differentiation and the socialization of severely retarded children. *J. Marriage & Family*, 27:37-42.

Vanggaard, T. (1968), Contribution to Symposium on acting out. *Internat. J. Psycho-Anal.*, 49:206-210.

Wender, P. H., (1972), The minimal brain dysfunction syndrome in children. I. The syndrome and its relevance for psychiatry. II. A psychological and biochemical model for the syndrome. *J. Nerv. Ment. Dis.*, 155:55-71.

West, D. J., (1969), *Present Conduct and Future Delinquency*. New York: International Universities Press.

Williams, R. M. (1965), *American Society* (2nd ed.), New York: Knopf.

Wolff, P. H. (1960), *The Developmental Psychologies of Jean Piaget and Psychoanalysis. Psychological Issues*, Monogr. 5. New York: International Universities Press.

Zeligs, M. A. (1957), Acting in. *J. Amer. Psychoanal. Assn.*, 5:685-706.

_____ (1961), The psychology of silence. *J. Amer. Psychoanal. Assn.*, 9:7-43.

NAME INDEX

Abt, L. E., 327
Aichhorn, A., 5-6, 63, 184-185, 289-293, 304, 310, 327
Alexander, F., 184, 288-289, 327
Alpert, A., 44n., 327
Altman, L. L., 4, 232n., 234, 327
Andry, R. G., 140, 327
Arieti, S., 284, 327
Atkins, N., 279, 327

Baldwin, J., 163, 179, 327
Balla, D. A., 137-152, 332
Barker, R. G., 106, 327
Bell, G., 331
Beller, E. K., 106, 333
Beres, D., 62, 272, 327
Berkowits, G. K., 334
Berman, L., 181
Bernfeld, S., 179
Bibesco, A., 171
Bibring, E., 108, 246, 327
Bird, B., 4, 233-234, 327
Blackwell, Dr., 24n.
Blos, P., xv, 76, 153-214, 247, 313-314, 324, 327
Bonnard, A., 164, 328
Boomer, D. S., 108, 330
Bowlby, J., 8, 137, 295, 328
Brenman, M., 108, 328
Brenner, C., 282, 320, 328
Briffault, R., 137, 328
Brunswick, R. M., 188, 191, 314, 328

Cantwell, D. P., 139, 141, 151, 328, 331
Carroll, E. J., 156, 328
Chance, E., 104-106, 328

Chien, I., 132, 328
Cloward, R. A., 138, 328
Cohen, A. K., 140, 328

Dare, C., 282-284, 334
Demaria, L., 328
Demos, J., 137, 328
Deutsch, F., 178, 192-193, 235, 328
Deutsch, H., 39, 233-246, 314-316, 328
Distler, L., 333
Dittman, A. T., 105-106, 329
Dittman, H. L., 334
Douglas, J. W. B., 141, 329
Duncan, P., 141, 329

Eissler, K. R., 329, 330, 332
Eissler, R. S., 108, 179, 329
Ekstein, R., 131, 233, 268-270, 329
El-Guebaly, N., 140, 329

Falstein, E., 234, 335
Fenichel, H., 268, 324
Fenichel, O., 1, 3, 6, 155, 223, 232, 257-263, 289, 303, 313, 324, 329
Ferenczi, S., 246
Fineman, J., 246-247
Finklestein, M., 334
Fliess, R., 328
Frank, J., 234
Freud, A., 45, 158, 179, 255-257, 272-275, 278, 297-305, 322, 328, 329
Freud, S., 23, 37, 139, 156-158, 178-179, 189, 232, 250-255, 297, 302-303, 305-306, 329

SUBJECT INDEX

43, 49, 255, 270, 275, 302, 324-325
and instinctual urge, 1-2, 6, 14
and regression, 94, 212
Defense mechanisms, 157, 219, 255-257
   see also Denial, Externalization, Internalization, Introjection, Isolation, Projection
Delinquency, 5, 25, 32, 45, 138, 167, 235, 270-271, 273, 276-277, 285-310, 318
   and crime, 21, 132
   and ego development, 55-79, 232
   father's role in, 137-152
   in girls, 5, 183-214, 241, 248
   and preschool years, 55-79, 130-131, 308
   see also Antisocial behavior, Criminality, Dissocial behavior
Denial, 3, 43, 118, 121-122, 157-158, 164, 219
Depression, 25, 169, 213
   and acting out, 133-134, 242, 257-260, 309, 324
   "infantile type," 185
   nuclear, 73
Dipsomania, 243-244
Discharge
   delay of, 37, 184
   and impulse disorder, 154-156, 173, 216, 228, 233, 257
   see also Motor activity
Displacement and acting out, 157, 175, 212, 257-258
Dissocial behavior, see Antisocial behavior, Criminality, Delinquency
Dora case, 156-157, 178-180
Dramatization, 2, 56, 65, 156, 263
Dream(s)
   and electroencephalogram, 281
   and wish for a baby, 193-194, 197-198
Drive
   and affect, 6, 14, 33, 56, 61, 161-162, 167, 172-173, 184-185, 323

and ego development, 203, 277, 305
   instinctual, 1-2, 15, 37, 40, 42, 82, 99, 126-127, 164, 171, 190-191, 270, 289, 292-294, 304, 309, 325
   see also Aggression, Libido
Drug abuse, 131-132, 243-245

Ego
   and acting out, 154, 222, 242, 260, 265, 273-274, 280-281, 325
   and defense, 126, 128, 255-257, 308
   fragmentation, 56
   and object relations, 159-164, 172-177, 179-182, 266-269, 277, 309
   and sense of reality, 48, 258
   and severe impairment, 24, 67, 161, 184-185, 247
   strength, 5-6, 9-10, 13, 225, 325
   and superego, 5-6, 41, 45, 128, 176, 255-256, 282, 287, 292-293
   and transference, 236-237, 240
Ego development, 34-35
   and acting out, 55-67, 71-74, 77-79, 221, 278-279, 315, 323
   and dissocial behavior, 55-67, 71-74, 77-79, 186, 203, 293-294, 296
   precocious, 73-74, 77-78
   and secondary-process, 35-38
   splitting, 43
Ego functions, 5, 51
   and impulse disorders, 287-288, 303
   and language development, 17-19, 23
   and object relations, 8, 46, 50, 61-65, 72, 77-79, 306, 320-322
Ego ideal, 201
   see also Superego
Electroencephalogram, 281
Emotional development, 4, 8, 28
   and acting out, 66-67, 264, 297
   and delinquency, 185-186, 201-